The Idea of Marathon

Also available from Bloomsbury

Homer's Iliad and the Trojan War: Dialogues on Tradition, edited by Jan Haywood and Naoise Mac Sweeney
Imagining Xerxes, Emma Bridges
Troy: Myth, City, Icon, Naoise Mac Sweeney

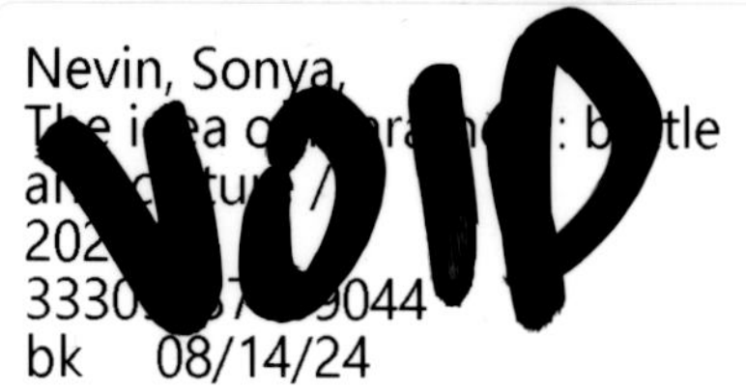

The Idea of Marathon

Battle and Culture

Sonya Nevin

BLOOMSBURY ACADEMIC
LONDON • NEW YORK • OXFORD • NEW DELHI • SYDNEY

BLOOMSBURY ACADEMIC
Bloomsbury Publishing Plc
50 Bedford Square, London, WC1B 3DP, UK
1385 Broadway, New York, NY 10018, USA
29 Earlsfort Terrace, Dublin 2, Ireland

BLOOMSBURY, BLOOMSBURY ACADEMIC and the Diana logo
are trademarks of Bloomsbury Publishing Plc

First published in Great Britain 2022

Cover design: Terry Woodley
Illustrations by Steve K. Simons
Cover image: line drawings by Steve K Simons of the Aristion monument,
National Archaeological Museum of Athens, Greece, and a spear-bearer
relief carving, Persepolis, Iran.

A catalogue record for this book is available from the British Library.

Library of Congress Cataloging-in-Publication Data
Names: Nevin, Sonya, author.
Title: The idea of Marathon : battle and culture / Sonya Nevin.
Description: London ; New York : Bloomsbury Academic, [2022] | Includes
bibliographical references and index.
Identifiers: LCCN 2021038674 (print) | LCCN 2021038675 (ebook) |
ISBN 9781788314206 (hardback) | ISBN 9781350157590 (paperback) |
ISBN 9781350157613 (ebook) | ISBN 9781350157606 (epub)
Subjects: LCSH: Marathon, Battle of, Greece, 490 B.C. | Marathon,
Battle of, Greece, 490 B.C.–Influence. | Greece–Civilization–To 146 B.C. |
Iran–History–To 640.
Classification: LCC DF225.4 .N48 2022 (print) | LCC DF225.4 (ebook) |
DDC 938/.03–dc23
LC record available at https://lccn.loc.gov/2021038674
LC ebook record available at https://lccn.loc.gov/2021038675

ISBN: HB: 978-1-7883-1420-6
PB: 978-1-3501-5759-0
ePDF: 978-1-3501-5761-3
eBook: 978-1-3501-5760-6

Typeset by RefineCatch Limited, Bungay, Suffolk
Printed and bound in Great Britain

To find out more about our authors and books visit www.bloomsbury.com
and sign up for our newsletters.

Contents

Illustrations

Acknowledgements

The Universities of Cambridge and Roehampton have my gratitude for facilitating this research. I would also like to thank Katarzyna Marciniak, Project Lead of the ERC-funded *Our Mythical Childhood... The Reception of Classical Antiquity in Children's and Young Adult's Culture in Response to Regional and Global Challenges*, which has given me the opportunity to explore new avenues. Further appreciation to Frances Foster, Susan Deacy, and Caroline Bristow.

My thanks to Alice Wright and Lily Mac Mahon at Bloomsbury who have been kind supporters of this work; also to Alex Wright who got it off the ground and to the anonymous reviewer for their thoughtful observations.

Many thanks to Hans van Wees for inviting me to talk on this topic at the Institute of Classical Studies. Hats off to Antonia Forster, Louise Maguire, Bridget Martin, Blaithin nic Giolla Rua, Anastasia Bakogianni, Philip de Souza, Amy Smith and Kathryn Tempest for their support. Thanks go to my parents, John and Joan Nevin, with added tribute to their multiple marathons (and even more triathlons). And special thanks to my husband, Steve Simons, for his constant practical and moral support and not least for the drawings and maps in this volume.

Abbreviations

Aesch.	Aeschylus.
Aeschin.	Aeschines.
Apollod. *Bibl.*	Apollodorus, *Bibliotheca.*
Ars Amat.	Ovid, *The Art of Love.*
Ath.Pol.	Aristotle, *Constitution of the Athenians.*
BICS	*Bulletin of the Institute of Classical Studies*
BNJ	*Brill's New Jacoby*, ed. Ian Worthington, Brill 2007.
Dem.	Demosthenes.
Diod.Sic.	Diodorus of Sicily, *Library of History.*
Diog. Laer.	Diogenes Laertius.
Dion.Hal.	Dionysius of Halicarnassus, *Thucydides.*
Hdt.	Herodotus, *Histories.*
I.G.	*Inscriptiones Graecae.*
Isoc. *Paneg.*	Isocrates, *Panegyricus.*
Lucian, *Laps.*	Lucian, *A Slip of the Tongue in Salutation.*
M.L.	Meiggs and Lewis (1988).
Ovid, *Met.*	Ovid, *Metamorphoses.*
Paus.	Pausanias, *Guide to Greece.*
Plut.	Plutarch
Ages.	*Agesilaus.*
Arat.	*Aratus.*
Arist.	*Aristides.*
Cim.	*Cimon.*
De glor. Ath.	*Were the Athenians More Famous in Wisdom or War?*
Dem.	*Demosthenes.*
Mal. Hdt.	*On the Malice of Herodotus.*
Per.	*Pericles.*
Them.	*Themistocles.*
PT.	Persepolis Fortification Tablets.
Res.Gest.	*The Achievements of the Deified Augustus.*
Schol. Pi. Ol.	Scholiast on Pindar's *Olympian Odes.*

TAPhA	*Transactions and Proceedings of the American Philological Association*
Thuc.	Thucydides, *History of the Peloponnesian War*.
Xen.	Xenophon
Ages.	*Agesilaus*.
Ana.	*Anabasis*.
Cyro.	*On the Education of Cyrus*.
Hell.	*Hellenica*.

Introduction

A day of blood and fire

A Greek soldier shifts his weight uncomfortably. The tension mounts around him. He waits with his fellow-soldiers, men he has grown up with whom he knows from home. They are nervous too; nervous and excited. Suddenly there is movement. The enemy are active. Archers' bows go up. He can see their faces now – the enemy – the Greeks defending their land.

War is a messy business, not only in farms burned and people cut down, but in split loyalties and conflicting ideas of what doing the right thing means. When the Persian Empire sent an army to mainland Greece, that army included exiled Athenians and other Greeks who had lived in the Persian Empire for years. Greeks would fight Greeks alongside Persians, Medes and Sacae from Central Asia.

The name of 'Marathon' would echo down the ages. It would be recalled as much as a clash of ideologies and cultures as it was a struggle of strength and skill. Yet it was not the straightforward struggle it can easily be taken for. This volume will explore the circumstances that led to the battle, what happened on the day that blood flowed and ships burned, and the stories of the mortals, gods and heroes who took part. We will see how Marathon influenced the lives of those who fought, and how it was replayed in family stories, in monuments, on the stage, in speeches, paintings, histories and biographies, in pageants and propaganda, and how it lived on in every age that followed, not least in modern film and literature and in the running events which bear its name. We will see how the battle came to hold the monumental reputation that it has; how it was drawn-on to teach young people and adults the values they should hold and how they should behave. We will see that these values were varied, sometimes outright contradictory. Marathon shaped world culture, but not always in the ways that we might think it did. This is not a simple history of Marathon, but a look at a world of wondrous variety.

Herodotus

To enjoy ancient history is to come to terms with uncertainty. There are so many gaps. The period of the Graeco-Persian Wars, the early fifth century BCE, is no exception. Much is unknowable and yet this is a period about which far more can be known than about any previous era. New habits and a rapidly-emerging sense of the importance of the events that had taken place means that more information is available about these wars and what people thought of them in antiquity than for almost any earlier conflict. We turn now to meet Herodotus, the person who did more than anyone to shape the way these wars have been thought about over the last 2,500 years.

Why are things as they are? What happened in the past that made things as they are? What does this mean for how we should live our lives? Who and what should be remembered? Herodotus and other early Greek historians developed the new genre of writing – history-writing, historiography – in order to address these sorts of questions. Other thinkers were using observation and reasoning to analyse the world around them. Historians did the same for events. In Herodotus' work, *The Histories* – literally *The Enquiries* – he explains that he looked into what had happened in order to explain why Greeks and 'barbarians', that is, non-Greeks, fought each other and to keep their great deeds from being forgotten. It was a ground-breaking work.

Herodotus was a Greek born and brought up in Halicarnassus in Asia Minor. He lived *c.* 490–420 (all dates BCE unless stated). His parents were Lyxes and Dryo. It is probable that Herodotus left his hometown after a failed revolt against the city's tyrant. He travelled widely and lived for some time in Athens before heading to Greek Thurii in Italy. He made it his business to talk to people about the Graeco-Persian Wars – what they had seen themselves and what they had heard. Sometimes he recorded the different versions of events as they were told in different places. There is no absolute version of history, even in this early foray into a new genre. Herodotus wrote up his findings in a work that spans the origins of the Persian Empire through to the Greek campaigns following the defeat of a second Persian invasion in 480. *The Histories* is also anthropological, full of interest in the traditions of different cultures. And it is a deeply moral work, woven together in a way that expresses the importance of moderation and the destructive forces of excess and boundary-crossing, whether in nature, in private life or in the great game of politics. *The Histories* has had highs and lows in popularity but it never became a forgotten text. It has survived and had an impact on every generation.

To Herodotus' *Histories* we can add all sorts of other evidence about this age and this battle. We will explore the work of other ancient historians, of orators, philosophers and other great thinkers. And we will take in material culture – the objects ancient peoples left behind – from inscriptions ordered by Persian kings, to administrative records, pottery, sculpture and bodies. And yet so much comes back to Herodotus and for that reason he appears again and again throughout this work.

1

Athenians at a Turning Point

Athens before the Graeco-Persian Wars

The victory at Marathon boosted the Athenians' confidence in their new system of government – democracy. What had been happening in Athens before the battle? How did the battle come about? Like most city-states in the Greek world, Athens had been run for centuries by an oligarchy of leading families. These elite families dominated virtually all aspects of society, owning much of the land and holding appointments in law, religion and civic decision-making. Birth and wealth determined eligibility for numerous senior posts such as the archonships and membership of the powerful Council of the Areopagus. Freedom from manual labour created opportunities for the elite to focus on public life. Members of aristocratic families tended to inter-marry with each other and with the elite of other city-states, a practice which extended their networks of influence and which maintained a degree of difference from poorer members of their own communities.

There was a certain glamour attached to these power-broker families – the Alcmaeonids, the Cimonids, the Philaids, the Ceryces, the Praxiergidai, the Peisistratids and more. They often claimed descent from mythical heroes and they could wow people with displays born of their wealth and with possibilities of favour. This system had its positives, but it frequently ran into problems. While its ideal form had the most capable people working together for the good of the city, its worst meant wrangling for power between those who selfishly looked not to the city's good but to their own short-term gain. No wonder elite men occasionally pushed themselves forward hoping to set the agenda and cut out the arguments. And no wonder the people of cities run in this way frequently hoped someone might offer decisive leadership that put the city first. Enter Peisistratus.

Where many had tried and failed, Peisistratus established himself as sole ruler, tyrant, of Athens. For almost twenty years, Peisistratus steered the ship of state alone but for the advice of his sons and his guiding goddess, Athena. Athens prospered and the people, the *demos*, benefited from reforms in law and land ownership. Building projects provided employment, brought amenities and beautified the city. Athenian rule of Sigeum at the Hellespont was re-established. Festivals were enhanced. This is the era in which drama was developing as a new art-form, emerging from choral singing. Athenian pottery was in demand all over the Mediterranean. Philosophers were finding new ways to ask questions and find answers. It was an exciting time to be in Athens.

'Tyrant' was not a dirty word then. To be a *tyrannos* was simply to be a sole ruler outside a framework of royalty and kingship. Many had done it in other Greek states. Some had done so successfully, bringing a welcome cohesion to their city's affairs. Welcome to some that is. While members of the wealthy families might cooperate with a tyrant in order to avoid clashing head-on, that did not mean that they would not look for ways to regain power. At Athens, Peisistratus exiled Cimon, son of Stesagoras, from the great house of the Cimonids. Cimon's uncle, Miltiades, had been 'encouraged' to leave Athens and go as tyrant to the Chersonese.[1] It is likely that Cimon was expelled for showing dissatisfaction with Peisistratus' rule. It has been suggested that he was a little too ostentatious in his devotion to chariot-racing – an aristocratic pastime which won the sort of popularity that tyrants jealously guarded.[2] While in exile, Cimon's team won the chariot-race at the Olympic Games and he declared it Peisistratus' victory. Peisistratus was charmed by this display of good will and Cimon was allowed to return home. It was a tricky balancing act for all of them.

When the politically astute Peisistratus died, his sons, Hippias and Hipparchus, succeeded. They were well-schooled in the ways of the city and they must have known that there were those who longed to see them fall. Some men were killed or encouraged to leave. One family, the Alcmaeonids, were expelled *en masse*, though they never stopped looking for ways to return. Cimon's victory had charmed Peisistratus, but his offences still rankled with the sons, who had him murdered. Cimon's son, another Miltiades, served as archon under the Peisistratids, but it must have been easier all round when he too left Athens to join the family firm in the Chersonese. For about seventeen years the brothers ruled without incident, but in the sort of episode that came to give tyrants a bad name, things began to unravel. The story is known largely from the Greek historian, Thucydides.[3]

Each year the citizens of Athens honoured their protector, Athena, with a great festival, the Panathenaea. The most striking feature of the festival was a procession through the city and up to the acropolis, the site of the goddess' sanctuaries. Crowds gathered to watch. The city as represented through its people was on display: people of both sexes, all ages, citizens and resident non-Athenians. Each had specific roles. Some carried baskets, jugs or instruments of sacrifice, others led animals to the altar. Riders displayed their horses and skill. Ensuring that these sorts of public ritual roles were taken by members of distinguished families provided a pressure release. They could display themselves and relish the prestige of being included – still eminent in a city where they were no longer *pre*eminent.

How ill-timed then, that in 514, Hipparchus used this as an opportunity for score-settling. Used to getting his own way, Hipparchus took it badly when a young man of good family turned down his advances. Harmodius already had a lover. Harmodius and Aristogeiton were about to become as famous a couple as can be imagined. A handsome young man might have more than one lover in his youth, but whether for personal or political reasons, Harmodius refused to leave Aristogeiton for the more powerful Hipparchus. Incensed, Hipparchus saw to it that Harmodius' younger sister was disinvited from the procession. It was a colossal insult to the family. It implied that the girl was sullied in a way that would mean her participation would sully the city. Few would hear of it without assuming that she had been sexually active outside marriage, a taboo likely to prevent her from ever marrying and which would shame her relatives. There was shame in the implied accusation and shame in the exclusion from what should have been a prestigious occasion. In a society where honour was paramount, this was a hard blow. There was no cultural imperative to 'turn the other cheek'; on the contrary, there was an imperative to defend one's friends and harm one's enemies. Aristogeiton stood by his lover. On the day of the Panathenaea the two men struck Hipparchus down, stabbing him to death amidst the gorgeous trappings of the festival.

Harmodius was killed on the spot. Aristogeiton died later under torture. Hippias grew harsher after his brother's death. There were executions.[4] But if Hippias grew more wary, so did the people of Athens. No elite families could feel safe. They had seen with concern how leading figures might be murdered or exiled without recourse to their peers, just as Cimon had been cut down. Murder, confiscation of property, exile, public shaming – all of these were anathema to the Athenian elite. As Hippias tightened his grip, he lost control altogether. In 510, tired of his over-bearing rule and inspired by 'the tyrant-slayers', the Athenians drove Hippias and his family from the city.

The Athenians and the Spartans that is. The Spartans had a reputation as the foes of tyrants. They were one of the few states with enough clout to interfere directly in other cities' business. They did so from time to time to secure sympathetic allies who would help when help was needed. Herodotus heard that the powerful Alcmaeonids bribed the Delphic oracle to tell all Spartan delegates to 'liberate' the Athenians. Such a liberation would mean the family's return from exile.[5] The Spartans acted, sending a force to shift the Peisistratids. They may well have been prompted by news that Hippias had married his daughter to the son of the tyrant of Lampsacus; a union intended to establish links to Persia.[6] Hippias and his family took shelter on the acropolis. Their resistance came to nothing. When the Peisistratids tried to smuggle their children out, they fell into the hands of the Spartan army. Faced with losing the future of their house, the Peisistratids came to terms and agreed to go into exile.[7] The Spartans, perhaps remarkably, went home.

The age of tyrants at Athens looked to be over, but was it really over and what would replace it? The extraordinary thing in Athenian history is not that the tyrants fell – their dynasties rarely lasted more than a generation or two – but what replaced it. The Alcmaeonids returned, delighted with the result of their patient scheming. Men of great family pushed their way back into the centre of the action. But the Athenians did not revert to the jostling oligarchy of former days. Instead, in 508, Cleisthenes, head of the Alcmaeonids, proposed wide-ranging reforms to welcome the *demos* into the political decision-making machine.[8] It would not be easy. Another figure on the scene, Isagoras, urged return to the old constitution and persuaded the Spartans to bring about a coup (again) compelling the Alcmaeonids and 700 associated families to leave. But Isagoras pushed his luck. He tried to rule through a council of 300 followers. The people pushed back. The Spartan king, Cleomenes, and his small band were forced to leave, and the Alcmaeonids and their allies were back. Isagoras left with the Spartans and was subject to some awkward rumours about his wife and Cleomenes.[9] The reforms could begin.

Cleisthenes remodelled the citizen body into ten tribes (*phylai*), instead of the traditional four. Athenian territory, Attica, was divided into 139 areas known as demes (*demoi*, from *demos*). The Areopagus remained, but not as a ruling body. All citizen men could contribute to discussions in an Assembly, which focused on decisions about going to war, making peace and appointing magistrates. Most power lay with a Council of 500 men, fifty from each tribe. Each deme, that is each community in Attica, now had its own political representation. Demes registered citizens, managed deme finances, oversaw many legal matters and carried out cult activities together. The army would be organised by tribe, so that men who fought together were members of the same local community as well as sharing wider Athenian identity. Each tribe elected its own general (*strategos*).

When call-ups occurred, the Council would nominate tribes to fight and the tribes would look to their citizen lists. The new system opened up responsibilities and decision-making to a wider group than ever before. Many men could now take a role in decisions that affected their lives. Cleisthenes might have been named after his grandfather, the tyrant of Sicyon, but he carried out a social revolution which granted power, *kratos*, to the people, the *demos*. Athenian democracy was in.[10]

The reaction outside Athens was not enthusiastic. Despite having set this ball in motion, the Spartans resented the rejection of their man, Isagoras, and launched an attack. The Boeotians joined in from the north, as did the Chalcidians from Chalcis on Euboea. The Athenians were to join success in politics with success in war. The Spartans argued amongst themselves and went home, leaving the Boeotians and Chalcidians out on a limb. The indignant Athenians achieved an overwhelming victory against the Boeotians, killing many and taking 700 prisoner. Chalcis fared worse. The Athenians crossed over to Euboea and defeated them in battle. Instead of looting and taking prisoners for ransom before heading home, the Athenians never went home. In an extraordinary move, they killed or evicted the Chalcidian elite and settled a staggering 4,000 Athenians on their land.[11] Athenian democracy's first flex of its power was to defend itself, then act imperiously. Democracy was not seen as being at odds with conquest.

One more element of this is worth mentioning for its significant repercussions. Herodotus offers an interesting detail about when the Athenians expelled Cleomenes and the other Spartans. The Athenians were nervous straightaway. This was a serious insult to a serious military power; it automatically put them on war footing. The Athenians decided to do what most Greek states would do in that situation; that is, they turned to a powerful neighbour – Persia. The Persian Empire now reached as far as the eastern coast of the Aegean, where they had replaced the eastern Greeks' former overlords, the Lydians. The governor, or satrap, Artaphernes, managed the region on behalf of his brother, Great King Darius I. This was a neighbour wealthy, powerful and far away enough that they need not be intimidated by Sparta. No mainland Greek states could say as much. With that in mind, the Athenians sent representatives across the sea to the regional capital, Sardis. There they delivered a request for alliance with Persia. Artaphernes must have been in the area a while, but he had not yet heard of the state across the water which now appealed to him:

> He asked in reply who these Athenians were that sought an alliance with Persia, and in what part of the world they lived. Then, having been told, he put the

> Persian case in a nutshell by remarking that, if the Athenians would signify their submission by the usual gift of earth and water, then Darius would make a pact with them; otherwise they had better go home. Eager that the pact should be concluded, the envoys acted on their own initiative and accepted Artaphernes' terms – for which they were severely censured on their return to Athens.
>
> Herodotus, 5.73.

The Athenians understood the significance of presenting the symbolic items. Greeks had similar customs as a practical yet ritual sign of transfer in a world where few could read and documents were rare. The envoys will have been expected to present actual Athenian soil and water to Artaphernes. As there is no indication that they went expecting to make this submission, we should imagine them agreeing that they would present it, but unable to do so then and there. Whether envoys returned with them to Attica or they themselves promised to return to Sardis, the Athenian Assembly's angry response suggests that no such formal submission was ever made. It is easy to see how this looked to Artaphernes – a small community wanting help at no cost; making promises and throwing them back in his face; offering friendship, snatching it back; shilly-shallying wasting his time. Whether they meant to or not, the Athenians had insulted the Persian Empire.[12]

The Cimonids

What of the Cimonids all this while? While some of the extended family and their related kin, the Philaids, were surfing the ebb and flow in Athens, the main branch of the family were riding a different wave across the Aegean in the Chersonese. As Herodotus tells it, the elder Miltiades had been invited there by the local Dolonci tribe, who wanted help against their neighbours. The Peisistratids urged him to go. It got him out of Athens and extended Athenian influence into an important area – the peninsular where Europe meets Asia along the sea-route down from the grain-rich lands of the Black Sea, with access to metal and timber in nearby Thrace. As is often the way, the community that invited an outsider in got more than they bargained for. Their tyrant was here to stay. He nearly ruined things by attacking Lampsacus across the water, but another tyrant, Polycrates of Samos, got him out of prison. Miltiades invited his nephew, Stesagoras son of Cimon, to succeed him. He succeeded but was soon murdered.[13] It must have been with a degree of trepidation that the

Fig. 1 A Scythian horseman accompanied by the words 'Miltiades kalos' – 'Miltiades is beautiful'. Line drawing of a plate made in Athens *c.* 520–510 BCE, Ashmolean Museum, Oxford, AN1879.175.

younger Miltiades sailed with his followers and young family to succeed his brother.

Rather wonderfully, an artefact survives related to this event. A ceramic plate was commissioned to mark the occasion. Decorated in the vibrant new red-figure style, it features a Scythian archer atop a horse, surrounded by the words 'Miltiades kalos', 'Miltiades is beautiful', the standard phrase of appreciation amongst the elite. The archer is the kind of warrior that Miltiades would soon encounter in the Chersonese. The detail captured in the figure's zig-zagged trousers, neat jacket, full quiver and distinctive cap, displays the Athenians' keen interest in this sophisticated nomadic culture which was based in Thrace and beyond, covering territory including modern-day Romania, Ukraine and beyond to Russia and Kazakhstan.[14]

Miltiades was about thirty-five years old when he sailed to the Chersonese in 516. He travelled in a trireme, a warship – a sign that he meant business. His father had been murdered less than ten years before. Since then he had served as archon. He had married an Athenian woman and they had at least one son,

Metiochus. Miltiades' mission was to govern the area and keep it within Athenian influence. Whether his wife was still alive at this point is unclear. Either way, when he arrived he married again, forging an alliance by marrying the daughter of King Olorus of Thrace, who ruled a region in what is now Bulgaria. Approaches to marriage were quite flexible in this period, so it need not have been taken as an insult to either wife or their families if Miltiades married bigamously.[15] We know the name of his new wife – Hegesipyle – her Greek name an indication of the Thracian king's hellenic leanings. Miltiades and Hegesipyle would have two children, born in the Chersonese: Cimon, given a family name, and a daughter, Elpinice, whose name means 'hope of victory'. Growing up, Metiochus, Cimon and Elpinice would have been thrown together without the usual array of cousins to play with. It was not a typical Athenian upbringing, but it was nonetheless a Greek one. As well as being a culturally Greek household, there were those who had come from Athens with them and there were Greek communities nearby. As the children of the man in charge, it would have been a comfortable life, perhaps more so than if they had been in Athens. But from time to time, life could get a little too interesting.

Only a few years after Miltiades and Metiochus arrived, Greek and non-Greek territories along the Aegean coast began to be occupied by Persian forces. Around 513, King Darius himself oversaw the bridging of the Bosporus up the coast from the Chersonese. This was the start of a bid to conquer the Scythians. A fleet went up to the Danube and the army marched to meet it. Miltiades marched with them. Like tyrants from other cities and islands along the coast, Miltiades judged it prudent to comply with the wishes of the major power in the area. It is likely that he had hosted Persian envoys and given earth and water on behalf of the Chersonese. Herodotus tells us the story of the invasion.[16] Miltiades appears in it once Darius has crossed the Danube, leaving the Greek tyrants and their troops on its southern bank.[17] Some Scythians appear, encouraging the Greeks to destroy the bridge and leave the Persians stranded. Miltiades persuades the others that this is exactly what they should do, but at the last minute Histaeus, tyrant of Miletus, destroys their resolve. He warns the other tyrants that they will lose their positions if Darius falls – the cities will prefer this new system, democracy. The appeal to self-interest works. Miltiades finds himself outvoted and the Greeks wait for Darius. This story is told by Herodotus as a dramatic set-piece and it expresses the competing interests that were at work. Where should your priorities lie? With your ethnic group? With the people you gave an oath to? With your city? Yourself? The eastern Greek tyrants did indeed rely on Persian backing. Did Miltiades really argue for abandoning Darius? Something like that is impossible to know, but it is striking that this story exists at all, likely a tradition passed down within his family, keen to distance him from his Persian-friendly past.

Herodotus presents Darius speeding back after an unsuccessful mission, abandoning his sick and wounded. From a different perspective the campaign went well. Although they could not expand north of the Danube, Thrace to its south became a satrapy. Darius went home leaving behind an army which could protect mining operations and submit more communities. As time passed, Byzantium and islands near the Chersonese became Persian territory.[18] More disconcerting still will have been the news of Hippias marrying his daughter into the tyranny of Lampsacus, his long-term rivals.[19] This was a slap in the face from Miltiades' supposed supporter at home and a signal that Hippias was conceding Athenian interests in the region. As if that was not enough, around the same time, *c.* 510, when Metiochus was about ten, the family was driven off the peninsular by a Scythian raid, most likely a response to the Persian activity in Thrace.

Miltiades and his family had been in the Chersonese around five years at that point. They left for a while, then managed to return, but by then Hippias was out and the Athenians had insulted Persia, straining relations all round. It was around this time that Cimon and Elpinice were born. Curiously, Hippias was now nearby, living in Sigeum where his half-brother was tyrant.[20] He would go on to Persia. More unrest would follow. Between 499–494, the eastern Greeks attempted to expel the Persians in what is known as the Ionian Revolt, which we will see more of in Chapter 4. Miltiades used the beginning of the unrest as a springboard to attack nearby islands, Lemnos and Imbros.[21] There was historical bad feeling between the islanders and Athenians. The citizens of one city chose to leave; the others were besieged, defeated and occupied. The Persians will have wanted these islands for themselves, so there was conscious defiance in taking them. Miltiades had chosen not to remain a Persian agent. Time passed. The revolt along the coast had its successes but the situation was precarious, especially once there was news of the Persian fleet approaching – actually Phoenicians, the great sailors of the Near East. Sensing overwhelming odds, Miltiades arranged for his family and followers to leave on five ships. They made a desperate escape, pursued by the expert Phoenicians. Only four ships made it. Metiochus, now around twenty-seven, was in command of the fifth. His ship was captured and the others were forced to sail on in the knowledge that they could do nothing to help.

There were rather different outcomes for father and son. Against expectation, it was Miltiades who was sailing into danger. Herodotus records the outcome for Metiochus:

> The king, however, far from harming Metiochus, treated him with the greatest liberality: he presented him with a house and property, and a Persian wife by whom he had children, who lived as Persians.
>
> Herodotus, 6.41.

Miltiades, on the other hand, was put on trial for his life on a charge of tyranny. A tyrant he had certainly been, albeit one who ruled with a council.[22] His tyranny had once been acceptable. The Athenians had sent him there, he had inherited the position, and after a bumpy start the Dolonci seem to have accepted him. But things had changed in his absence. Tyranny was now profoundly out of vogue in Athens and some things had stayed enough the same that there will have been rival families who were less than pleased to have an old enemy stride back into town. That Metiochus had essentially become an honorary Persian cannot have helped, especially combined with Miltiades' service with the Persians years earlier. Still, the knowledge that Hippias had had Miltiades' father murdered may have balanced out suspicions about his loyalty and there was no doubt that he had fled the Persian advance. It is hard to be sure how sincere the charges were, but the trial was real enough and it must have come as a great relief to Miltiades and his supporters when he was acquitted. In a striking twist of fortune, his tribe then elected him their general. He was now in his late fifties. His eldest son had just been lost to him and he was back in a city that had changed enormously since his youth.

Not shy of controversy, Miltiades soon clashed with the archon, Themistocles. Both opposed Persian expansion into Greece, but Themistocles was playing the long game, beginning walls at Piraeus, the future harbour, and arguing for investment in the fleet to lean Athens towards sea over land. *Not quick enough*, Miltiades argued, *the Persians will be coming any time now. The walls will not be finished and, besides, walls have never kept the Persians out. When they come, we must be prepared to fight*. Miltiades won the argument. Themistocles was in the political wilderness for several years.[23] For now, the Athenians were on notice that trouble was coming.

Why have we spent so much time with the Cimonids? The answer is that no family was more involved in the Battle of Marathon and its legacy and no family's involvement with it was more intriguing. Their relationship with Athens is extraordinary and adds a satisfying complexity to the picture. For Miltiades, the trial was a wake-up call that his situation was precarious. His ancestry, wealth, experience and perhaps his charisma and ability made him a leading figure, but that could be snatched away at a moment's notice. Whether or not Hegesipyle was still alive and returned with him is unclear, perhaps unlikely. If she did, what a welcome to a new land! The same might be said for Cimon and Elpinice. Now in their teens, they had just experienced the loss of their home and their brother. We must imagine them at home anxiously awaiting the outcome of their father's trial and the relief of the verdict. Had he been executed it would have meant disaster for them all. They had fled to Athens, but it had yet to prove safe.

Wider society

Greece was a relatively poor country; a small land divided into smaller communities, mountainous, with a low percentage of land available for cultivation. There were few prospects of widespread enrichment and even those who did inherit or accumulate wealth were not wealthy by comparison with the elite of Egypt or Persia. Thucydides would later have a Corinthian voice the opinion that Athenians had a great love of novelty.[24] What could be more novel than goods which had travelled many miles to reach Athens? Products and motifs from the south and east had long carried a certain cache and still did in the early years of the fifth century.[25] There was interest in Persia and its people. The earliest surviving image of a Persian in Greek pottery dates from *c.* 520. It depicts a satrap or perhaps the Great King himself, seated, attired in the intriguing turban and trousers of the east.[26]

The Athenians, like other Greeks, lived in a world rich in the supernatural – nymphs inhabiting pools, heroes presiding over land around their graves, deities taking an interest in human activities when they cared to – pleased to see performances and material works of art. Religious activity accompanied all aspects of life. Frequent festivals offered opportunities for singing, dancing, spectacle and a feeling of belonging. Animal sacrifices were made on behalf of the whole community, or one's tribe, deme or household. Offerings of other foodstuffs or libations – liquid offerings of wine, milk and honey – were made on all manner of occasions. No serious decision was made without divination – interpreting omens. There were sceptics. It had already been observed that people imagined gods like themselves much as a horse might imagine a horse god. Some took their scepticism further, but these were a tiny minority.[27] It was widely and thoroughly accepted that the divine was a real and present actor in human lives. Priests and priestesses were not a special class. Many people could serve in those roles, often for only a set time rather than for life, and anyone could make a sacrifice or offer their opinion on an omen, whether it was the look of a liver, a dream, a sneeze, a rainbow, an oracle from a sanctuary, a bird, a chance word or anything that seemed like it might have more to it than met the eye. And if the gods noticed dance and song, of course they noticed battle – where human struggle was laid bare in raw form; a struggle for life and death. Every Greek had heard how the gods had watched the war at Troy. Euripides would later describe blood flowing from warriors' wounds as 'The chill, gory libation offered by Ares/Received as his due by the god of the dead'.[28]

Violence was familiar. The communal aspect of sacrifice meant that people were not shielded from the origin of the meat they ate; they saw the throat cut and the blood flow. Those with means enjoyed hunting. Bloodsports were popular, especially cock-fighting. It was a slave-owning society. Slaves' bodies were not their own and could be raped and beaten without recourse. Wives and children could be struck. It must also be said, however, that by the standard of the time Athenian society was not particularly violent. A complex legal system controlled violence between free men and against women by men who were not related to them. The Athenians were proud that it was not their custom to carry weapons in the street or at meetings – a practice they considered rather vulgar. Nonetheless, violence was commonplace. War was a frequent feature of life. Unlike many modern societies, Athenians and other Greeks lived in communities where most men had killed someone, albeit someone from outside the community.

As is typical, the Athenians had most experience of fighting their neighbours. Veterans in this period might have fought their enemies across the water on Aegina, or been north to clash with the Boeotians. Some might have fought the Spartans. Then again, some might have been further afield, fighting the Mytilenians for control of Sigeum or making money as mercenaries in the armies of the wealthier kingdoms round-about. Campaigns typically took place in spring and summer. They were frequently border disputes and they were a valuable opportunity for looting – the descendent of an older raiding culture. War was conducted by unwritten but widely acknowledged norms around the declaration of war, the treatment of heralds and of the dead, and the avoidance of the sacred spaces of the enemy.[29] But as the rules were unwritten and ownership of territory disputed, there were often differing opinions on whether or not these rules had been followed. The development of history-writing and drama would soon change people's relationship with the morality of warfare. Stories that had once been told only within the community or sent as accusations delivered by heralds could now be dwelt on and articulated with new clarity and shared with a wider audience. The Graeco-Persian Wars are remarkable precisely because we can see the ancient Greeks reflecting on what happened.

The star of the Athenian military in the Marathon era was the hoplite soldier. The hoplite was a heavy infantryman. There was no uniform or state provision; people wore what they preferred and could afford. The hoplite's most distinctive piece of kit was his heavy wooden shield, typically made of ash and built with an interior strap for the forearm and handle at the rim. These features made it responsive and helped the bearer to take its weight. That said, in this period one might still find the occasional use of a Boeotian shield, with a figure-of-eight shape and the same strap and rim-handle on the interior. Some carried their shield in combination with a metal bell cuirass protecting the body, but these were not universal.[30] The shield provided so much protection that a lighter yet still-effective linen or leather corselet was usually preferred. These would be made by women of the fighter's family, laying layer-upon-layer of fabric. They were easier to move in and not so hot. Based on the number of them dedicated

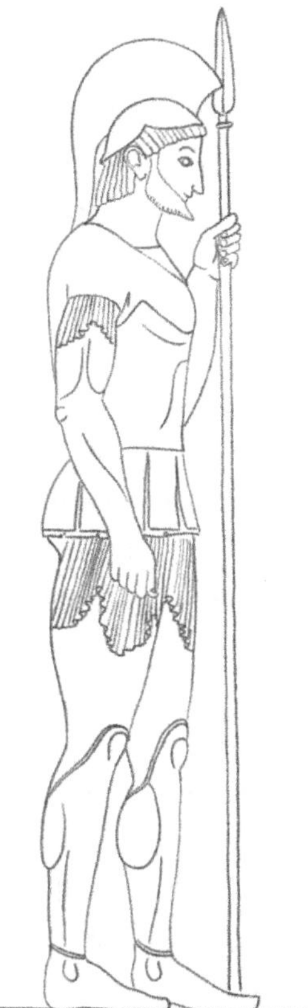

Fig. 2 Line drawing of the Aristion Stele, depicting Aristion as a warrior. Found near Marathon. Made by Aristocles *c.* 510 BCE. National Museum of Athens, 29. A copy now stands on the Marathon Plain.

in sanctuaries, around one in three hoplites wore greaves. They added weight but were useful against arrows or a low-swipe from a blade. The head was typically protected by the iconic Corinthian helmet. These were beaten from a single piece of metal. They protected the face as well as the cranium and they looked fantastic. The primary hoplite weapon was a heavy thrusting spear. A pair of lighter spears might be preferred, useful for thrusting and for throwing. To these one might add back-up swords and daggers according to individual choice.

The weight of this equipment has been much debated. Estimates range from *c.* 30–15kg. Some imagine that hoplites could hardly manoeuvre in their armour, but this is surely an exaggeration even if we picture the man who chooses to wear heavy versions of all the kit. Running in armour is unlikely to have taken off as a sporting event, as it did, if the competitors were passing out after a few meters.[31] Then there were those who were even less heavily armed. The hoplite gets all the glory, but there were also those who had little or no armour, light or no shields, who fought primarily with light spears or simple projectiles. In the Classical period, these fighters were gradually excluded but in the era of the Graeco-Persian Wars they were still very much part of the scene.[32]

There were no specialist units of archers or cavalry. These would be adopted later, but again, at this stage things were less formally organised. The same can be said of the phalanx – the fighting unit. These would become more organised into formal ranks and rows in the Classical period, but this was some way off. Instead, picture an irregular crowd of light and heavy infantry spread out in a wide line. Only the first couple of men at the front can engage, reaching and stabbing with their spears while keeping as much behind their shields as possible.[33] Here and there someone with a sling or a throwing spear rises between the infantrymen to release a projectile. The men behind the front-fighters provide physical and moral support, but they are not shoving them forward.[34] When a man is killed, wounded or exhausted, someone behind him will step forward to take his place – hopefully – otherwise this could be the beginning of a rout. The rout is the most dangerous part of the battle for the defeated side. Momentum and cohesion are lost, panic has set in and men can be picked off as they try to flee. These are not professional soldiers. Little in the way of training happens. Precise group manoeuvres are impossible. But these men are tough; born and raised in a culture that values skill and bravery in war, fighting for gain or to stave off disaster. And besides, the gods are watching. If you are fortunate, they will help you. If not, it could be your blood that provides 'the chill, gory libation offered by Ares/Received as his due by the god of the dead'.

2

The Greek World

On being Greek

Ancient Greek culture developed on the islands as well as the mainland. At the time of Marathon, Greek communities could be found all over the Mediterranean, in places to the west such as Emporium in modern Spain, Naples in Italy, in the east down the coast of what is now Turkey, to the north around the Black Sea and to the south at Cyrene in Libya. These settlements had been thriving for several hundred years. The eighth century in particular had seen cities launching groups of energetic citizens, keen to lay hold of land and opportunity. As far and wide as these people settled, they continued to regard themselves as Greek and acknowledged in each other a shared identity. What made someone 'Greek in this period?[1]

If you had asked an ancient Greek of the Archaic period, they are likely to have answered with some of the things that Greeks thought of themselves as having in common, such as shared blood (i.e. descent), shared language, customs and gods. This might be called an 'aggregate identity', comprised of things that have been added together. In time, many Greeks would develop an increasingly 'oppositional identity' – the sort of identity defined by reference to another group of people, saying 'we are not like them'; but that is a matter for later on.

The Greeks – or to use the term that they used themselves, the Hellenes – thought of themselves as descendants of Hellanus, the son of Deucalion. Deucalion was the man who survived the Great Flood, a myth that is better known through its biblical version, Noah's Ark. This shared mythical ancestor bestowed a sense of kinship. The Greeks knew that they were not all the same, however, and the tension between sameness and difference was expressed through perceived tribal groups. The tribes were thought of as descendants of the various sons and grandsons of Hellanus: The Aeolians from Aeolis, Dorians from Doros, Ionians and Achaeans from grandsons Ion and Aeachus and so on. The Spartans were Dorians, the Athenians Ionians, but both recognised each other as fellow-Greeks.

Language was another unifier. Wherever they lived, Greeks spoke Greek. That gave them a practical bond which facilitated trade and cooperation. That said, there was again difference within unity. All Greeks spoke a language that was descended from early or 'proto' Greek, but that language had morphed in different ways, resulting in numerous dialects. These were a component of tribal identity. Aeolians spoke Aeolic or Arcado-Cypriot Greek, Ionians spoke versions of Attic-Ionic Greek, and many other forms of Greek fell into what can be termed the Western Greek language family.[2] Nonetheless, speakers of different versions of Greek could readily understand each other. Many Greeks will also have spoken additional non-Greek languages, particularly in areas with a lot of interaction between communities and where the mother of the household was non-Greek. While the mythology of shared descent was important, many Greeks had Carian, Lydian, Samnite mothers or Thracian mothers – as Cimon son of Miltiades had.

Shared custom reinforced shared identity. Custom is a vague phenomenon that is easily identifiable and yet so full of variation that it can seem to collapse as a concept. Some customs were shared all over the Greek world. Households had a similar structure. Cities had similar features, including an agora, the market-place, where items were exchanged, workers recruited and news and ideas shared. Pastimes and clothing were similar, albeit with a degree of local preference. All Greek communities were slave-owning and all of them very patriarchal. Forms of agriculture, whether arable or pastoral, were recognisable across Greek communities. Other forms of production were also done in similar ways, from weaving to pottery, with certain 'Greek' shapes recognisable.

All Greek communities valued skill in warfare. There were shared practices for ravaging landscapes, sea-raids, pitched land battles, declarations of war and the arranging of peace treaties. Not all Greeks fought the same way. The Thessalians, with their broad plains, were famed cavalrymen when most Greeks had little or no cavalry at all. Different communities placed more or less emphasis on projectiles, although it is fair to say that where they were used, these tended to be stones rather than bow-and-arrow. The Spartans are famous for their dedication to war, but it is easy for this idea to get out of hand. They did revere military skill and focus their education on it, but even in antiquity it was noted that their difference came from the amount of training that they did. They were not super-soldiers and by modern military standards they were still rather amateur. The famous heavy infantry kit, the hoplite panoply, was widely used in the Greek world. As such it became a shared custom, but we should not put too much store in this as an expression of Greekness. It was a custom shared by neighbouring cultures and Herodotus actually tells us that the Greeks adopted it from the Carians. When Greek hoplites served abroad as mercenaries, they were useful because they added more heavy infantry, not because they were the only heavy infantry on the market.[3]

The seasons and their agricultural tasks drove the rhythm of the year and with that came the rhythm of festivals. Worship of shared gods meant a whole host of shared customs, rituals and a shared way of looking at the world. The epic poems *The Iliad* and *The Odyssey* created a shared vision of the gods, not priestly texts. These key works featuring the war at Troy and Odysseus' long return also offered shared values and a shared core myth. Greeks shared the idea that gods might take interest in human activities and delight in human performance. There was also a shared idea that gods liked to see moral behaviour from mortals, even if the gods themselves could behave as they liked. Gods might punish humans for their wrongdoing, but it was unpredictable. Punishment might be delayed and fall on a wrongdoer's descendants.

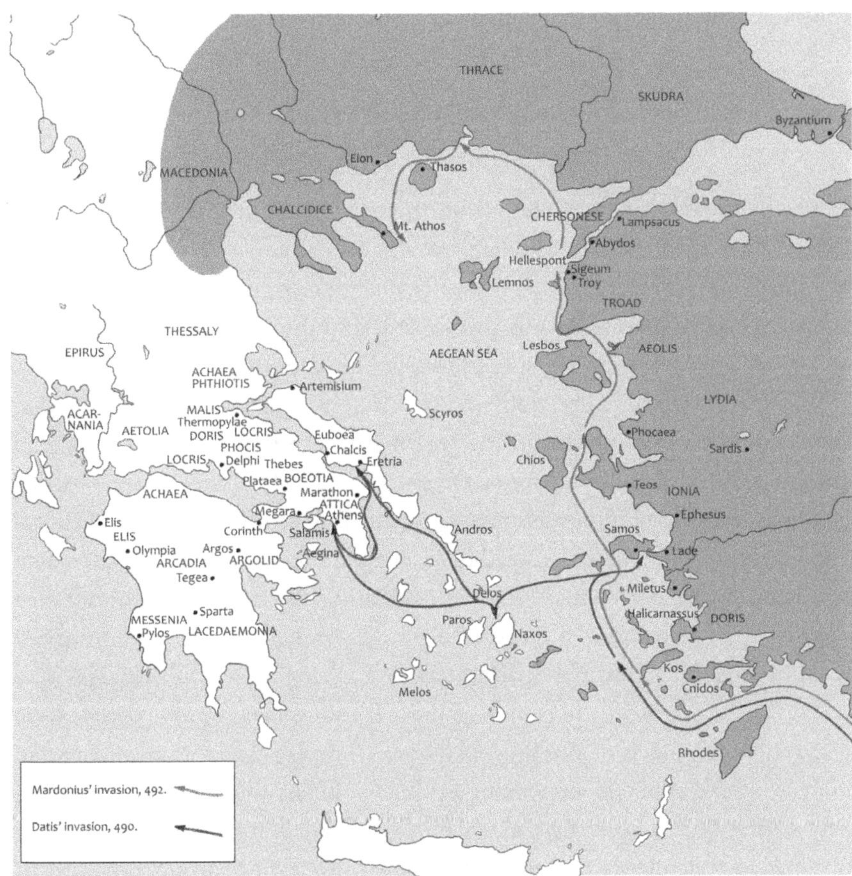

Fig. 3 Greece, the Aegean and Western Asia Minor.

As well as local sanctuaries, there were regional ones, shared sites of worship and display. These included the sanctuary of Artemis and Apollo on Delos, open to all Greeks but mostly attended by Aegean islanders and Athenians. There was the Panionium in Asia Minor attended by Ionians. And then there were the panhellenic sanctuaries. All Greek communities valued success in the games there. The big four were the sanctuaries of Zeus at Olympia and Nemea, of Poseidon at Isthmia and of Apollo at Delphi. Open all year, they really came into their own at festival time. When the sacrifices took place, when athletes performed and the spectacles were seen, festival-goers were actively doing something as part of a 'Greek' community; for a time they were actively part of something bigger than their local state or their tribe. Different dialects, different political systems, different levels of patience with intellectual debate, even different versions of the same gods – there was a lot that fed into the sometimes bitter divisions between Greek communities. Nonetheless, there was still a recognisable Greekness that enabled Greeks to acknowledge shared bonds between them.

Life in Sparta

Athens is the capital of modern Greece; around one in three inhabitants of Greece lives there. Athens' modern dominance makes it challenging to 'un-imagine' its importance, yet that is exactly what must be done when considering Archaic Greece. Athens was not always central to the Greek experience. In the era of the Graeco-Persian Wars, Sparta was indisputably the most powerful state.

The Spartans lived in the southern Peloponnese, with Mt Taygetos rising into the sky on the western horizon. The region around Sparta is Lacedaemonia; in ancient texts the Spartans are frequently referred to as 'the Lacedaemonians'. The Spartans' social revolution was long past by the fifth century. The semi-mythical Lycurgus was said to have designed their constitution, establishing Spartan men as equals, forming a council of elders, initiating the *agoge* – the communal upbringing of male children, and creating the dual kingship – one each from two royal households.[4] Those in Spartan territory who were not full citizens were known as the *perioikoi*, the people who dwell round-about. These people were responsible for much of the manual labour. They also supported the Spartan military as servants and sometimes as fighters. Below them in status were the helots, Messenian Greeks held as a slave population whose agricultural labour the Spartans relentlessly exploited. This hierarchy left the Spartans free to focus on other matters, such as hunting, athletics, military training and politics. They had established a series of alliances (now known as the Peloponnesian League) with several communities such as the Tegeans and Eleans. This was an unequal alliance in which the Spartans could call on the allies for military help; in exchange they supported more or less broad oligarchies in those allies' cities.

Spartan life has a reputation for grim austerity. To a degree this is fair, but inevitably it is much exaggerated. Friends and foes of Sparta alike have enjoyed telling tall stories about its horrors, creating what is now known as 'the Spartan mirage'. True, men and boys ate communally for the most part rather than at home, coinage was disallowed and the beautiful architecture of Athens was not seen in Sparta. But military service was required in other states too, the exposure of unwanted babies happened across the Greek world and beyond, and life in Sparta had its pleasant aspects. Like elsewhere, there was a culture of athletics and games. Spartan women seem to have had more freedom and property rights than those in other states. There was a fine tradition of dancing and singing by choirs of men, boys and girls. The move from wooden to stone temples happened at the same time as it did elsewhere in Greece despite the expense. There was also no shortage of well-crafted items amongst the Spartans, as indicated by offerings left in those sanctuaries. These include beautifully-carved ivories, when ivory was purely an imported material. Lead figurines dedicated throughout the seventh and sixth centuries include eastern-style winged goddesses indicative of the Spartans' contact with the east. Masks dedicated at these same sites suggest the influence of Phoenician religion and other Near Eastern cultures. Perhaps even more tellingly, fine pottery has been found which suggests that while the communal meals were frugal, family meals based around cult activities could be rather more opulent. Some of this pottery depicts people in Lydian clothing, demonstrating knowledge of the customs of that kingdom. It was not all gruel and chilblains in Sparta.[5]

That said, despite their absorption of Near Eastern goods and ideas, the Spartans had been on-notice about the possibility of Persian aggression from the 540s and they had been quite consistently anti-Persian in their response. Cultural exchange is one thing; conquest is another. The Spartans joined a loose defensive alliance with Lydia, Egypt and the island of Samos. When the Persians approached Asia Minor, the Spartans sent a message ordering them to leave the Greeks alone, although they did not venture forth when the message was ignored. That changed in 525. When the Persians conquered Egypt, Samos submitted to Persia. The Spartans responded this time, encouraged by Samian exiles. They attacked Samos, but failed to oust the island's pro-Persian tyrant.[6] The Spartans had more success in 517 expelling a pro-Persian tyrant from the island of Naxos, near

Delos. They installed an oligarchy of elite locals in his place as was their usual custom. This was followed by the events we have seen in Athens: the Spartans heard that Hippias had sacrificed Miltiades to pro-Persian interests and at the first hint of encouragement they ousted Hippias. Their relationship with the Athenians went sour pretty quickly, but the removal of the tyrant was characteristic. This also explains why we see them back in Attica when the new democracy approached Persia, then backing off once that negotiation stalled. The Spartans then attacked their enemies at Argos, probably in response to the Argives' friendliness with Persia. They hit them so hard that it was said the city survived only because the poet Telesilla persuaded Argive women to dress as soldiers and defend the walls.[7] In 491, the year before Marathon, the Spartans went as far as to execute Persian heralds requesting earth and water. They then promptly attacked their former ally, the island of Aegina, when Aegina offered its support (and ships) to Persia.[8] This was some fifty years of push-back against Greeks siding with Persia.

Through all of this, the double kingship was going through a rough patch. The kings at the time were Cleomenes of the senior Agiad house and Demaratus of the junior Eurypontids. The dual kingship worked much of the time, but it was vulnerable to personality clashes. Cleomenes and Demaratus both had big personalities, so there was potential for explosive trouble. Trouble came when the two kings campaigned against Athens' new democracy. Cleomenes had felt the burn of the insult when the Athenians had essentially thrown him out. He returned with the army to teach the Athenians a lesson. The problem was that this was not a sound reason for a war. The allies demurred and King Demaratus agreed with them. An angry and public quarrel ensued. This was not the clear, determined leadership that the Spartans prided themselves on. The campaign collapsed and everyone went home. Back in Sparta, the council determined that from now on, only *one* king would go on campaign at a time.[9]

This was an unprecedented breach. It is likely that behind it lay a more fundamental difference of opinion on foreign policy. The rift deepened under the stress of developing circumstances. The Spartans were approached by more communities attempting to draw them into their conflicts. According to Herodotus, once Cleomenes was dead, the Spartans said that he had died because he had learned to drink his wine neat under the influence of visiting Scythians (the Greeks drank their wine heavily watered).[10] These Scythians were planning to attack the Persian homelands from the north and they urged the Spartans to head east and meet them. It is likely that these are the same Scythians who drove Miltiades out of the Chersonese briefly. It is also likely these Scythians came at the same time as another important visitor: Aristagoras of Miletus arrived, urging the Spartans to join in a conflict in Asia Minor.[11] His plan was very similar to the Scythians' and he offered riches to sweeten the deal. The Spartans stayed at home on that occasion. Anti-Persian feeling was one thing. Heading across the Aegean for war was quite another, especially after the embarrassing failure on Samos.

The difference in policy was confirmed when nearby Aegina submitted to Persia in 491. Athens requested that action be taken. Cleomenes tried to oblige. Demaratus foiled it.[12] Two kings. Two policies. It was unsustainable. Cleomenes seems to have been quite widely disliked – a strange man who could be aggressive.[13] But enough people must have shared his views on Persia inching closer. They were all too ready to agree when Cleomenes began saying that Demaratus was actually born illegitimate and should never have been king at all. The Spartans consulted Delphi. Delphi confirmed Demaratus as illegitimate and the Spartans dethroned him.[14] Demaratus made a run for it and, like Hippias before him, settled in Persia, where he was welcomed at court. As Cleomenes had planned, Demaratus was succeeded by one Leotychides, a senior member of the Eurypontids with a grudge against Demaratus.[15] So it was that in 491, Leotychides became King Leotychides II. By 490, Cleomenes was dead.[16] He was succeeded by his half-brother, Leonidas, of Thermopylae fame. It was a turbulent time at the top in Sparta. Cleomenes had maintained the anti-Persian position. What Leonidas and Leotychides would do was still to be seen.

Life in Boeotia

North of Attica was Boeotia and, to the east, the island of Euboea. Beyond Boeotia were still more Greek states, but it is Boeotia and Euboea which have a particular bearing on the Marathon campaign. There were several cities in Boeotia. The largest were Orchomenos and Thebes, separated by Lake Copais. Smaller players Plataea, Thespiae and Tanagra were also Boeotian. The region's cohesion was boosted by shared ethnicity (Aeolian), a shared dialect (Aeolic) and shared cults and festivals. There were several impressive sanctuaries in the region. At the oracle of Trophonius in Lebadia, questioners ventured into underground caves and were washed out by streams to obtain insights from the divine. To the west of Thebes there was a cult of the Cabiri, brought to Boeotia from Asia, probably in the eighth century.[17]

Boeotia had its claims to fame, not least the poet Hesiod, creator of *Works and Days* and *Theogony*. Thebes had a particularly rich role in mythology of panhellenic significance. It was the traditional birthplace of Heracles and Oedipus. The story of Oedipus – cast-out as a baby only to return with ... consequences, unfolds in Thebes, as do the myths of his children – Eteocles, Polyneices and Antigone.[18] Polyneices campaigned against Thebes with six of the greatest heroes from across Greece, battling to expel his brother. This campaign, the Seven against Thebes, was a hugely celebrated myth that fostered panhellenism in a similar way to the myths of the Trojan War. Boeotia had its own Trojan War connection too. The expedition was said to have set sail from Aulis on the coast following the grisly sacrifice of Agamemnon's daughter.

A Boeotian Confederacy had existed since at least the late sixth century. This enabled cooperation between the oligarchies of the Boeotian cities. It was not an equal confederacy. Thebes was the major power in the sixth and fifth centuries and from time to time they were considered overbearing, inevitably leading to conflict. It was not for nothing that the plains of Boeotia were known as the 'dancing floor of Ares'. In the late sixth century, Plataea so resented Thebes that when Cleomenes was in the area the Plataeans requested to become Spartan allies. Cleomenes, then unconcerned about Athens' power, told the Plataeans that they would be better off with the Athenians as they were closer. The Plataeans took his advice and were accepted by the Athenians as allies. The Thebans responded predictably with an invasion, but the Corinthians stepped in to arbitrate.[19]

As Athenian allies, the Plataeans maintained an uneasy stand-off with the Thebans. The alliance exacerbated an already tense atmosphere between Athens and Boeotia. As neighbours they had often looked enviously on one another's lands. Borders frequently shifted. When Cleomenes came with Demaratus to attack the Athenians, the Boeotians eagerly supported him. As we have seen, the Spartans then abandoned the campaign, leaving the Boeotians and Chalcidians to absorb the Athenians' vengeance. Chalcis fared worst, its land occupied. Euboea had a long history of strife between Chalcis and Eretria, its two great cities. In the end it was not *that* war which ruined Chalcis but the Athenians' devastating attack. The Eretrians must have been delighted.

Ionia

By now we have had several encounters with the territory across the Aegean from mainland Greece, Asia Minor. By 500 there had been Greeks settled along that coast for hundreds of years. The region could be divided into sub-regions. Miltiades had been in the Chersonese on the European side of the Hellespont.

Across the water, into Asia, was the Troad. South of that was Aeolia. The mid-coastal region below that was Ionia, and the southerly section, Doris. To the east of Ionia was wealthy, non-Greek Lydia. East of southerly Doris was non-Greek Caria. All the Greek areas of the coast might be rolled into the term 'Ionia', even if strictly speaking that was only part of it. There were many vibrant cities, such as Smyrna, Ephesus, Magnesia, Halicarnassus and Miletus – 'the Versailles of Ionia', the greatest city of the region.[20] There had been Greeks at Miletus for over 500 years and though once a colony itself, it had since sent out its own colonists to found cities around the Black Sea.

The Greeks told each other that these areas had been settled by Greeks from different tribes; Aeolia by the Aeolians, Ionia Ionians and Doris Dorians. Naturally the reality of settlement was messier than the rhetoric. These relationships are more usefully thought of as a projection into the past rather than a memory of long ago. All the tribal groups were represented in Asia Minor creating a cosmopolitan mix. It was easier for people from different Greek backgrounds to marry there. Marriage between Greek men and Lydian or Carian women was also extremely common.[21]

Since the seventh century, things had been booming in Asia Minor. There was trade to be done with the Greek mainland and with major islands nearby – Samos, Chios, Lemnos, Lesbos and Rhodes – and still more to be done with the wealthy kingdoms round-about. There were the Lydians to the east and the Medes beyond them, the Egyptians to the south, Thracians to the north, the Neo-Babylonians from Babylon to Damascus and the Elamites and Persians east of them. There was work as mercenaries in the armies of these rival kingdoms. Trade brought wealth and the exchange of goods and ideas. The Greeks in Asia were uniquely placed to engage with the cultures of the Near East as well as with their fellow-Greeks.

The Greeks of Asia were famous for their intellectual pursuits. This was where *The Iliad* and *The Odyssey* developed.[22] While these epics became definitive Greek works, the influence of works from further east, particularly the Babylonian *Epic of Gilgamesh*, has long been recognised.[23] The Greeks were interested in the differences and similarities between themselves and their non-Greek neighbours. It is entirely consistent that our main correspondent was a man from this area – Herodotus of Halicarnassus. He was an original writer, yet he developed his work from a tradition of ethnographic writing that had emerged in the sixth century, exploring what non-Greeks were like and why they did what they did. This intellectual endeavour was fed by the impressive philosophical, scientific tradition of the Greeks in Asia Minor, which valued observation and recording.

That in itself had been nourished by the scientific traditions of Babylonia. The grand temple architecture of Asia Minor has led to the suspicion that the eastern Greeks meant to impress their non-Greek neighbours and to demonstrate their distinctive Greekness, yet other aspects of material culture show their use of items from across the Near Eastern world. Even the famous Temple of Artemis at Ephesus had a many-breasted statue of the goddess that looked rather un-Greek and more akin to Anatolian deities such as Cybele.[24]

The wealth, opportunity and ideas bubbling away in Asia Minor made it an attractive centre to interact with. Seventh and sixth-century Athenians had been keen to foreground their Ionian identity, naturalising close links with Ionians (and others) in the east. As we have seen, the Peisistratids were keen to hold land on that side of the water. They were involved in the Cimonids' occupation of the Chersonese, they re-established Athenian rule at Sigeum and they forged links with nearby Lampsacus. Beyond the tyrant's family, many Athenian men will have had links with the Ionian cities and visited for trade and other business.[25]

Lydia

Life in the Greek cities of Asia meant some degree of familiarity with Lydia. This kingdom was ruled by the Mermnad dynasty between *c.* 700–546 from its capital, Sardis. Lydia covered much of the Anatolian plain, up to the Halys River in the east. Although different from Greek, its language was an Indo-European one, as Greek was, meaning that it was not a huge leap for people in either community to learn the other's tongue. Lydian religion had similarities with Greek practice – sacrifice, dedications, festivals, oracles and in the conception of deities. The Lydians' main deity, Cybele, was descended from the Hittite Great Mother figure and Lydians and Greeks saw similarities between her and Aphrodite or – as in Ephesus – Artemis.

Lydia was a famously wealthy kingdom. Its wealth came from two pieces of good fortune: trade and tax opportunities from the roads connecting the coast and the Anatolian interior, and the Pactolus River – a source of gold. No wonder this area was thought to be the home of the mythical King Midas of the Golden Touch.[26] With its access to precious metal, its oversight of trade and its need to pay diverse people for a variety of services, Lydia was the natural place for a huge cultural innovation – coinage. The first gold, silver and electrum coins were minted in Lydia and the Greeks were quick to pick up the habit.

The last king of Lydia was Croesus, whose fabulous wealth gave us the expression 'as rich as Croesus'. Previous generations of Lydian kings had compelled a handful of Ionian cities to pay tribute. Cyme, Smyrna and Ephesus moved in and out of Lydian control, although the much-sought Miletus escaped them. Under Croesus that control expanded until almost all of the eastern Greek cities became tribute-paying. While the initial conflict and sieges must have been terrifying, the transition into empire was otherwise uneventful. The cities maintained their basic independence. Croesus did not install garrisons or interfere in governance. Cities with oligarchies retained their oligarchies; cities with tyrants kept their tyrants. Indeed, the lifestyle of the Ionian tyrants was essentially modelled on the Lydian court.[27]

Ionian culture had many Lydian elements and Lydian culture adopted aspects of Greekness. Croesus himself had a half-Greek brother with an Ionian mother, while Croesus' own mother was Carian.[28] The brothers competed for the throne and the fact that Lydia could have had a half-Greek king gives a good sense of the permeability between communities. The Lydian kings were known for making dedications at Greek sanctuaries. Croesus made dedications at the two major sanctuaries in Ionia: that of Apollo at Didyma near Miletus and that of Artemis at Ephesus – one of the wonders of the ancient world. More remarkably, Croesus sent dedications to the Greek mainland – to a shrine in Boeotia dedicated to one of the Seven against Thebes and to the most important sanctuary in the Greek world, that of Apollo at Delphi.[29]

Croesus' interactions with Delphi were intricately related by Herodotus, his story offering one of the most memorable twists in his history.[30] Croesus had been king for about ten years when Persia began to expand. Herodotus tells us that in order to deal with this new threat Croesus consulted the Greek oracles. Typically this would be regarded as a good move, but Herodotus tells us that beforehand Croesus tested the oracles: pragmatic or hubristic depending on your point-of-view. All of this heralded trouble. Delphi apparently gave a satisfactory response, so it was to them that Croesus appealed for advice on whether to strike the Persians pre-emptively. The oracle replied that if Croesus attacked the Persians then a great empire would fall. He was delighted, but – the twist – the great empire which fell was his own.

Croesus allied with Babylonia, Egypt and Sparta against Persia, but he attacked Cappadocia in Persian-held territory with only those mercenaries who were readily available. Herodotus added more warning signs: Croesus ignored an advisor who pointed out that he had more to lose than to gain by the attack. He sent his army over the River Halys to achieve it. Croesus had by now a despot's 'craving' for more and he enslaved what Herodotus calls the 'innocent' people of the region.[31] All of these things – ignoring sound advice, craving more, crossing natural boundaries and attacking innocents – are Herodotus' indicators that pride is about to come before a fall. In *c.* 546, the Lydians and their mercenaries clashed with the Persian army at the Battle of Pteria.[32] Croesus withdrew towards home. He did not expect to be pursued as the campaigning season was coming to an end. The Persians came on. Sardis fell and the Lydian Empire collapsed. Croesus had added to an already enlarged empire. It must have looked set to thrive for years to come. That was not to be. Far from collecting money from their neighbours, the Lydians became tribute-payers themselves. Sardis was now the Persians' capital in the west.[33]

Persians in Ionia

The fall of the Lydian kingdom caused shockwaves across the Greek world. It had been a powerful and apparently ever-expanding force for longer than anyone could remember. And now . . . what? It was a new and uncertain time. Back on the mainland, Peisistratus was securing his tyranny in Athens. Miltiades, Cleomenes and Demaratus were young children in this era. The mainlanders will have waited anxiously to hear the unfolding news.

It was Cyrus II, known as 'the Great', who had swept into the Greeks' view with a Persian army buzzing with success. The people of Miletus, who had held out so long against Lydia, were the first to go to him for an audience. They asked to be friends and to stay on the same loose terms that they had enjoyed under Croesus. Cyrus obliged, although he was apparently much sharper with subsequent envoys. He had tried to tempt the Ionians and Aeolians to join him and they had kept their heads down. Cyrus was quick to remind them of that when they later asked for lenient terms. He had a story to tell: do you recall the flute-player who tried to tempt fish from the water with his music? The fish ignored him so he caught them in a net. The fish flipped and jumped in the net and the flutist told them there was no point dancing now – they had had their chance.[34]

Cyrus left subordinates to secure the Greek cities. A satrap was installed in Sardis, however Cyrus so prioritised stability over change that he left a Lydian in charge of the treasury. That should keep things running smoothly and would perpetuate Lydian arrangements with the Greeks. The treasurer hired mercenaries and started a rebellion. What a dilemma this presented for the Ionians. Should they join in and liberate the Lydians? Success could mean a return to paying *them* tribute but escaping potentially greater Persian demands. Failure could mean the full wrath of Persia. No Greek cities officially joined, but the mercenaries were said to be drawn from 'the coast', meaning a high percentage must have been Greek, much as many Greeks will have been in the army that had faced Cyrus at Pteria. Their caution proved wise. The revolt was short-lived. The Persians' response was to prevent the Lydians from carrying arms or training for war. The Lydians soon ceased to be a military power at all.[35]

The Greek cities' dilemma shifted. Now the question became whether to resist the Persians, submit or try something different altogether. Two cities chose the latter option. The people of Phocaea and Teos took what they could carry, climbed aboard their ships and sailed off for a new life. The one settled in Italy after a few false starts, the other in Thrace. Miletus had already made its arrangements with Persia and stayed out of what followed. One by one the other cities were besieged and fell to the Persian army. Caria succumbed to the same fate.[36]

As frightening as this must have been, life still did not change hugely for the eastern Greeks after the Persian conquest. It is a period about which too little information is available, yet what there is indicates attempts to facilitate a smooth transition. There does not seem to have been a major sacking of cities or mass enslavement. Neither Cyrus nor his successor imposed Persian rulers or even Greek tyrants. Politically things seem to have continued much as they were. The decision to leave a Lydian in charge of the Lydian treasury, while it proved a mistake, demonstrates the continuity that some places experienced. The fact that coinage remained the same – with Lydians, Greeks and others still using Lydian coins – is another indicator of continuity.[37]

Things were different, however. The Greeks of Asia Minor were now subjects of the Persian Empire. A new set of personalities were in charge. Contacts between the Lydian and Greek elites that had grown over generations were no longer guaranteed to be valuable and in some cases will have fallen away altogether. A Persian called Tabalus now ruled in Sardis. Two cities' populations had simply disappeared. This would have made it easier for the satrap to give land and property as rewards, but would have been disorientating for others round-about. For some the new power in Sardis meant trouble; for others, opportunity. For the most part, this was the first time that Greeks were in direct contact with Persians. A handful would have met Persians by venturing further than most on trading missions. More would have fought them during the Lydian campaigns. But now Persians were living nearby and governing the region. Communities now considered whether to make a show of loyalty, as Miletus had, or to keep a low profile and hope to keep as much independence as possible.

As old networks disappeared, new ones were opening up. From this time on there is evidence of Greeks at work in various Persian contexts. Records from Persia itself show Greek women working on irrigation systems and Greek men at work transporting materials and working in numerous crafts. Their technical knowledge was valued and Greeks worked as masons at Susa. In the Persian court, a Greek doctor, Democedes, served the royal family.[38] When Cyrus' successor readied an invasion of Egypt in the 520s, the Ionian Greeks did well out of those preparations financially and again in serving as mercenaries and sailors. This latter aspect continued the Lydian and Carian practice of hiring Greeks for military service; there was simply a new employer to get used to.[39]

For Miletus this was a good time. The Milesians had long wanted rid of the Lydians and that wish had been unpredictably granted. They remained the most powerful Greek state in Asia Minor. They retained their governance – a tyrant from a Milesian dynasty of tyrants, ruling with the consent of the elite and the demos. The Milesian elite remained in charge of the sanctuary at Didyma. It was symbolically and pragmatically important that Miletus remained one of the few places in the empire exempt from tribute.[40] If the Milesians had been asked for their view on the Persian conquest, it is fair to say that most of them would have been in favour. It is time we met the Milesians' new best friends, the Persians.

3

Persia

Who are the Persians?

Darius the Great was the Persian Great King at the time of the Battle of Marathon. It was unlikely that he would become king, yet he managed it. The empire that he ruled was vast, yet it had not existed just a few generations before. The Persian Empire was a phenomenon. For nearly 200 years it spanned much of the known world, from Bulgaria to north India, from Egypt to Kazakhstan. What do we know about this great empire and its culture? Why was the Persian army on the field at Marathon in 490?

That last question touches on one of the challenges around ancient Persia. The Persians were not involved in historiography of the sort that the Greeks were developing. For that reason, we are disproportionately dependant on Greek sources – on what Greek writers had to say about the Persians, their culture and their motives. That brings with it all the problems of biased outsiders. The Greeks were disproportionately fixated on ideas around Persian wealth and power, about moral failings caused by wealth, about the comings-and-goings of court culture and – for reasons of geography and self-interest – in matters to do with the Persians' western frontier, where the Persians met the Greeks. This does not mean that the Greek sources are nonsense – indeed, they frequently show genuine knowledge and interest and record real events. Nonetheless, it means that those sources must be handled with care and accepted for the kind of material that they are. It also means that it is important to combine what the Greeks say about the Persians with what can be gleaned from other avenues. Monumental inscriptions, administrative records – particularly what are known as the Persepolis Fortification tablets, the records of others who encountered the Persians, such as Babylonians and Egyptians, archaeology, art and architecture all convey a huge amount of information.[1]

The Persians had not always been in Persia. They were part of a movement of Iranian-speaking cattle-herders who moved over many years in the ninth and eighth centuries from Central Asia down into the region we now know as Iran, around the Zagros Mountains. Society consisted of smaller groups speaking different versions of Iranian – which is an Indo-European language, as Lydian and Greek are. Some settled in the Zagros region itself. They became known as Medes, their region Media. Others settled in an area that corresponds to the modern region of Fars, a little further south, closer to what we now call the Persian Gulf. Fars, 'Parsa' in Old Persian, gave its name to the 'Persians'. Fars was then part of the ancient kingdom of Elam; the Elamites had a city there known as Anshan although settlement there dropped off. Much of this is known from the records of the Neo-Assyrians, who took a keen interest in who was doing what in the Near East. In 646, 100 years before the fall of Croesus, Ashurbanipal, King of the Neo-Assyrians, led a formidable attack on the Elamites at Elam and Susa. The Elamites were permanently weakened and ceased their claim over the territory around Anshan. The Persians now asserted their ownership of it and began to build a state. The leading family, the Achaemenids, named for an ancestor, Achaemenes, became its ruling dynasty. The area was still known as 'Anshan' in inscriptions made some 100 years later, but that name gradually gave way to 'Persia'.[2] The Greeks, who loved etymology no matter how retrospective, later decided that the 'Persians' were probably descended from the hero Perseus.[3]

Despite Persian, Lydian and Greek sharing the same root, significant differences had occurred in the passage to different languages. The vowels e and o were dropped from Old Persian. This and issues such as the inflexibility of the Greek alphabet for dealing with new sounds mean that Persian names transliterated into Greek and so, transmitted to us, can look significantly different from their originals, with Persian 'Baga-' rendered as 'Mega-' and so on. The name 'Cyrus' in Old Persian was 'Kurush' and curiously does not have an obvious meaning. 'Darius', on the other hand, is more typical, 'Darayawaush' meaning something like, 'he who holds firm'. There has been some suggestion that this was simply a throne name, and if that is the case then his personal name has been lost. As far as public documents go, a type of cuneiform was used to write Old Persian, but this exists mostly in monumental inscriptions and was little used beyond that. Those inscriptions appeared accompanied by translations, typically some combination of Elamite, Babylonian, Akkadian or Egyptian hieroglyphs. This multi-lingual approach is a testament to the multi-ethnic nature of Persian society.[4] Aramaic was already widely used in the Near East. It was Aramaic which became the most important administrative language in the Persian Empire, used across all regions. Other languages and scripts continued to be used, but Aramaic had a special place in facilitating communication. The Persians never campaigned for the mass adoption of the Persian language.[5]

Persia under Cyrus II

The first king of Persia was Teispes, from *c.* 650. His son, Cyrus, succeeded him. This was a time of state-building, confirming the move from herders to a more settled and formally-run society. Teispes' great-grandson was also called Cyrus and it was this Cyrus II who was the empire-builder, known as 'The Great'. Within twenty-five years, Cyrus and his son had conquered all of the neighbouring kingdoms – Media, Elam, Lydia, Babylonia and Egypt. There were difficulties and set-backs, but it was a staggering success. The Medes were the first target. This was a natural step. Cyrus himself had a Median mother and the Persians had always been the junior in the relationship. Cyrus toppled Astyages, King of Media (Croseus' brother-in-law). Herodotus tells us that the Median king relied for defence on one Harpagus, a Median noble whom the king had been cruel to. Harpagus took the opportunity for revenge and gave Cyrus an easy conquest. It was this same Harpagus who Cyrus would later trust to bring the eastern Greeks into line. Cyrus' record of events gives us something similar if less personal: Astyages invaded Anshan, followed by a mutiny of his army, which meant short work for Cyrus; he captured Astyages and took the Median capital.[6] As we have seen, after Media, the Persians came on and the Lydians came out to meet them. The Lydian capital, Sardis, fell in 546, followed by many of the Greek cities of Asia. Cyrus added Babylon to his territories in 539, followed by parts of Central Asia, then Phoenicia, the great sea power of the Levant. The conquest of what we now know as Afghanistan had its difficulties. Cyrus and his army were cut off and reduced to cannibalism when they campaigned in what is now Helmand province, but they were relieved and the local Bactrians joined the empire. Cyrus was killed in 530 attempting to conquer the nomadic Massagetae, led by Queen Tomyris. This was a blow, but Cyrus had sired the necessary heir and spare along with several daughters, so the throne passed smoothly to his eldest son, Cambyses, who added wealthy Egypt to the empire in 525.

It is hard to get a clear sense of Cambyses. The Greek tradition is that he was quite mad. The Egyptians present a mixed picture; the image of the mad king likely has roots in Egypt, yet he is sometimes spoken of well there. In Egypt he was named a full pharaoh; there and in Babylon he was praised for carrying out key rituals expected of a legitimate ruler.[7] This was consistent with the approach Cyrus had taken and would, for the most part, be followed by subsequent Persian monarchs. Those who talk of the 'tolerance' of the Persian Empire perhaps go too far. There were simply not that many Persians in relation to the vast lands and populations that they quickly came to rule. There can have been no real expectation amongst the Persian elite that they would be able to restructure the political systems and religions of all the regions that they occupied. It was practical and efficient to fit themselves into the systems that already existed and to let subject populations carry on their religious practices as they chose. This was essentially the only approach possible in the circumstances and it was besides the one least likely to prompt revolt. When it suited them, the Persians might punish rebels by looting their sanctuaries, but when things went smoothly the Persians were content to let people pursue whatever religious practices they chose. So, in Babylon the king did as a Babylonian king did and in Egypt he did as a pharaoh did. A Persian court culture amongst the Persians themselves was rapidly evolving, as was their own religious practice.

There were no sacred texts and no Persian-authored accounts of their religion, but inscriptions, iconography and administrative records reveal that the Persians were polytheists, like most of their neighbours.[8] Inscriptions refer to the god Auramazda. This name is related to the Ahura Mazda of later Zoroastrian religion, but there is no firm evidence that the Achaemenids or other Persians were Zoroastrians as such.[9] Administrative tablets refer to rations being sent from the royal treasury for the worship of further Iranian gods as well as the Elamite god Humban and Babylonian Adad. These are the main-stay of Persian polytheism. Auramazda features in this list, but is by no mean the most prominent, with Humban receiving more.[10] Tomb reliefs seem to show kings worshipping fire and Greeks witnessed fire-worship in Ionia. Sacrifices to all the elements are mentioned by Greek writers and confirmed by administrative records, which cite sacrifices to rivers.[11]

Animal sacrifices included sheep and goats, with grain, cakes, fruit, beer and wine, oil, milk and honey amongst the non-blood offerings. An intoxicating drink, *haoma*, was made, but whether this was consumed within a spiritual framework is unclear. When it came to death rituals, bodies would ideally be exposed for birds to remove the flesh prior to the bones' storage in an ossuary. This prevented polluting either earth or fire with unclean remains. Nonetheless, the great number of burials found in Iran from the first millennium BCE indicates that there was no significant taboo against burial. For simply practical reasons, those Persians who died on campaign away from home must frequently have been buried rather than enjoying the lengthy process of exposure and collection.

Herodotus describes aspects of Persian religion, including aspects familiar to the Greeks such as animal sacrifice and consumption of sacrificial meat, but also differences, including the absence of sacrificial paraphernalia such as flute music and garlands. He cites the use of a priestly caste, the importance of the sun, moon and the elements, as well as the adoption of gods from other cultures.[12] Herodotus also says that the Persians made no use of statues, temples and altars. While much of the former information shows his familiarity with Persian culture, this latter claim shows either a major hole in that information or a preference for a contrast with Greek culture over accuracy. Other evidence indicates that the Persians *did* use altars and temples, although there is no indication of statues of gods.[13]

Herodotus and Plato tell us that the Persians placed considerable emphasis on truthfulness; in fact Herodotus claims that elite Persian education consisted of archery, horsemanship and learning to tell the truth.[14] Royal inscriptions bear this out. They place great emphasis on truth and lies, or rather, liars, for those who rebel against the empire are regarded as perpetuating disorder and 'the great lie'. Zoroastrianism would come to emphasise this dichotomy between truth and lie as the foundation of human and divine order. Empire, for the Persians, was an extension of divine, cosmic order. It was the constant order of the planets and the stars manifest on earth; order brought to chaos. To rebel against empire – to transform your promise of obedience into a lie – was an offence against the divine as well as the state. This is communicated again and again in royal inscriptions in what might be regarded as a 'mildly messianic tone'.[15]

Clothing and arms

> Trained am I both with hands and feet. As a horseman I am a good horseman. As a bowman I am a good bowman both afoot and on horseback. As a spearman I am a good spearman both afoot and on horseback.

When Darius the Great died, this inscription was carved upon his tomb. Royal inscriptions indicate the high regard in which horsemanship and martial skills were held.[16] Herodotus thought that the Persians adopted riding dress from the Medes, while Xenophon, another Greek writer interested in Persian custom, suggested that the Persians knew little about horses until the time of Cyrus.[17] Herodotus adds that the Persians had no substantial cavalry until after their conquest of Lydia, during which camels had been more in play, frightening the Lydians' horses. If this is not exaggeration, it reinforces a pattern seen elsewhere in Persian culture of willingness to adopt new ideas and technologies.

The Persians decorated the walls of their palaces at Persepolis and Susa with large carved images of themselves and their subjects. These splendid scenes offer insight into the dress and arms of Persian and non-Persian men alike in this

Fig. 4 Line drawing of a spear-bearer from the relief carvings at the palace at Persepolis, Iran.

region and era. The Persians at Persepolis wear two forms of dress. One is a closely-fitted, belted trouser-suit, known as the 'riding costume', although clearly it was acceptable at court as well as in the saddle. This is the costume that Herodotus believed to have come from the Medes. Trousers presented a cultural gulf between Greeks and Persians. Greeks had seen them before on the Scythians, but unlike many eastern novelties they were not generally adopted by the loosely-clothed, tunic-loving Greeks. Because of their rarity, trousers and the distinctive Persian hood became key features to indicate Persians in Greek art. Across the Near East and further north, trousers were unremarkable. The second style of Persian clothing was looser, a long gown worn with long, wide sleeves. This is known as 'court dress'. Even footwear is picked out in the reliefs, with Persians in low-cut shoes in contrast to ankle-boots worn by the Elamites.[18]

Some key persons are picked out by name in the images. One caption at Persepolis reads 'Aspacanah [Greek "Aspathines"], bow-bearer, holds the battle-axe of Darius the King.'[19] This indicates the high status of the king's weapon bearer. It also gives insight into weaponry. We have the bow, supporting the emphasis on archery in the king's tomb. The bow is depicted via a fine bow-case, worn on the shoulder. The other named item is the battle-axe, a formidable weapon to accompany the bow and the spear. Battle-axes were also used by the Sacae of Central Asia, although whether they were adopted from them is less clear. At his hip Aspathines wears a short-sword, an *akinakes*. The Sogdian delegate from Afghanistan and the Median delegate are shown bringing further *akinakes* as gifts. The Medians also offer a pair of daggers, always useful in a close encounter.[20] The Persians are famous bow-users, so it is valuable to get these insights into the range of other weaponry that they used.

The Persepolis reliefs and further depictions provide information about another aspect of military-ware – shields. Two main forms were used. The first is a type of dipylon shield, a large oval with a hole cut on either side. These were descended from a Bronze Age model used widely across Greece and the Near East. They take their name from the Dipylon Gate in Athens, where a good deal of pottery depicting them was found. They were made from a bull's hide stretched taut across a frame. The distinctive side-holes were initially not cut out at all, but a result of pulling the hide in tight. The hide and its frame were then fitted with a metal rim and boss. These shields were light yet strong and durable. They seem primarily to have been used by palace guards.[21] The same strength and durability can be found in the other form of shield used more widely by the Persians – the wicker shield. These were not as flimsy as they sound. The base was once again raw hide and the wicker would be woven through the hide to add an extra layer of protection. The infantry used long ones while the cavalry carried shorter ones. They offered flexible, tough and lightweight defence.[22]

Persian depictions of their troops include cuirasses – armour for chest and back. These are sometimes shown with groin coverings hanging down and with guards for the back of the neck akin to a high reinforced collar.[23] These depictions and the snippets of literature that support them are significant because of the widely held but under-examined belief that the Persians fought without armour. Herodotus embedded this idea by suggesting that the Persians lost the Battle of Plataea against the Greeks because the Greeks were heavily-armoured while the Persians were essentially naked.[24] Not every Persian will have turned out in the best armour, but various options were certainly available, and despite his comment about lack of equipment, Herodotus himself provides some of the evidence for it. He refers, for example, to iron scale-armour worn by the infantry along with a felt cap, sleeved tunic and trousers.[25] The scales would be small slips of metal stitched overlapping onto leather. This armour would be effective yet lighter and more mobile than a sheet of metal. Herodotus also describes Persians wearing the 'Egyptian cuirass'; it is not entirely clear what this refers to, but is likely to be a reference to linen armour – another light yet effective protection.[26] The Persians seem frequently to have worn their armour beneath a coloured tunic. This will have helped to reduce over-heating in the sun. It may also have added to the impression that the Persians fought without armour.[27] It has been estimated that around one in ten Persians had the full equipment; the rest had some elements of it. That rate is similar to that suggested for Greek forces, some of whom would have a full panoply and many of whom would have had only parts of it.[28]

As we have seen, a Persian infantryman would likely be equipped with a spear, dagger, perhaps an axe, and the piece for which they are well-known – the bow. Archery was held in higher regard in Persia than amongst the Greeks and the archers beautifully depicted at the palace at Susa are thought to be infantry from the elite unit known as the Immortals.[29] They were said to take their name from the keenness with which the number of their unit was kept up; should one man die he would be immediately replaced, giving the impression that the unit was deathless – immortal. They were also known as the Apple Bearers after the

Fig. 5 Persians with bow, sword and neck-guard fight Sacae armed with bow and axe. Line drawing of the imprint of a Persian Cylinder Seal. Delaporte (1910) 403.

distinctive apple shape of the bottom of their spears.[30] One thousand of the 10,000 Immortals served as the elite guard. Elite and non-elite alike carried weapons for distance and hand-to-hand combat. We should imagine the Persian infantry forming a phalanx of around ten men deep, the front ranks putting their shields down to form a wall, arrows being loosed over the top, then combat switching to spears, axes and daggers as the battle closes in.[31] The infantry were protected by the highly mobile and forceful weight of the cavalry.

Darius' tomb emphasises skilled horsemanship. Cavalry in the Persian military wore bronze or iron helmets and they bore similar arms to the infantry, with the shorter shield. Modern-style saddles were unknown, but skilled horse riders were accustomed to manoeuvre effectively from an animal skin across the horse's back. Sophisticated bridle and reins were used, while some also adopted thigh covers.[32] The Medes were famous horsemen and their absorption into the Persian military may have provided the first impetus to become serious about riding and cavalry. Once adopted, the numbers seem to have been kept at *c.* 30,000 troops.

As new peoples were added to the empire, those peoples were obliged to render a set amount of military service and they did so in their own style, each bringing their own equipment and skills. Once again this was a matter of practicality as well as ideology. The Persians of the sixth century could not equip and train people from across the empire and, besides, there was strength in diversity from allowing different warriors to act in the specialist ways that they had trained all their lives. The same went for mercenaries. Like the Near Eastern kingdoms which had gone before them, the Persians made extensive use of mercenaries on short-term contracts. They fought with the weapons they were used to, incorporating into the Persian military as specialists in whatever field they were accustomed to.

The military was managed on a decimal structure. Each regiment had 1,000 soldiers. That regiment was divided into smaller units, sabata, of 100 men, each sub-divided into units of 10. A group of 10 regiments – 10,000 troops – was a baivarabām, the most famous of which was the Immortals. There were commanders at every level, so whether you were in a group of 10 or 10,000, you knew who was in charge. Each region of the empire – each satrapy – was expected to provide a baivarabām when called on to do so.[33] This was a well-organised, multi-skilled and flexible fighting machine. Its efficiency was multiplied by the outstanding road system of the Persian Empire, which enabled troops, supplies and messengers to move across the landscape at phenomenal speeds.[34] Under Cambyses the Persians added a fleet of sixty ships to their fighting power. The Persian military was a force to be reckoned with by land and water.

The rise of Darius

The Persian Empire ran on a straightforward administrative model. The empire was divided into regions which reflected the kingdoms which existed before their incorporation into the empire. Aside from some participation in military campaigns the Great King typically stayed in Persia, ruling from Susa, Persepolis or from Ecbatana in Media. The king's subordinates, usually his sons, ruled on his behalf as 'satraps' in approximately twenty regions beyond Persia.

The dazzling expansion of Persian territory under Cyrus placed strain on the system of governance even as it created new opportunities for wealth and culture. One flaw, present in perhaps all monarchies, was the sheer attraction of the top spot. There was a problem with internal unity, meaning that when a king died there was frequently instability as leading candidates vied for power. The events surrounding the death of Cambyses and his replacement on the throne tested the Persian system to the limit.

Herodotus describes Cambyses dying from an accidental leg wound, self-inflicted as he rushed back to Persia from Syria following news of a coup at home. It seems certain that some sort of coup was unfolding. It is less clear who was leading it. As Herodotus tells it, Cambyses had killed his brother, Smerdis, and the coup was led by two Magi (learned men), one of whom was imitating Smerdis. The so-called False Smerdis was rumbled through a fabulous fairy-tale

Fig. 6 The Persian Empire.

style ruse, and with both brothers dead, the seven men who exposed the Magi determined the future of the government.[35] Other traditions suggest that Cambyses had not killed Smerdis and that the revolt was really one brother against another. Few now believe that there really was a usurping Magi; more think that Smerdis rose against his brother, apparently with the support of many Persians and Medes, before meeting his end. The death of Cambyses is not without its own questions. Was it an accident? Did Smerdis arrange for him to be killed? Did 'The Seven' arrange it?[36]

Darius was one of the Seven. He was well-placed within Persian society. His father, Hystaspes, governed Parthia in north-eastern Iran. Darius was born around 550, so he grew up through the heady years of Persia's first expansion and was coming into adulthood around the time of Cyrus' last campaign. As a young man, Darius served as spear-bearer to Cambyses and although Herodotus called that as a position of no account, it is more likely that it was a high position which enabled Darius to study the course of high politics and form alliances. He married well to the daughter of a man named Gobryas, a relative of the satrap of Babylon and a man in high esteem at court.[37]

The other members of the Seven were also well-placed Persians: Hydarnes, Intaphernes, Otanes, Megabyxus, Ardumaniš and Gobryas, Darius' father-in-law.[38] Darius would later celebrate them all in his famous Behistun inscription, an account carved into a mountain-side of how they struck down the false Magi and put down the revolts that followed Darius' succession. Herodotus used the Seven's situation to air the pros and cons of different constitutions. Otanes speaks in favour of democracy and lists the short-comings of monarchy and tyranny, Megabyxos argues for oligarchy and critiques democracy, Darius champions monarchy. Darius won the argument and the group agreed that they would take their horses to the outskirts of the city and whichever neighed first after sunset would be king. Darius' groom used a cunning ruse to ensure that his master won. Herodotus' Constitutional Debate is an intellectual experiment rather than a literal record of events although, odd as it sounds, the reliance on the chance noise of a horse is not especially unlikely in the context of Persian religion, which placed great significance on chance.[39] However it was done, by October of 522 Darius was king and his co-conspirators stuck by him.

Some have suspected that the Seven acted to end attempts to draw the Medes further into governance.[40] Inscriptions from Darius' era suggest that he placed more emphasis on his Persian ethnicity than Cyrus or Cambyses had ever done. Nonetheless, neither Persians nor non-Persians reacted well to the coup.

Uprisings erupted across the empire. In a year of chaos, there were nationalist revolts in Media, Elam, Babylon, in Armenia, Afghanistan and in Central Asia. There were also risings in Persia itself as rival claimants and supporters of the late king and his brother reacted in shock to the sudden deaths and replacement of the sons of Cyrus. There may have been risings in Ionia, Lydia and Egypt, but there is a tantalising lack of information.

Darius and the other six swept into action. The initial rising in Elam was repressed by threats alone, but Darius was compelled to lead the army against revolt in Babylon, conveying troops across the Tigris and reoccupying the city and its vital treasury. Hydarnes took an army of Medes and Persians to supress Media; he made inroads but found himself cornered. Darius had with him the experienced army that had fought with Cambyses in Egypt. Mercenaries were in high demand between the factions. Darius' enemies had seized the treasuries in Media and Persia, but holding Babylon meant that Darius still had the cash to compete. With a combined force he swept up from Babylon, putting down a nascent revolt in Elam on his way to relieve Hydarnes in Media. As Media was brought to heel, a Persian and Median army crushed the revolts in Persia. Babylon saw opportunity in Darius' absence and rose again. This time two of the Seven, Gobryas and Intapernes, ended their bid for freedom. Babylonian independence was over. Dadarshish, satrap of Bactria, supported Darius and put down revolt in Afghanistan and Turkestan. There were nineteen battles in little over a year, with nine enemy leaders executed. It was a colossal achievement. Against the odds, the Persian Empire was still intact and Darius was its king.[41]

Adding to empire was a key method of maintaining momentum and discouraging conspiracy at the top. Following the suppression of revolt in Turkestan, Darius instigated a campaign of conquest in that eastern region, successfully conquering the semi-nomadic Sacae in 519. Soon north-west India, part of what is now Pakistan, was added to the empire. This eastern action was followed by a turn towards the western frontiers. Darius continued Cambyses' Mediterranean policy, projecting Persia's naval power. Mighty Samos submitted, its people captured 'like fish in a net'. More Greek islands fell.[42] We have seen how a Persian campaign was launched across the Hellespont and into Thrace, with Greek tyrants, including Miltiades, lending their weight. Alliances were made with Macedon.

Much of what we know of this period comes from Darius' own account. The Behistun inscription was carved in *c.* 520, highly visible on the main road from Mesopotamia to Ecbatana. Of his conquest of the Sacae, the inscription reads:

> I smote the Sacae exceedingly; another (leader) I took captive; this one was led bound to me and I slew him. The chief of them by name Skunkha – they seized and led him to me. Then I made another their chief as was my desire.[43]

In addition to the text, Darius is depicted in a carving almost 2m tall. At his feet are the leaders he triumphed over – the liar kings as he calls them, reinforcing the moral and religious perspective on rebellion. The text was written in Elamite. Darius then arranged for a new script to be developed to express Persian so that Persian and Akkadian versions could be added. Behistun itself was a spot with sacred associations, adding profundity to his claims. For those not using that route, alternative versions were copied in numerous languages and sent around the empire. The inscription asserted Darius' hold and emphasised the empire's Persian nature.[44]

The inscription featured another way of declaring Darius' authority – it asserted his right to be king. This was not easy in the circumstances. Darius was not a particularly close relative of Cyrus, if indeed he was a relative at all. Cyrus' sons were dead, but there were many cousins, second cousins and more who could claim a closer tie to Cyrus than Darius son of Hystapses could. He began the inscription by laying out his genealogy. Rather unusually in royal terms, Darius' father and grandfather were still alive when he became king. It was necessary to go back to the long gone Achaemenes to find an ancestor in common with Cyrus. Darius' repeated and insistent declaration of his Persian-ness was

Fig. 7 Line drawing of the Behistun Relief. Image and text describe Darius the Great's defeat of his enemies. West Iran, *c.* 520 BCE.

essentially another way of declaring his closeness to Cyrus and his fitness to be leader. One more critical tactic in the quest for legitimacy was a dynastic marriage. Darius was not one to miss an opportunity.

At the time of his succession, Darius was a married man with three sons. Having sons is useful to a monarch. Once old enough they can serve in vital roles and they represent dynastic stability. Darius' father-in-law, Gobryas, was a high-status Persian who had backed Darius in the coup. On the other hand, he did not add anything to Darius' dynastic claim. For that, Darius turned to the daughters of Cyrus, Atossa and Artystone. Their high status under Cyrus was a matter of course and Cambyses had capitalised on it by marrying Atossa, for all that she was his full sister. This is disconcerting to the modern reader, but it is by no means evidence of madness or depravity. Marriage between full siblings was normal amongst royal Egyptians and in other parts of the Near East. While it was taboo amongst the Greeks, they too indulged marriage between half-siblings so long as they shared a father not a mother. It was a matter of consolidating wealth and power, not one of affection. Atossa was married to her brother to shore-up his position and now she was married to Darius to provide him with that same critical link to the founder of the empire. What she or her sister thought of all this is impossible to know. They were marrying someone who was implicated in the murder of their brother Smerdis and possibly in that of Cambyses too. It was unlikely that either sister had much choice; such scenarios tend to mean being married or murdered. The royal sisters would not have been allowed to live to marry a rival claimant. If they could bear to marry Darius in those circumstances there were benefits. Rather than being disappeared they would retain their wealth and status. It is possible that Atossa secured at this time the promise of another benefit – becoming mother to a future king. Darius had three sons already, but it was Xerxes the son of Atossa, grandson of Cyrus, who would succeed Darius when the time came. It was through his mother that Xerxes could make his claim to the legacy of Cyrus. Darius had completed a crucial manoeuvre in claiming legitimacy and building a dynasty.

Darius showed enormous skill as a leader. He managed the competing demands of the Persian nobility, who were still adapting to the existence of the empire, and he fostered loyalty to himself as king. As an unexpected successor, he was essentially a 'new man'. He lacked the inherited loyalty that a Crown Prince enjoys. Darius tackled this by creating a revised network of supporters. He put close associates in key positions, building a new network and sweeping the Cambyses era into the past.

Key personalities

Who were some of the key figures around Darius? His new wife, Atossa, was certainly a crucial figure. As well as connecting Darius to Cyrus, as his most prestigious wife she was a focus of proceedings concerning other women of the aristocracy. Greek writers were not complimentary, but as members of a patriarchal society moving away from monarchy, it is no surprise to find them critical of women who achieved power through their royal relationships. Hellanicus of Lesbos criticised her by implying that she was too manly, she 'concealed her female nature and was the first monarch to wear the tiara and trousers; she also established the service of eunuchs and the issuing of judgements in writing. She subdued many peoples and was extremely warlike and manly in all her accomplishments'. There is hyperbole here and it is unlikely that Atossa led campaigns, yet the basic premise that she had some authority and held land in her own right is fair. It is worth noting that the images at Persepolis and Susa feature only men. Persian society was deeply patriarchal and Atossa's power was drawn largely from her relation to the men in her life – Cyrus, Cambyses, Darius and later Xerxes – yet she was valued and had a degree of power and the ear of Darius, perhaps even encouraging him to invade Greece.[45]

Less is known of Atossa's sister and co-wife, Artystone. The Persepolis tablets indicate that she had influence at court; she certainly owned large estates in Persia. She had children with Darius, including three sons and a daughter, Artozostre. According to Herodotus, Darius favoured Artystone above his other wives and had a statue made of her in gold.[46]

Darius' paternal uncle, Pharnaces, became Darius' treasurer, a role that required someone of total loyalty. Pharnaces is depicted in the relief carvings at Persepolis. He received a huge ration from the royal treasury; enough for his household, for gifts and patronage, with some left over for sale. Only one man received more: Gobryas.

Gobryas, Darius' first father-in-law, was appointed Darius' spear-bearer (*arštibara*). He is represented in that position on the Behistun inscription and on Darius' tomb. Gobryas had proved his usefulness in recapturing Babylon; he put down rebellion in Elam and was made satrap of that region. The Persepolis tablets show Gobryas to have been the most highly paid man in the empire, indicating a status exceeded only by the king and Crown Prince. Darius had married Gobryas' daughter and now Gobryas married Darius' sister, making Gobryas Darius' father-in-law *and* brother-in-law. Families can be complicated.

Mardonius, the son of Gobryas and Darius' sister, would become one of Darius' most trusted generals.

By the time Marathon was approaching, Mardonius had entered adulthood. As Darius' nephew and the half-brother of one of the king's wives, he will have enjoyed a good education and the trust of the monarch. The familial connection was extended when he was married to Artozostre, the daughter of Darius and Artystone. As we will see, Mardonius performed well when placed in charge of Ionia and he was entrusted with an invasion of Greece. He was initially successful against Macedonia; however that success was marred by the loss of the fleet – wrecked off Mt Athos. He was not chosen to lead the later campaign which led to Marathon, but he avoided long-term disgrace and was a major figure of Xerxes' campaign ten years later. This use of close relatives bound closer by bonds of marriage was typical of life at the top of the Persian nobility. Herodotus calls Mardonius a young man recently married at the time of his expedition. The Persepolis tablets indicate that he was already married to Artozostre by 498, so 'recently married' is a bit of a stretch in 492, though the characterisation of him as a young groom adds a curiously endearing quality.[47]

As well as a plentiful supply of uncles and cousins, Darius also had younger brothers: Artabanus, Artaphernes and Artanes. Little is known of Artanes. Herodotus tells us that he had only one child, a daughter called Phratagune. She was given in marriage to her uncle, Darius – as an only child she was a gift, Herodotus says, equivalent to giving his brother his whole estate. Darius and Phratagune had children together. Two of their sons were killed at the Battle of Thermopylae serving their half-brother, Xerxes.

Of Darius' two other brothers, one represented him in the east, the other in the west. Artabanus was the east. He received the important eastern satrapy of Bactria, modern Afghanistan. He is familiar from Herodotus' *Histories*, where he plays the thankless role of 'wise advisor' – a figure who tries to urge moderation and is generally dismissed for being gloomy. After failing to caution Darius in Scythia, he would be similarly dismissed by his nephew, Xerxes. Three of his sons would command troops at Thermopylae.[48]

In the west was Artaphernes, satrap of Lydia from 513–493. Artaphernes was most likely another younger brother. There is no reference in the Behistun inscription to him contributing in the war of the succession, so it is likely that he was then too young. He is represented quite neutrally by Herodotus, who depicts him listening to envoys at Sardis and never associates him with the sorts of cruelty or avarice which colour the images of so many Herodotean rulers. When the time came, Artaphernes was succeeded to the satrapy of Lydia by his son, also called Artaphernes. It was the younger Artaphernes who would lead the campaign to the west.

Another rising star at court was Datis, a senior Mede. He was given numerous posts requiring competency and loyalty. Through his successes he worked his way up and was eventually made commander of the King's forces. He would join Artaphernes leading the expedition to Greece, and Datis appears to have been the senior party. He is said to have spoken Greek, albeit, allegedly, badly.[49] He had children, at least two sons. Datis is depicted in a handful of Greek sources in which he speaks sense and shows respect for Greek sanctuaries.[50] His representation in Persian sources is necessarily less characterful, but it is curious to see references in the Persepolis tablets to his various journeys, a reminder of the mobility of intelligence and key personnel within the empire. As someone who was not directly related to the king, Datis was more pressed than most to prove his worth and secure the high status he had gained.

The Persians had seen colossal change within just a few generations. Darius settled into a reign with family and close confidants in senior roles across a vast territory. He was not known as 'the Great' for nothing. As well as maintaining and expanding his lands, he became a great builder of palaces, notably at Susa, Persepolis and Parsagadae. These building projects saw him embed a distinctive Persian artistic style. His introduction of currency and a system of weights streamlined trade and the collection of taxes. He supported engineering projects, completing a canal connecting the Nile to the Red Sea. There was prosperity throughout much of the Persian Empire, although it must be said that far in the west there was dissatisfaction in Ionia with how Persian rule was panning out. It is to that tinderbox that we now turn.

4

Revolt in Ionia

By 500 BCE, the vast majority of Greek cities in Asia had been through conquest and oversight from the Lydians and re-conquest by the Persians. Dissent was risky, yet in this period we see mass revolt across the region. What happened?

Under Cyrus and Cambyses, things had not changed a great deal in the Greek cities. They left the administrative structure alone and there was even a period of prosperity as Cambyses prepared to invade Egypt. Greek mercenaries continued to provide manpower. Likewise, the Persians were now a market for luxury goods produced by the Ionians, who could sell to them where once they had sold to the Lydians and Egyptians. It has sometimes been assumed that paying tribute to Persia created impoverishment and resentment in Asia Minor, yet many Greeks were making good incomes and the increased use of coinage reflects a move to make trade easier, not a medium of tribute.[1]

Things changed with Darius and we begin to see shifting attitudes. It is during Darius' reign that the coinage changes. Persian *darics* and *sigloi* replaced Lydian coins for the first time – not a matter for revolt, but an indication of permanence and reorientation. Tribute was now extended to include the islands off the coast, such as Samos, Chios and Mytilene on Lesbos.[2] Trade had continued, but then again there is a decline in Greek pottery in Egypt from 525–500. Some Ionians were losing out. The Greek cities were now obliged to contribute troops to the Persian military, a service common in ancient empires but nonetheless a source of resentment. Perhaps more importantly, Darius appointed his own tyrants to rule the Greek cities. As we have seen, Darius had given people close to him most of the top spots in the empire, so appointing his own men to these posts was more of the same. For the communities subject to these appointments however, it was more of a shock. Mytilene had elected a man as their general for Darius' Scythian campaign, but it was still disconcerting when Darius appointed him tyrant. Similarly, the Chians governed themselves through a form of democracy. No wonder that they bitterly resented the imposition of a new tyrant.

Tyrants had once gained their posts by working their way up the ladder in their communities, winning popularity and holding on to power through acts of civic munificence. They rarely lasted more than a generation or two before passing to someone from a different house. They were posts worth aspiring to, though there were fewer of them as communities began to favour democracies or broad oligarchies. Now, instead of tyrants rising from within, they were imposed from without. And instead of organising works of public benefit, they were preoccupied with collecting tribute.[3] Little wonder that there was not much love for the Persian-backed tyrants. Herodotus has Histaeus voice the truth of this during the account of the Scythian Expedition (see p.12): *we cannot get rid of Darius without risking our positions.*

These tyrants were Greeks who had chosen to make the most of the political climate that they found themselves in. Persian authority was a reality and they were working with it. They remained Greek by ethnicity and culture, but the cultural aspect was flexible. While there were differences across language, gods, cuisine and any number of other areas between Greeks and Persians, there was room for adaptation. Miltiades may have left the Chersonese when the Persians approached, but his eldest son Metiochus had lands in the Persian Empire and lived 'like a Persian'. Compromise was possible, as it always had been between Greeks, Lydians and Carians. Aristocrats in particular had choices to make about how much they wished to adapt and how much they wished to curry favour, but all the while the presence of the tyrants was a reminder to the elite of their loss of significance.

The temptation of Naxos

Miletus had held out against the Lydians for many years and welcomed the Persians as a breath of fresh air. Their tyrant was Histaeus. His success is another example of Greeks who prospered under Persia. At some point Histaeus was called inland to Susa – most likely as an honour, to become an adviser, although he would later claim he was a prisoner. Histaeus was not deposed when he left; his nephew and son-in-law, Aristagoras, would rule on his behalf. Aristagoras had become the most influential Greek in Ionia, with the ear of Artaphernes at Sardis.

Aristagoras looked for ways to increase his standing with Artaphernes. A good way to do that was to help the Persians acquire territory. Darius had proved his interest in going further west with the Scythian campaign of 510 and the conquest of the east Aegean islands. As Herodotus has it, Aristagoras was approached by aristocrats who had been expelled from the island of Naxos on the adoption of a more democratic government.[4] These were the aristocrats who the Spartans had installed as an oligarchy some years before. Naxos sits in the Aegean, half way between the Greek mainland and Asia Minor. The Naxian aristocrats urged Aristagoras to help them return to power, pointing out that this would also reclaim the islands under Naxian influence, including valuable Paros and Andros. Aristagoras fancied this as an opportunity to become tyrant of Naxos. He replied that he did not have the resources to help alone, but that he had a friend who did – if he could convince Artaphernes to fund a campaign, nothing could stop them. By implication, Naxos and the surrounding islands would become Persian, ruled by the returning aristocrats or, as Aristagoras hoped, himself. Artaphernes loved the idea and the game was afoot. The fall-out would change the balance of power.

Perhaps if Aristagoras had been able to plough ahead, things would have worked out differently. Instead a power struggle during the campaign destabilised things. Darius introduced a Persian rival to Aristagoras' authority – Darius' cousin, Megabates. He was most likely a son of Megabazus, a satrap who was Histaeus' main rival in Thrace, so there was already a certain tension between the two parties.[5] Megabates was appointed to command the Persians and the other non-Greeks. As many must have predicted, Aristagoras and Megabates clashed. It took the form of a scandalous public showdown over who was entitled to discipline whom. Aristagoras objected to the conspicuous punishment by Megabates of one of Aristagoras' Greek friends; it was a struggle between the two camps enacted over the body of one unfortunate man. The divided expedition was a disaster, with none of the looked-for benefits. Artaphernes, overseeing this debacle, needed someone to blame. It would be easier to challenge Aristagoras than to take on the king's cousin, and after all it was Aristagoras who had got them into it. The bill for the failed expedition was presented to Miletus. Aristagoras could only argue that Miletus had done its bit and that it was Megabates who had spoiled things. Pressure on Aristagoras was building. He could not keep refusing Persian demands for a refund, but nor could he persuade the Milesians to pay for the expedition – the costs of which should have been covered by the spoils of success. If he could not persuade his fellow Milesians to pay, perhaps he could persuade them to revolt. What had essentially begun as a struggle for favour with the Persians ended in revolt from their authority.

Finding allies

Aristagoras needed to persuade the people of Miletus to follow him on his daring course of action so that they did not expel him altogether. According to Herodotus, there was another prompt for the revolt: Histaeus. The story is too infused with folk-tale tropes to be literally true, but it is likely to be a retelling of the stories Herodotus was told. Histaeus was eventually accused of instigating the unrest, so whether he did or did not, he might as well take credit for it. As Herodotus tells it, when Histaeus was in Susa he determined that Miletus should be free. Histaeus sent Aristagoras a slave with a secret message tattooed onto his scalp urging revolt. Reeling from the mess at Naxos, Aristagoras welcomed the message and acted. Pre-empting deposition and demonstrating his commitment, Aristagoras relinquished his tyranny and instigated popular government. Senior Milesians were consulted. There was some call for caution, the philosopher Hecataeus noted the Persians' great resources, but the majority were on board. The revolt was on.

The Ionians began operating in loose cooperation, now known as the Ionian League. The Panionium sanctuary offered a practical and symbolically powerful place for leading figures to meet, debate and plan. Before the revolt was known, they organised the seizure of key pro-Persian military figures. Other cities and islands registered support. Across the region tyrants were expelled in largely bloodless coups. The readiness to remove the tyrants confirms the unpopularity of these figures. Aristagoras ordered the cities to pick generals in preparation for the backlash that would inevitably come. He then sailed to the Greek mainland to call forth support.

Herodotus' story of Aristagoras at Sparta is some of Herodotus at his finest. The story is driven by the personalities involved, yet it is full of political factors and psychological truths. Aristagoras meets with King Cleomenes. Aristagoras tempts him with powerful rhetoric. He refers to the 'slavery' of the Ionians, calling it a shame to all Greeks – especially to the Spartans, the Greeks' leaders. A bit of flattery can get you a long way. He asks Cleomenes in the name of the gods to end this slavery of the Spartans' kinsmen – an appeal to their shared culture and ethnic ties. He then switches to a different tack, insisting that the Persians (who had destroyed armies of Elamites, Babylonians and Lydians) have little taste for war and with their bows and ridiculous trousers can be easily defeated by real warriors like the Spartans. He goes on to temptation, describing the colossal wealth of Persia and the riches that are Sparta's for the taking. Honour and wealth from an easy victory. This is the moment when Aristagoras goes too far. He reveals a map which shows the Persian Empire: the lands of the Lydians, Phrygians, Armenians, Syrians and on to Persia. *Why not help the Ionians defeat the Persians and take all of this?* Aristagoras asks. Cleomenes questions him, asking how long it would take to march across those lands. Herodotus says that if Aristagoras had lied at this moment he would have had Cleomenes and the Spartans in the bag. His truthful answer – three months – appals Cleomenes. This is risk on a scale that the Spartans are just not interested in. Seeing that the game was almost up, Aristagoras turned to hard cash. He follows the king home and offers him fifty talents to join the revolt. At this point the king's young daughter, Gorgo, notes with a child's frankness that Aristagoras is attempting to bribe him. Cleomenes recognises the truth of what she says and leaves Aristagoras standing alone in disappointment.

The appeals to status, kinship and potential gain are all plausible as motives that might be put forth to tempt the Spartans, even if we receive them through a lively tale. It is curious that Sparta rejected the appeal and a reminder that the history of Greece and Persia is not one of consistent opposition. The Spartans had no love for the Persians. We have seen their history of opposing pro-Persian Greek states. But the failed attack on Samos had cautioned them and they must have known that the Persians were not the poor soldiers that Aristagoras made them out to be. Herodotus' image of Cleomenes' recoiling at Aristagoras' map reflects a general policy. Until almost the fourth century the Spartans were reluctant to stray far beyond the Aegean. A more active opposition to Persia would develop once the Spartans' long-time rivals on Aegina became Persian subjects, but for now there was no joy for Aristagoras.

Aristagoras would have more success in Athens, where he headed next. The city was riding high after the removal of their tyrant. Launching their democracy had not been easy, however. There had been pressure from their neighbours. As we have seen, the Athenians had sent envoys to Artaphernes for support. Those envoys had been rebuked for agreeing to submission. That was a commitment too far and they never formally made it. That made for bad feeling; worse was to come. Hippias had long been bending Artaphernes' ear, asking that the Persians support his return to Athens. Artaphernes agreed at last and sent word to the Athenians that they should reappoint Hippias as tyrant – just a suggestion but they might like to bear in mind who was making it. Nothing could be further from what most Athenians wanted. They refused and their refusal put them in open conflict with Persia.[6]

This was the situation when Aristagoras arrived seeking support. The Athenians had strong links with Ionia and many Athenian men would have spent time in Miletus or the cities nearby. Aristagoras played on this and repeated the arguments he had made at Sparta. Perhaps the appeals to kinship, honour and booty alone would not have been enough, but having opposed Persia's demand they were already on a collision course. With a surge of enthusiasm the Athenians voted for conflict. They would send twenty ships to Ionia. Herodotus notes wryly that such is democracy that it is easier to persuade a crowd to do something than an individual. Nearby Eretria voted to send five. Herodotus calls these ships 'the beginnings of evils for the Greeks and barbarians', echoing the sentiment in Homer's *Iliad*.[7] This has a tremendously ominous feel, although it was likely that conflict would have unfolded sooner or later even without the twenty-five ships.

Revolt unfolds

The revolt would rumble on over five years, but it got off to a flying start. Greeks in Asia mustered and, with their Athenian and Eretrian allies, marched inland to Sardis where they ravaged the former Lydian capital, the seat of Persian power in the west.[8] Artaphernes and his supporters survived the attack by retreating to the acropolis that towered above the city. Things below escalated quickly. The opportunity to sack the city was curtailed, Herodotus tells us, by a soldier lighting a fire that swept through the city. Artaphernes and his inner circle must have looked down grimly on the flaming chaos below. *So this was the Athenians who had messed him around about submission? These were the ones that Hippias was always complaining about?* The risk was dangerously real, including to Artaphernes' son, another Artaphernes. Unable to escape, the Lydians and any Persians below found themselves channelled by the fire into the marketplace where they attempted to defend themselves. The combination of fire and armed resistance stemmed the Greeks' momentum and they withdrew. The fire had taken such a hold that the Temple of Cybele was burnt to the ground. Herodotus adds some curious details. He notes that Sardis' buildings were made of reeds, which is what caused the fire to spread beyond anyone's intention. The burning of the temple was an accident. The unnamed common soldier and the flimsy buildings are offered in mitigation of what was a serious moral failing. Herodotus notes that the Persians used this as a pretext for burning Greek temples – a pretext because the Persians did it on purpose whereas the Greeks had done it by accident. This would be more compelling if archaeologists had not confirmed that the majority of buildings in Sardis were brick with ceramic roof tiles, not the flammable reeds offered in defence.[9] It is possible that the destruction of the temple was not initially intended, but we should not accept as literal truth the notion that the fire was an accident of circumstance and primitive urban design.

The Greeks withdrew from Sardis to Ephesus. The Persians regrouped, met them there and inflicted a heavy defeat. Aristagoras had promised that it was easy to fight Persians, but the Ionians and Athenians got a taste of something harsher. Herodotus records that many prominent men were killed, including the leader of the Eretrians, a celebrated athlete called Eualcides. The Eretrians cared for his body and made their way home. The Athenians too had lost their taste for the conflict and left. If booty had motivated them, there was little to stay for. The Ionians had no such option unless, like the Phocaeans and Teonians, they abandoned everything and sailed away. They fought on. From disappointment came hope. New allies joined the revolt – Byzantium and communities in Caria and across Cyprus.

It is not really possible to piece together what happened over the next few years in a clear narrative. The Ionians' actions were not entirely unified. That may well have been deliberate. When disparate communities take on a coordinated imperial power, sporadic resistance across a wide area can be highly effective, making it difficult for the empire to know where to focus next. Our perception of the Ionians' efforts is coloured by Herodotus writing with hindsight of their ultimate defeat. It was a personal story for him in the sense that many of his own relatives and other community members will have either taken part or, more often, would have been the children and grandchildren of participants. The events, successes and failures of those years must often have been debated by his circle. What may have seemed a good idea at the time could hardly seem so several decades afterwards, especially as Ionia was never again so powerful or so prosperous. So it is that Aristagoras in Herodotus' *Histories* appears something of a shifty good-for-nothing. There is no love lost when he and Histaeus meet their deaths, Aristagoras in Thrace, Histaeus attempting to re-enter Miletus, where he dies with Herodotus' tell-tale sign of a tyrant's death – a fatal wound to the leg.[10]

Persian retaliation was intense. The Hellespont was retaken. Cyprus was retaken. There, in addition to Herodotus' account, evidence of the siege can be seen in the archaeology of Paphos. In 497 the Carians fought and were soundly defeated at the Marsyas River. The survivors, sheltering in a sacred grove, were relieved by the army of Miletus, which arrived in the nick of time like the proverbial cavalry riding to the rescue. The celebrations proved short-lived. In a second clash at Labraunda the Milesians were wiped out alongside the Carians they had come to save; a neat victory for the Persians, who had once again proved themselves a match for Greek arms and armour.[11]

Rhodes had a different experience. They were not part of the empire, so their involvement was not as rebels. However the position of their large island makes it an important gateway into the Aegean from the Near East and that attracted the Persians' interest. An inscription puts Datis there. The Chronicle of Lindos, one of the city-states of Rhodes, describes the Lindians standing a siege in 495. The water ran out and they grew desperate. A magistrate dreamed that he saw Athena pleading with her father Zeus for water. Heartened by this, the city requested a five-day armistice, after which they would surrender if there was no rain. General Datis laughed and agreed. Laughter in ancient sources almost always comes before a fall. The next day it rained and a humbled Datis agreed a truce and left dedications for the goddess.[12] The inscription was carved many years later, but we can be confident that it reflects local traditions about how Rhodes resisted submission – at least until 490 that is – an island so important could not hold out forever. The Persepolis tablets list extra rations given to Datis at this time and refer to him carrying documents for the king and travelling between Sardis and Persepolis. These references to his presence in the area, combined with the testimony of the Chronicle, make it likely that he really was in charge of the Rhodes offensive and perhaps of the wider suppression of the revolt. It is likely that Datis oversaw what followed at Lade.

The Battle of Lade, near Miletus, saw things come to a head in the autumn of 494.[13] After further meetings at the Panionium, around 70,000 allied Greeks gathered in over 350 ships, under the overall command of Dionysius of Phocaea, a man with a long history of seafaring, trading and piracy. Communities contributed different numbers of ships according to their size and wealth. The overall numbers are huge by the standards of the time and a testament to the wealth of the eastern Greeks. The smaller contingents did not have the clout of the big islands, but they represented a high percentage of the able men of their communities and many of the hopes of those communities will have been bound-up in those men and in the expensive ships themselves. Herodotus gives Dionysius a speech in which he presents the outcome of the battle as a contrast between freedom and slavery – a few hours' effort to win a lifetime of freedom and the only way to avoid punishment for rebelling.

The situation must have been daunting for the Ionians. The Persian Empire had greater resources to call on and had assembled a fleet of 600. Herodotus gives us one more prompt about the self-interest of the Greek tyrants. Dependent on Persian success to regain their positions, they write to prominent members of their former cities urging that they can escape ruin by capitulating, whereas defeat will bring fire, enslavement, castration for boys and deportation to Bactria for girls. But Herodotus adds that because the recipients of the letters thought that they alone had received them, they buried them deep and resisted. This is another case of him stressing that the individual can be harder to convince than a crowd. There was an exception, however, and that would prove crucial. Aeaces, former tyrant of Samos, succeeded in persuading some Samian commanders that it would be safer to desert.

The two fleets approached one another. Each ship would wish to get close to an enemy and have its contingent of fighters board and occupy the other. To seize or disable the enemy target was the brutal aim. Triremes had rams which provided protection and a means of attack. They could break oars and pierce weak points. Wood would be splintering all around amidst the clash of spear, sword and shield, the cries of wounded men, and the struggles of those trapped or already drowning. The Samian ships deserted. It was a big force to see go from a fleet that was already outnumbered. The fleet from Lesbos despaired when they saw their neighbours go and they too extricated themselves from the battle as best they could. Other cities fought on, but without success. Herodotus notes the Chians for their bravery, but also for the horror of their end. Those of their ships in trouble made their way to the coast, pursued by their enemies. It must have been a last adrenaline-fuelled surge of effort from rowers who had been going for some time. They made it ahead of their enemies and ran inland. There they were mistaken for raiders by the people of Ephesus and massacred. It is entirely possible that this story is literally true, yet it is fair to say that Herodotus includes it as a final sorrowful example of the Ionians' disunity. The battle was over and with it the revolt. Now was time for the Persians to re-establish their authority.

The fall-out

When the Persian army conquered a new city, it frequently acted with restraint. Not so with rebel cities. In order to maintain fear and obedience in their subjects, imperial forces frequently punish uprisings in a striking manner. In the case of Persia, such pragmatic ruthlessness was compounded by the belief that rebels were offending against the divine order of things.[14] Both these factors resulted in brutal retaliation against the Greek and Carian communities which had revolted; nowhere more so than at Miletus.

Miletus was besieged by land and sea. There was no route for escape, especially once mining and rams caved the walls in. Most of the men of this wealthy, cosmopolitan city were killed at once. Huge numbers of women and children were enslaved and removed to destinations around the empire. Those men who were not killed were deported, taken to Susa, then settled far away on the Persian Gulf. Herodotus recalls a chilling oracle which refers to this disaster: Miletus, 'a feast for many, a splendid prize,/Your wives shall wash the feet of many a long-haired man/And others shall care for our shrine at Didyma'.[15] The Persians, he explains, were the long-haired men, and the splendid sanctuary of Apollo at Didyma – with its recently rebuilt temple – was plundered, burnt and passed to new hands. The city was attacked as a physical space, as a political and financial entity, as a population, in its family units and in its function as a religious community. The destruction was profound and remains traceable at both the city and the sanctuary. Although the sanctuary was repaired and reopened, its oracle remained out of use for 160 years. Its priests were exiled to Bactria, where their descendants would later meet Alexander the Great.[16]

News of the fall of Miletus soon reached Athens. Herodotus tells us that the Athenians expressed their distress in many ways. The most striking was to have an effect on the subsequent development of drama. The playwright Phrynichus staged a play called *The Capture of Miletus* which brought the audience to desperate tears. Phrynichus was fined 1,000 drachma for reminding people of their troubles and the play was never staged again.[17] These were very early days of drama and it focused from then on upon myth and allegory. The only surviving play explicitly exploring a contemporary topic is Aeschylus' *Persians* – a play that deals in Greek victory not shattering defeat. Whether what moved the Athenians most was pity for their distant kin, disappointment over plans in the east, guilt over their withdrawal from the revolt, or fear at the prospect of things to come is a hard question to answer. We might recall the women captured at Troy who wept for Patroclus and at the same time for themselves, one feeling merged with another.[18] Someone like Miltiades, and his children Cimon and Elpinice, must have counted their lucky stars that they made it out of the east when they did. They had been back in Athens about two years by the time of the Battle of Lade, although of course Miltiades' elder son had not made it. It was the end of an era for Miletus, as it was to be for many cities along the coast. Samos was the only place involved in the revolt to survive unscathed – yet even for the Samians it was a turning point. The community survived because of their capitulation, yet many felt unwilling to return to life under tyrant and empire; they departed, taking with them what refugees there were from Miletus. The atmosphere aboard ship must have been tense, but ultimately they settled successfully on Sicily.[19]

For those who had dreamed of a return to Greek independence in Asia, the Ionian Revolt was a bitter disappointment. The fall of Miletus sent shockwaves around the Greek world. Greeks in Asia Minor faced a long period of recovery and reconstruction. As for the mainlanders, Herodotus leaves us in no doubt that this was all bad news for Athens. He paints a vivid picture of the court of Darius after the burning of Sardis.[20] The Great King hears of the revolt and destruction. He knows that the Ionians will get their comeuppance, but not who the Athenians are. After receiving the answer, he notches an arrow and looses it into the air, praying aloud that he might punish them. From that point on he bids his servants say to him three times at every meal, 'Remember the Athenians'. It is a little hard to accept as literally true, but Herodotus' meaning is clear – the revolt put Persia on the path to Athens.

There were, on the other hand, more positive outcomes from the revolt. Anyone who went into it with more modest expectations might well consider them met. When all was said and done, different communities had different priorities and different relations with Persia and each other. Within those communities there were further differing priorities and desires. We have already seen that it was the elite who were most put-out by changes imposed under Darius. It was this elite which did worst out of the revolt, but there were others who eventually benefitted. A year later, Artaphernes summoned representatives from the Greek cities. They were obliged to swear an oath that they would settle disputes through arbitration (rather than the all-too-frequent piracy and raiding of old) and he announced that their regions would be reassessed for tribute. Rather than a punitive tribute hike, the new level was similar and arguably fairer. This is his last known act as satrap before he was succeeded by his son, the younger Artaphernes. More was to come. The following year Darius appointed a new commander in the region: his nephew and son-in-law, Mardonius. With the backing of the fleet, Mardonius evicted the tyrants and installed democracies in the Greek cities. It may justifiably be said that it was a Persian who brought democracy to a huge number of Greeks for the first time. With the punishment phase over, these economic and political changes secured peace and stability for the region for a long time; exactly what an empire wants in its territories. This was also agreeable to the majority who lived there. The Ionian Revolt brought, if not complete freedom, a sort of freedom.

The Ionian Revolt had also bought time for the Greeks further west. Following the failure to take Naxos, the Ionian Revolt provided a distraction that prevented further attempts there or at other west-Aegean settlements. This did not mean that plans to expand west had been retired. Once Ionia was settled, Mardonius took his fleet and a large army up and across the Hellespont. Herodotus tells us that he was seeking retribution against Athens and Eretria.[21] This is possible, although they were perhaps some way down the priority list. The immediate targets were the north Aegean island of Thasos and Macedonia, both of which were added to the empire. However, when Mardonius attempted to go further, the fleet was caught-out in the dangerous waters around Mt Athos. Thousands drowned in a terrifying storm. The beleaguered force tried to return the way they had come, only to be devastated by fleet-footed nomads. Mardonius himself was wounded, although he survived to coordinate further retreat. It had been a disaster and the remains of the force limped back to Asia. This was a further reprieve for the mainland Greeks, but there must have been a sense of impending trouble. Persia would be coming west and the Athenians and Eretrians had raised their hands as enemies.

Motives

Why was the 490 campaign launched? Multiple explanations are out there and it is of course likely that there were overlapping factors. Personal factors are cited. Herodotus has the Greek doctor at the Persian court wishing to get home and seeing an invasion of his homeland as the way. He pressures Atossa to pressure Darius, and she obliges out of gratitude, telling Darius that she wants more Greek slave girls. Another writer tells us that Darius was fond of Attic figs and keen to tap the source.[22] Such personal motives are obviously not the full picture. Personal motives play a prominent role in early historiography and naturally tend towards stories of this sort. On one level they have an engaging behind-the-scenes quality. On another they belittle the nation or leader involved by trivialising their reasoning; such stories are a common way of indicating the arbitrary nature of monarchy. That said, this does not mean that personal, even petty, motives never play a role in people's reasoning. Perhaps it suffices to say that if such traditions are true they require combination with more substantial motives.

Herodotus places greater emphasis on Darius desiring to punish the Athenians and Eretrians for their part in the revolt. His suggestion that this was a pretext has often been accepted; however the intense emphasis placed on loyalty in Persian imperial philosophy means that, taken with the Athenians reneging on their agreement to submit, a punishment campaign of some sort is not implausible. Revenge may not have been the only motivator, but it was a real one all the same.

Herodotus adds a third reason which was widely accepted in antiquity: Darius wished to expand the empire and conquer all the Greeks who had not yet submitted. This fits the Herodotean view of imperial behaviour – an autocrat always wants more. It also fits with the wider picture of this particular empire's recent behaviour. Darius' reign had seen Persia expand within Egypt, Nubia and western India, suggesting that conquest was very much on the agenda. The creation of the satrapy of Thrace and the conquest of Macedon also indicate a push further west. Sooner or later that would mean mainland Greece.[23]

A finer question remains. Was the 490 campaign just for punishment, an attempt to secure Athens, or a mission to fully conquer Greece? It is certainly possible that a thorough ravage and looting spree on the mainland would be regarded as satisfactory in the short-term, especially if some of the islands could be secured more permanently. On the other hand, the presence of Hippias suggests that capturing Athens was a serious intention. Pickings in Attica alone would be worth having. It was a source of silver and marble as Hippias had no doubt told Artaphernes. Miletus had once helped the Persians extract silver from other Mediterranean sites; Attica could join the list. Just as importantly, Athens offered a foothold on the mainland. Once secured, Athens and Eretria would make practical bases for follow-up campaigns. An attempt to conquer the whole of Greece in this campaign seems unlikely, but this was surely the longer-term goal. It is possible that Hippias was intended to draw the rest of the Greeks into the empire without much more Persian help.[24]

Exactly what was planned we cannot be sure, but there is no reason to doubt that punitive mission and longer-term resource grab could be usefully combined. Herodotus' reference to a 'pretext' is interesting. A great imperial power can proceed with conquest without condescending to give a reason, yet in a world of alliances, treaties and networks of patronage, having a reason to put forward – a grievance to address – was still a useful way to discourage opposition and encourage compliance. Either way, the Persians had reason to be confident. Medes and Persians had now met Greek forces in land battles at least twice – at Ephesus, against Athenians and Ionians, and at Labraunda, against Mytilenians and Carians. The Persians had come off best both times. There were motives and there was a good chance of victory. Mission on.

5

The Plain of Marathon

These days Marathon is a fairly short journey from Athens by bus or car. There is an annual run between the two, although it is not a route that many would run more frequently than that as the *c.* 26 miles from east to west Attica is challenging terrain. Mountains encircle the Marathon plain, and the plain slopes down to where the land meets the sea. The coast around Attica is typically steep and rocky. The Bay of Marathon offers a rare spot where ships can pull in with little risk. Key roads – once little more than paths – then take you from the plain through the mountains into the rest of Attica.

This sort of topographical information was presented to the Persian military by Hippias son of Peisistratus. Ever since his expulsion from Athens in 510 he had looked to the Persians to reinstate him. Once their support was engaged, his knowledge and that of his circle could help secure a smooth landing and swift success. Herodotus notes that the plain was good for cavalry and he is explicit that it was Hippias who directed the fleet.[1] The Peisistratids had roots there. Years before, Peisistratus had gone into self-imposed exile when his allies and enemies joined forces once his father-in-law discovered that Peisistratus had been sleeping with his new wife in 'an unnatural way'. He took Hippias and his brothers with him to Eretria on Euboea. They gathered forces, hired mercenaries, made alliances with Thebes, Argos and Naxos, then they travelled back to Attica, stopping first at Marathon. Eventually their rival Athenians marched out. The armies met near the sanctuary of Athena Pallenis on the way from Marathon to Athens. Peisistratus ordered an attack while the other Athenians were resting. The result was an overwhelming victory and Peisistratus secured his tyranny. This Battle of Pallene, fought in 546/5, around the time Sardis fell to the Persians, will have loomed large in Hippias' memory as he began his return to Greece.[2] It is possible that he hoped for support from Thebes and Argos once again, and he had been able to call on the famous cavalry of Thessaly in years gone by.[3] The accessibility, the topography, the support the Peisistratids had found there all made Marathon a natural destination for Hippias and his Persian backers when they made their way over from the ashes of Eretria. The city where Hippias had spent much of that exile was now in ruins.

Momentum builds

Things had moved on since Mardonius had brought his beleaguered forces back from the north Aegean. In 491, Darius had sent heralds to the Greek states asking for submission. Several agreed, including Aegina. The Athenians were convinced that the Aeginitans would try to use this new alliance to crush them once and for all.[4] The heralds came to Athens. Datis played the genealogy game with a message arguing that as the Medes were descended from Medus, son of Aegeus, half-brother of Theseus, it was the Medes who had the true claim to Athens. Not so, came the answer from Miltiades. If Aegeus' son founded the Medes, the Athenians should rule *them*. A droll but firm answer, perhaps the kind that only takes shape years after the event.[5] Further heralds were thrown to their deaths. The Spartans' reaction was similar, the herald died at the bottom of a well.[6] These incidents were a gross violation of international practice, in which heralds were supposed to move freely. Their killings suggest a desire for a loud statement of intent, and perhaps at Sparta for an irreconcilable action that would end debate.[7] Shortly before, the kings of Sparta had clashed about Aegina. There could be no going back now.

As the heralds travelled across Greece, in Susa Darius issued orders for the eastern Greeks to prepare warships and transport ships. The transports would bring cavalry horses amongst other things; a most ambitious plan.[8] Darius made changes at the top of the military. Mardonius was relieved and two men were appointed to command the westerly expedition: Datis the Mede, who had put down the Ionian Revolt, and Darius' nephew Artaphernes, who had most likely witnessed the sacking of Sardis and who had governed the region for some time.[9]

Mardonius had demonstrated the hazards of entering Greece via the land-route along the north Aegean. This expedition would do things differently and travel via the sea-route through the mid-Aegean. It was a shorter, quicker route. It would require control of at least some of the Cyclades to source water and harbour in bad weather. The Cyclades may themselves have been the major target; after all, a great deal of effort had been wasted attacking Naxos only a few years earlier. Datis and Artaphernes mustered Medes, Persians and Sacae from Central Asia. They led them to Cilicia to meet the fleet, where some 20–25,000 troops plus crew embarked. Getting the horses safely aboard must have been easier said than done, requiring ingenuity on the part of those responsible. This was all very novel. Even experienced Median and Persian soldiers will have spent little time at sea. The Sacae will have spent even less, having perhaps not even seen a body of water bigger than the Caspian Sea, let alone sailed on one. It was a long way west for all of them and they were far more accustomed to the long marches of land campaigns. Herodotus reports 600 triremes, although it is likely that this figure includes transports. Still a large force by any reckoning.[10]

This time there was no reprieve for Rhodes. Despite coming to terms a few years earlier, they were now submitted. The fleet proceeded to Samos. More troops were taken on board, then it was across the Aegean to the Cyclades. There was no resistance at Naxos. People fled into the hills above the city – a defence against raiders which had served them in troubled times for centuries. Some escaped. Others were enslaved or pressed into service. The city and its sanctuaries were torched.[11] The same happened on other islands: a trail of destruction, men seized for service, children taken as hostages. The exception was at Delos, the holy island. The people had fled. Datis sent a messenger to tell them that he was surprised by their fear (showing that gas-lighting has been around a lot longer than the expression). He would not harm such a sacred site but instead left 300 talents, some seven tonnes, of frankincense as an offering.

This was a striking gesture that looked to the future of Greek-Persian relations. Herodotus has Datis announce that even without the king's orders he would have done the right thing. Sanctuaries had already been damaged on this campaign, but Delos was different – the birthplace of Artemis and Apollo, important to all Greeks. Sparing Delos was the carrot to the stick of looted cities. We can infer from Datis' remark that Darius knew of Delos and its reputation and had given orders to preserve it. It would have been known to them at least since the earlier campaign against Naxos, when the prospect of controlling 'other islands' was put forward as a motive. The Persian fleet's absorption of Cycladian Greeks into its force was another reason to act carefully at this special site. The Persians used might and terror but they could act at different registers and use restraint where it would serve. Nonetheless, the Delians reported an earthquake soon after, though they had never been troubled by one before – a sign of trouble and a motif used by Herodotus to mark a shocking aberration from the norm.[12]

The Eretrians were in trouble and they knew it. They withdrew within the well-fortified city, but they could not defend it forever. They had appealed to the Athenians, who now shared the island of Euboea with them, and 4,000 had come to their aid. It is a little chilling to think how many Euboeans from Chalcis had

Fig. 8 Attica and Euboea.

been displaced to provide those 4,000 with their farms. Amongst the Eretrians, opinion was split, as it was in so many states over whether to concede and hope for leniency, or to hold out and hope that the Persians would be drawn away. Divisions became so stark that one Eretrian, a man called Aeschines, advised the Athenians to leave and save themselves. They did so, and were some of the last people to see the bustling city before it was destroyed. The siege lasted seven days before two men betrayed the city. This was not 'betrayal' in the figurative sense of surrender; it was a betrayal that admitted the Persians who burned the city, sacked the sanctuaries, demolished the gates and enslaved the people. Many were killed, while almost 800 men, women and children were taken aboard ship. Those who had favoured resistance and those against were all subject to the onslaught. Survivors must have reeled in horror at the fate of themselves, their loved ones and their city.[13]

After settling affairs on Euboea, Datis and Artaphernes looked south to Attica. For Hippias and his circle the long hoped-for dream was becoming real. It was over fifty years since Hippias had made this journey with his father. Just a short trip across the strait and the fleet landed at the eastern coast of Attica. They anchored off the beach and encamped nearby on the Plain of Marathon.

The plain

The Bay of Marathon meets the long Schoinia beach at its northerly end, and the beach in turn was backed by an extensive marsh. The marsh could not be camped on, but the spring at its northern edge would be a vital supply for horses and humans alike. Beyond the perimeter of the marsh a road leads north-east towards Rhamnous, skirting Mt Stavrokoraki. Stavrokoraki and Mt Kotroni sit to the west of the plain with the road into the village of Marathon and on to the main body of Attica sitting in the valley which separates them. Mt Agrieliki and Mt Aphorismos sit to the south-west, with a spring and small marsh at the base of Aphorismos and the sea meeting the base of Agrieliki beside a coastal road. 'Marathon' is Greek for 'fennel'; perhaps the herb grew well there. This complex natural landscape was complimented by an equally complex sacred landscape with rich mythological relevance. There had been buildings and tombs in the area since the Neolithic period and these remained sites of ritual over subsequent generations. The plain and its large deme bore the name of the hero Marathon. The Bull of Marathon had wreaked havoc there and a fatal accident involving a prince of Crete trying to capture it led to the famous grudge held by King Minos. He demanded a tribute of fourteen young Athenians tossed into the labyrinth from then on. The hero Theseus defeated the Bull, which became the constellation Taurus. He then defeated its progeny, the Minotaur, before including Marathon amongst twelve towns he united to create Attica.[14]

Heracles, who had inadvertently released the Marathonian Bull, was honoured on the site. There is reference to a *temenos* – a sacred space – devoted to him, and there was perhaps a small temple. Other heroes were worshipped at tombs on the plain. Depictions of heroes apparently rising to fight in the battle show them climbing out of a tomb, and various offerings have been found. The most dominant sacred space belonged to Athena. As Athena Hellotis she had a sanctuary and temple there which would have been the focus of cult activity and festival celebrations for the local community. Her association with the area was deep. She is even described in the *Odyssey* landing at Marathon on her way into Athens – a well-worn route.[15]

The plain was an ideal spot. The gentle beach created a safe point to disembark people and animals. Supplies could be brought in from various directions – from Euboea and other islands and from Boeotia if necessary. Springs provided water

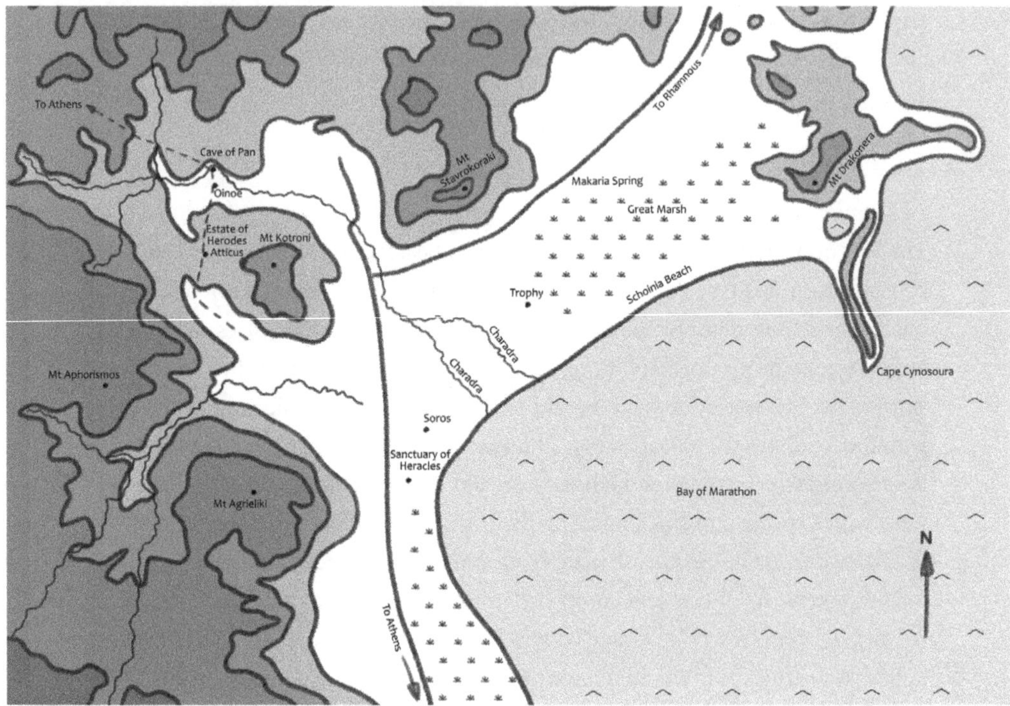

Fig. 9 The Marathon Plain.

and we should picture the Persian army making camp to the north of the Great Marsh at the base of Mt Stavrokoraki, where they had space, access to a spring and control of the road. In later years the travel writer Pausanias was shown stone mangers used by the cavalry and marks in the rock where Artaphernes' tent had been secured.[16] We should imagine Hippias leading sacrifices to Athena before her temple, perhaps in the company of Datis and Artaphernes, certainly in the company of his loyal circle. There seems to have been no attempt to secure the sanctuary beyond that, but as gods and heroes in Greek thought are bound-up in location, it would be natural to appeal to the goddess with influence over the plain. Meanwhile the cavalrymen would be caring for their horses; Persians and Medes alike checking bow-strings and other weapons; Sacae sharpening their axes; the Ionian Greeks and islanders with them were perhaps processing mixed feelings as they made their preparations. There would be meals to prepare, time for storytelling and jokes, games to play. Armies spend a lot of time waiting and this army like any other will have found ways to kill time and diffuse some of the stress of a possible battle.

Final decisions at Athens

News of the fall of Eretria arrived in Athens in September, in the Athenian month of Boedromion around the time of a festival in honour of Artemis Agrotera and Apollo. The Persians' arrival at Marathon was confirmed soon after. The big decision could be postponed no longer. And there certainly was a decision to be made. There was no consensus in *any* city on what to do about the Persian Question and Athens was no exception. There were those who were not averse to the return of the Peisistratids; those who disliked the radical reforms had reason to feel optimistic about Hippias' approach. There were those who had no love for tyranny or Persia who nonetheless regarded Persian defeat as inevitable. To them resistance may well have seemed a sort of betrayal of the population who would face the consequences. Then there were those who did wish to resist, but these too were divided between those who thought it wisest to stand a siege and those who favoured marching out to fight. Another option was to abandon the city; to sail away and start again as people from Phocaea, Teos and Samos had before them.[17]

At this stage in his narrative, Herodotus reintroduces Miltiades. He is more positive about him than he was earlier; there is no emphasis on his tyranny or his service in Darius' army. We are reminded of how Miltiades' father was banished by Peisistratus then murdered on Hippias' order, of his escape from the Persian fleet, although not of his son Metiochus, who we might recall was now 'living as a Persian'. There is a reminder that once Miltiades 'escaped' punishment for tyranny he was elected general of his tribe, Oineis.[18] His election to general would prove decisive. We find Miltiades as the main advocate for marching out. The debate must have been raging in homes and at the agora as well an in Assembly for a long time beforehand, ever since the Aeginetans' submission made invasion seem real and inevitable. The final decision was made in Assembly by adult male citizens; male and female slaves, resident foreigners, children and free women such as Elpinice, Miltiades' daughter, would wait poised to hear the outcome.

When it came down to it, the city was not fully walled. Only a fraction of the citizens could take refuge on the acropolis and even they could not hold out long with the city burning below, even if pro-Peisistratids did not betray them first. A siege was doomed. Submission was opposed by many and that ship might be thought to have sailed, given recent events at Eretria. Those who favoured tackling the invasion head-on won the day. It was risky, but options were limited and this gave them a chance. They chose to march out and risk death on the battlefield rather than risk death coming nearer their nearest and dearest. Perhaps by meeting the enemy at the border they could prevent the torching of Attica and the arrival of the Persians at Athens itself.

Message carriers – long distance runners who could cross mountains faster than horse-riders – left to request assistance.[19] The Spartans might respond, but the Athenians had few friends at the moment and even the Spartans could not be expected in less than four days. Miltiades proposed decrees for adult men of fighting age to gather provisions and muster. It is likely that male resident foreigners were called-up too. In a decision that put survival above all else, the decree proposed that male slaves be offered their freedom if they would join the army. This was novel, but the Athenians voted for it. Men came forward, willing to take the risk for so great a reward. The state seems to have offered compensation to their former owners.[20] Arms and armour would be checked and provisions gathered. There will have been sacrifices and omen readings in council and in homes as men took their leave. Miltiades' son, Cimon, was just too young to fight. He, Elpinice and others like them would be considering what possibilities there were for defence or escape should their father's plan fail. The army mustered at the gymnasium of Apollo Lyceus. They took an oath to fight to the death and to obey their generals. They promised Artemis Agrotera, goddess of the hunt, that for every Persian killed a goat would be offered to her. Blood magic in perilous times.[21] The army hurried as fast as it could to Marathon.

6

The Fight

Gods at war

On the plain of Marathon the two armies met. The gods sent signs to both sides, revealed in sacrifices, indicating that it was the right time to begin. Miltiades called the Athenians to run into action and the heroes of Attica rose up to assist. Marathon, the hero of the plain was there, wielding his spear. Theseus rose up from the Underworld and charged ahead to cut down the foe. Cecrops, founder of Athens, appeared fighting with a great rock. Other heroes entered the fray, Echetlus, Codrus and Neleus. There were supernatural forces at work for the Persians and Medes. A heavy-armoured giant stalked through the crowd, cutting down Greeks. One man who saw him was blinded though untouched by any weapon. Heracles put heart into the Athenians, as did the goddesses Hera, Hecate, Demeter and Core and Athena. Apollo played his part, and above all his sister Artemis saved the day. She fired the Athenians with the skill and bloodlust of the hunt to help them take down their prey. General Callimachus was skewered by so many spears that his body was held up by them, yet like some god he continued to slay the enemies around him. At last the god Pan unleashed a Panic amongst the invaders who, overcome by the irresistible fear, broke and fled. Once again the goddess of the hunt aided the Athenians in pursuing their targets, this time to the beach where they called for fire and set ships aflame. The remains of the fleet sailed off with the last of the Persians scrambling aboard. The battle was over; the Greeks had won. This was no surprise to Hippias, who had received a discouraging omen before the battle had even begun.[1]

It is no easy thing to get at the literal truth of what happened at Marathon. Greek accounts of the battle were infused with religious traditions from the start, to which more were added as time went on. Herodotus' description was written fairly close to the events and his narrative is the standard to which details from other sources are sometimes added along with conjectures based on what happened on other occasions, the lie of the land and what seems plausible. But we should not anticipate a great deal of certainty. Herodotus' version is extremely brief and even if we stick to only the non-supernatural aspects of his account it is clearly influenced by the idealisation that crept in over time. That said, the combination of Herodotus' innovate work and the information generated owing to the sheer fame of the battle means that more can be deduced about this clash than any previous battle. While certainties are limited, there is a lot to be gained from considering the possibilities.

The armies prepare

Herodotus tells us that the Athenians encamped in the sanctuary of Heracles. It is impossible to be precise about where it was despite numerous attempts to identify it, but it is safe to say that it was south or south-west of the plain. Another author has them cutting stakes from trees on the mountainside to protect the camp. The best news for the Athenians was the arrival of the Plataeans – much-needed allies who had responded to the call. The Athenians had fielded around 9,000 hoplites; the arrival of around 1,000 Plataeans added a decent percentage. To the hoplites we must add a few thousand more to include the freed slaves and the fighting poor, ready with slings, rocks, perhaps daggers or a spear, but little armour if any.[2] There was no sign of the Spartans. For this reason we should accept Herodotus' description of a wait of several days before the battle. The Athenians' presence prevented the Persians from going further in-land, so it was worth waiting to see if the Spartans would show. This adds credence to the tradition of the re-enforcement of the camp. The Athenians and Plataeans would have provisions, there was a spring and they were well-placed to source extra if needed. Later authors would have the Athenians fighting as soon as they arrived, but this seems like an adjustment to create a more dramatic impression.[3] The Persians were under greater time constraints. They had a lot of people to manage: Persians, Medes, Sacae and Greeks. They could receive provisions, but it was already September and the seas would be getting rough. Anyone who remembered what happened to Mardonius' fleet would know that if they could not secure Attica swiftly, then it was worth returning to safe shores before too long.

The Athenians were commanded by ten elected generals. In overall command was Callimachus of the Aeantis tribe, the polemarch or war-archon, who had also been elected to his post. Herodotus heard that the generals took turns to preside, a day each. Decisions were made by a vote of the ten, with the polemarch casting the deciding vote if things were even. This is probably anachronistic – a projection into the past of how things had become. Callimachus was in charge, advised by the generals.[4] Nonetheless, as most authors have it, including Herodotus, Miltiades carried a lot of influence. This made sense. There was force of personality of course, but beyond that he seems to have been the chief motivator behind the campaign and he had experience of the Persian military.

Callimachus, joined by seers, would be leading sacrifices and omen-readings. Military leaders were expected to have this ability, but it was usual to get the support of more experienced seers who would be fighting alongside everyone else before long. A liver could not tell anyone their future, but it could help answer simple questions. They might ask '*Is it wise to continue waiting?*' A healthy enough liver would indicate 'yes'. One was expected to consider the circumstances when reading omens. These sorts of sacrifices also resulted in meat that could be eaten by the army, although the final sacrifices before battle – the *sphagia* – were not considered edible. Athena, Heracles and Artemis must have had a good share of these offerings and the heroes and other gods will have been called-on too. Sacrifices might bring guidance and help and they offered an outlet for fraying nerves as the hours stretched on.[5]

We know by name several of the men in the Athenian camp in addition to Callimachus and Miltiades. Aristides son of Lysimachus was there as general of the Antiochis tribe. His cousin Callias was there, a wealthy man and a torch-bearer at Eleusis. Aeschylus the playwright was there with his brother, Cynegeirus. Stesilaus was another of the generals. Themistocles son of Neocles was there, though he was no friend of Miltiades. Xanthippus who had married into the Alcmaeonids was there, another man without much love for the Cimonids. And Hipparchus of the Peisistratids was there. He had not left when the bulk of his family went into exile. How strange to have them coming back. The Plataeans were led by a man called Arimnestus. Members of the Athenian elite would know him and other prominent Plataeans already.

Miltiades and his followers had last seen serious action on Lemnos. Other Athenians will have last fought against Chalcis. Some of them will have fought the Persians at Ephesus, without much success. It would be a strange time for the former slaves. A week ago these Athenians had them enslaved; now they were sharing a camp. There cannot have been time to organise them into a fighting unit of their own so they will have been readied to mix amongst the rest of the army.[6] Were they more comfortable socialising with each other? Was that even permitted? Everyone must have felt anxious. Losing a battle for border territory could mean one's own death, the loss of some land, and the exposure of territory to ravaging and pillaging. The stakes this time were far higher. This army knew what had happened at Miletus and Eretria. Defeat would most likely mean extensive killings, rapes and executions, the burning of the city, destruction of the countryside, and the mass enslavement and deportation of the population. Their whole community was depending on them.

Datis and Artaphernes were unambiguously in command of their force. Each baivarabām of 10,000 had a commander reporting to them, and that continued down in a decimal structure to the units of 10. More sacrifices, more omen-readings, more prayers as they waited. The Medes, Persians and Sacae were a long way from home – especially the Sacae. There would be tension about being on foreign soil with sea behind them, but on the whole the campaign had been going well and there was every reason for a buoyant mood.

Cavalry

Perhaps the greatest challenge that the Greeks faced was how they could manoeuvre on the plain without being routed by cavalry. Infantry light or heavy are vulnerable to the weight and manoeuvrability of a cavalry unit. Used freely, cavalry can attack the flanks and rear of a phalanx. The Persians also positioned cavalry in front of their centre to devastate approaching forces. Horses are generally reluctant to charge dense spear-armed units, but no such ordered horse-repelling phalanxes were likely at Marathon. Herodotus had told us that Hippias recommended Marathon for this very reason – that it could be dominated by horsemen if the Athenians came out to fight. Other traditions place horses there too. Ancient images of Marathon, which we will see more of later, depict an infantry battle yet include horses here or there. In his first-century BCE biography of Miltiades, Cornelius Nepos refers to an over-the-top 10,000 cavalry fighting in the battle. The orator Aelius Aristides, in the second century CE, claimed that the Athenians captured Persian horses. And as we have seen (Ch. 5), Pausanias, in the same era as Aristides, relates how visitors were shown mangers and thrilled with stories of ghost horses neighing around Miltiades' monument.[7] Clearly horses were part of the battle traditions, although we do not know how many really were present. It is one of the mysteries of Marathon that when Herodotus came to write his battle narrative, he made no mention of the cavalry. So intriguing. Their absence has prompted speculation over the years.

In the late nineteenth century, the scholar J. A. R Munro proposed that Datis and Artaphernes divided their forces, with one staying and the other taking the cavalry and half the infantry towards Athens. Getting wind of this, the theory goes, prompted Miltiades to attack when the cavalry left. Another commentator imagines that the Persians divided because they heard from Greek traitors that the Spartans would soon arrive. The division is an attractive idea as it explains the cavalry's apparent absence and why the Athenians did not wait indefinitely. In other respects it is unsatisfactory; it relies on invention and has little basis in ancient sources. No ancient writer says that Datis and Artaphernes split up; Herodotus gives the opposite impression. The closest tradition is found in Nepos. He refers to the Persian force being 200,000 – colossal hyperbole meant merely to indicate 'a lot' – however he then refers to only 100,000 fighting. Munro and others use this as inspiration for the theory that half the force had left, taking the cavalry with them. The weakness is that Nepos never says that the 100,000 left and he explicitly has the cavalry fighting in the battle.[8] It offers a flimsy basis to build the re-embarkation theory on.

A second source may support the theory. A dramatic scene can be painted. The Athenians wait nervously in camp. Across the plain the Ionian Greeks wait too, wracked with shame at the thought of the position they find themselves in, reluctant to attack their fellow Hellenes. The cavalry leave. The Ionians can take it no longer. They come through the tree-cut stakes and alert the Athenians to what is happening. The Athenians recognise the significance of the moment and leap into action, attacking once the cavalry are gone and winning their famous victory. Novelists sometimes seize on this idea and convey it with all the atmosphere of Priam crossing the Greek camp to Achilles. The weakness of the tradition lies in the tenuousness of its origin and the difficulty of thoroughly understanding the text. The story comes from the *Suda*, a lexicon from the tenth century CE which includes excerpts of ancient texts and commentary by ancient scholars. It is a valuable resource, providing snippets of scholarship which would otherwise be lost. But it was not tasked with being reliable on historical matters; that is not its purpose. The story is listed to explain the term 'choris hippeis', 'the cavalry are apart'. The phrase and the context are confused. J. A. S. Evans has highlighted some of the linguistic difficulty in his translation of the passage:

> When Datis invaded Attica, men say that the Ionians, when he had withdrawn (or *gone away*), came up inland to a wooded area (or *climbed trees*) and told (or *signalled*) the Athenians that their horses were apart (or *away* or *brigaded by themselves*, or possibly *off on a separate mission*). And Miltiades who took note of their departure (or *understood what they were up to*), attacked and won a victory. Thus the aphorism is said of those who break up (or *destroy*) battle order (or *an army detachment*, or possibly even *an army*).[9]

It is hard to know exactly what is meant and there is reason for caution about what the entry describes. It does confirm that there was at some point a tradition that the Ionians had in some way encouraged the Athenians to strike when the cavalry was doing something. Vague as that is, it is an enticing prospect. It appeals to our love of daring and to the thought that the Ionians were loyal to their kinsmen despite the circumstances. On the other hand it is such a good story it seems unlikely that Herodotus would have left it out had he heard it. It has all the sort of vibrancy he enjoyed and enlivened his work with. Equally it seems impossible that he would not have heard it, when he himself was Ionian. It is unlikely that this story was being told in Athens in the mid-late fifth century. It is more plausible that this story developed in Ionia well after the event to mitigate the uncomfortable and well-known reality of their having fought on the 'wrong' side. *Yes, our fathers(?), grandfathers(?), ancestors(?) fought for Persia at Marathon, but they did what that they could to help the Athenians and gave them the key to victory*. It is intriguing to know that this tradition circulated, but it would not do to put too much weight on it.

So we know that cavalry sailed with the expedition, but not how many. The evidence that they were away is weak, but the evidence that they were there *en masse* is weak too, and it is hard to see how a sizable cavalry would not have routed the Greeks almost at their leisure. Is there a way of resolving these differences? The answer might have to be 'yes' and 'no'. 'No' because there is unlikely to be any definitive new evidence coming to light, although never say 'never'. 'Yes' is driven by the emergence of further theories. Loathe to invent the cavalry leaving, yet reluctant to consider a battle in which they stood by and did nothing, Peter Krentz has speculated on a compromise. Suppose the Greeks had for days observed the movements of the Persian camp: the daily routine as they woke, prepared arms and horses for battle, and how they deployed with fighters and horses making their way from camp to plain for another day of waiting. Suppose the Greeks realised that this took a while. There was a crucial time when much of the army was on the field while the cavalry were still making their way down the narrow path. Suppose they saw that as their chance, until eventually they acted on it, striking the Persian infantry when the cavalry was not yet there to defend them. The cavalry is *at* Marathon, and yet *not* at Marathon.[10] There is a tradition of observing the enemy and attacking before they are ready; Peisistratus and Cleomenes both had form for it.[11] We might also wonder if the Suda's 'cavalry are apart' refers to this distribution rather than to re-embarking. It has a lot to recommend it, although this theory also involves a lot of supposition.

The other thing to reconsider is numbers. It is difficult to transport horses by sea. Nepos' 10,000 is clearly absurd. Some have suggested that we should be picturing only very few horses.[12] If we imagine not thousands but *c.* 100–200 they could have been present yet less than usually effective. If we imagine a small force delayed in transition or actually leaving, it is even easier to picture their usual effectiveness being reduced. There is simply no certainty on this issue; however it is clear that cavalry did not play a decisive role in the battle.

Horses were not the only animals on the plain. Sheep and goats travelled with ancient armies, providing mobile access to sacrificial offerings and meat. Donkeys were necessary pack-animals. Athenian commemorations of the battle included at least one dog and we might picture more. Dogs were not a standard part of an army, but a campaign close to home might be a different matter. These would belong to private households, kept for hunting. They would be good company in camp and could source extra food if the campaign dragged on. When the time came, their hunt experience would be good preparation for battle, much as it was for humans. This was especially the case when things moved to a rout.[13]

Debate

As always with the ancient Greeks, there was debate. Herodotus presents a split between the generals over whether to fight. He may well be revisiting arguments that were heard in Athens, but it is not implausible that there were generals who never approved the plan to fight and those who liked the idea less once they saw the assembled enemy. They had reason to be nervous. Greeks had come off worse when they had met Persians in the field before. Herodotus gives Miltiades an inspiring speech to Callimachus. He bids him support an attack: *It is up to you whether to enslave Athens or make her free.* He reminds Callimachus about the impending return of Hippias and evokes the glory of Harmodius and Aristogeiton, men of Callimachus' own tribe, who had challenged the tyrants. *Not fighting will mean disaster, whereas if we fight we can win – if God* (meaning Zeus) *gives fair play – a win would make Athens the foremost city of the Greeks.* Anxiety must have been through the roof. Callimachus made his decision and the fight was back on.[14]

We are told that the generals who supported Miltiades gave up their command days to him but that he waited for his own day to fight anyway. This is probably another anachronism. This tradition most likely arose from later people trying to make sense of the delay and interpreting it in a way that reflected well on Miltiades. We have seen that the Athenians and Plataeans were waiting for the Spartans. We have seen that it is possible, though uncertain, that they waited until the cavalry left. Herodotus has the Athenians take the offensive. There has been suggestion that Miltiades and Callimachus attacked before the Spartans arrived because each day increased the risk of medising – pro-Persian activity – at home, perhaps even in the army. As we saw at Eretria and earlier in the Ionian Revolt, there were many Greeks who thought it advisable to join the empire and be done with it. Hippias clearly had high hopes of finding supporters. As it is he seems to have grossly overestimated that support, but that is not to say that there was no chance of things going his way.[15] It is possible that the Greeks saw some indication that the Persians were going to attempt to advance inland; perhaps simply signs of increased activity, perhaps them thundering boldly towards them taking the initiative. Something, whether fears of medising, other concerns, or being attacked, pushed the Athenians to fight without Spartan aid.[16]

Herodotus' battle narrative

A great deal of discussion has been had over the position of the armies, but fundamentally it is unknown. The Persians and their allies either had their backs to the sea with the marsh, the camp and their ships to their right, or the marsh and so on was behind them.[17] Herodotus describes the deployment of the Greeks:

> The right-wing was commanded by Callimachus the polemarch, for it was then the Athenian custom for the polemarch to have the right-wing. Next to him came the tribes in order of their number; and finally, the Plataeans were on the left-wing. Ever since that battle, when the Athenians bring sacrifices to the assemblies held at the five-yearly festivals, the Athenian herald prays that all blessings may fall on the Athenians and Plataeans alike. Once the troops were deployed at Marathon the lines were of equal length to the Medes so the centre was only a few ranks deep – the weakest part of the line – while the wings were stronger. The battle-line arrayed and the sacrifices (*sphagia*) being favourable, the Athenians were released straightaway and ran towards the barbarians. They were not less than a mile away. The Persians, seeing them come running, prepared to meet them, thinking the Athenians mad to attack at speed with no horsemen or archers.
>
> Herodotus, 6.111–2.

It is worth noting the reference to army forming up in tribes. These were the building blocks of Athenian society. They had elected their own generals; they had mustered, travelled and would fight together. This familiarity would be beneficial once battle began. Men would find reassurance in fighting alongside people they knew well, people unlikely to abandon them, people they may wish to protect. There is also the value of peer pressure. It can be motivating to perform in front of those whose opinions you value most; those who will celebrate your deeds back home. Even feelings like anger and grief might be channelled in this system. There is no one way to react to, say, seeing your cousin run-through, but it could spur some on for vengeance. From a different perspective, men do not wish to be shamed in front of their friends and family; those who could spread the word at home and hold it over their heads. It is a negative motivation, but could reduce the inclination to hold back or bolt. A further practical result of this order was the impact at home. If one part of the line suffered heavily, the bereavement would be confined to one or two tribes rather than spread across the population as a more disruptive force. Plutarch gives us a slightly different picture, presenting Themistocles and Aristides fighting side-by-side in the centre despite belonging to different tribes. Yet even he stresses that they were central precisely because their tribes were central – Leontis and Antiochis. Plutarch's motive in this passage is to stress the virtue of cooperation, which the two men show here, so with that in mind there is no reason to abandon the tribe-by-tribe formation.[18] Across the plain a similar principle was observed on a larger scale: Medes fighting in units with other Medes, Persians with Persians, Sacae with Sacae, and Greeks with Greeks. This put friends and countrymen beside one another, supportive and, usefully, speakers of the same language.

It is common to read that the Athenians and Plataeans ran into battle to avoid Persian arrows, spending as little time as possible in range. There is a certain logic to this of course, although it is not something that Herodotus offers as an explanation. We have also seen the idea that they hurried to beat a delayed cavalry – another possible but un-evidenced theory. If, however, the Persians initiated the attack, then the Athenians were matching like-for-like by hurrying to meet them. It has concerned some scholars that troops could not keep a tight formation running even a relatively short distance; however the density and regularity of the phalanxes of this era have been much exaggerated. We should not picture orderly ranks running or fighting, but a much looser crowd.[19] We should picture non-hoplites in that crowd too. Herodotus describes the Persians looking on in wonder as the Greeks attack without archers or cavalry. While there was no formal archery unit, the Athenian army was still not an exclusive hoplite domain. The former slaves and light-to-unarmed troops would be in amongst the hoplites, looking for their chances to contribute. The exclusive hoplite phalanx came later and was projected back upon Marathon, pushing the poor out of the picture.

First blood has been shed – the last-minute *sphagia* sacrifice taken with the prayer *We kill. May we kill.*[20] The armies are on the move. Persian archers proved ineffective. The Athenian and Plataeans' shields will have taken the brunt of anything incoming as they did on later occasions when Greeks and Persians met.[21] Those without shields will have fared worst, but even they will have gained some protection from the shields round-about them. The casualties were not enough to disable the attack. The armies get closer. Soon individual faces of the enemy can be made out, before, still shockingly, blows are exchanged at the front. Herodotus goes on:

> The Athenians closed with the barbarians and fought in a way that deserves telling. For they were the first Greeks, so far as I know, who charged their enemies at a run, and the first who could stand to look at Median clothing and the men who wore it; for until then the Greeks were frightened of the very name of the Medes.
>
> The fighting went on for a long time at Marathon. The barbarians were victorious in the middle of the line, where the Persians and the Sacae were arrayed. With this victory the barbarians broke the Greek line and pursued them inland. On the wings, however, the Athenians and Plataeans were victorious. With this victory they then allowed the defeated barbarians to flee and they drew their wings together to create a single unit to fight those who had broken through the centre.
>
> Herodotus, 6.112–3.

With his usual clarity, Hans van Wees notes that the Athenians were not at all the first to run into battle: 'blatantly untrue since running into battle had long been common practice'. van Wees also observes that the claim to have run almost a mile is eight times further than an army would usually run – a little less than 200m is more likely.[22] It is entirely plausible that people soon began to exaggerate how far they ran and how fast. If we picture them hurrying on the double as it were and rushing as they neared the enemy we would probably have a fair picture.

What Herodotus presents after that is a pincer effect; the Athenian right-wing under Callimachus and the Plataeans on the left defeat their opponents and then turn to destroy the Persians and Sacae in-between them. The Ionian Greeks disappear from the narrative at this point, so who knows where they were positioned. The Athenians in the centre had a rough ride, but plenty of them survived to tell the tale. For some, this battle narrative 'inspires confidence' in credibility. Others have called it an 'unimpeachable' narrative heard from veterans themselves.[23] This is over-optimistic. It is rather to some extent 'a story of ideal hoplite behaviour pushed to heroic extremes'.[24] It is tempting to take the description literally when it is so rare to have an account of a battle of this period. The chief reason to be cautious, however, is that Greek armies were never again able to accomplish such a well-orchestrated manoeuvre; not when they were more experienced, not when they trained more. Archaic Greek soldiers were not professionals. With the odd exception they did not practice together. More detailed accounts of later battles make clear it was a frequent problem that victorious sections would pursue their victory, leaving defeated sections of their line vulnerable. They were not heartless, it was simply too chaotic to organise much once the fight was underway – the noise rising, the dust flying and the adrenalin pumping. Those who picture Miltiades carefully planning this tactic in advance and deliberately thinning the centre to achieve it are putting romance above likelihood. Miltiades was never famed as a tactical genius and innovator; he was famed for his brave determination. Not that he had *no* tactical ability, simply that it is unlikely that he would rely on a tactic that no Greek army had ever managed. Nor does Herodotus even claim it. He does say that the line was thinner in the centre, but we need not infer from that that this was planned and, perhaps more compellingly, this could well be another retro-fit to make sense of the tradition that developed of the perfect hoplite battle. There might be some sense in letting go of the idea that we can read this as a literal account altogether. We could perhaps compromise and consider that if we accept the Athenian centre gave way first, the wings may have been close enough to maintain the fight, but in a less organised orderly way than is suggested by talk of them reforming and re-engaging in a pre-planned manoeuvre.

What was the scene like where the fighting occurred? Xenophon, rather gruesomely, has a man argue that hand-to-hand fighting is a work of enthusiasm rather than precision.[25] Enthusiasm the Athenians and Plataeans must have had by the load. The orator Isocrates would later say that they fought as if their souls were not their own – that supernatural element suggested again.[26] We should picture their opponents fighting with plenty of enthusiasm too. They were an experienced army and besides it is dangerous to fight half-heartedly, especially with the sea as your only exit.

Archery is simple enough to picture. The range of ancient bows was fairly short. When the armies were at the extreme ends of the plain, the archers could not reach. By the time they were around 200m apart it would be a different story.

Many Persian arrowheads have been found on the plain, so there is no doubt that they were flying fairly thick at some point. As we have seen, they do not seem to have been powerful enough to effectively penetrate a hoplite shield. A linen, leather or metal cuirass might well keep them out too; far more dangerous for the lightly-equipped. An arrow ripping into the lungs would disable and likely kill you – a painful, gasping death. One to the head would be similarly bad news. Without a helmet you would be vulnerable; even with one a lucky shot might catch you in the face. Arrows to the limbs might be disabling, but if you could get out of trouble without further wounding you had a good chance of surviving. Once the Athenians were close, the archers would switch to other weapons.

Hand-to-hand battle was an exhilarating, ferocious affair. The spears of both sides had good reach. A fighter is looking for a vulnerable gap. A downwards stab into the throat would be fatal, further down to the thighs or buttocks might also bring a man down and prove fatal if he was caught in the artery near the groin. Those with shields and cuirasses had good protection for their torso; those without them were vulnerable to horrible injuries to their vital organs. The same can be said for the head. A Corinthian helmet gave excellent protection; Greeks without them and Persians, Medes and Sacae in caps were more exposed. Anyone who fell would be vulnerable to those Greeks with spikes on the base of their spears – *sauroters*, lizard-killers. Many a helmet and breastplate at Olympia reveals the tell-tale square puncture-hole of these spikes.[27] More Greeks than Persians or Sacae carried durable thrusting spears. Both sides carried lighter spears which could inflict similar stabbing and slashing injuries and which could pierce someone horribly when thrown. These were more likely to snap, however. Of the Battle of Plataea, Herodotus describes the Persians deliberately trying to grab at spears to break them.[28] There was space to manoeuvre as the phalanxes were not rigidly packed. While overarm thrusts are more frequently depicted in Greek art, underarm thrusts can also be seen and we should imagine people fighting according to personal preference and the necessities of the moment.

There were the other blades to look out for. Some Greeks carried swords and the Persians and Medes had their *akinakes*. These had a shorter reach than the spear but the longer blade could inflict nasty slashes and stabbing injuries. Again, the neck, the head, the thighs and the groin would be targets, with torso and limbs worthwhile alternatives. Some added axes to the mix. These can generate a lot of power and a hacking blow from one of them could end someone or leave a deep wound. And let us not forget the most lightly-armed: the former slaves and the poor. As the most vulnerable to blades, they would be trying to avoid hand-to-hand confrontations for the most part. Within the phalanx they would be releasing rocks from slings and dispatching with daggers any unfortunate wounded who came their way.

Once the fight was on, it was chaotic. You could not tell what was going on beyond a small group around you. Danger came from many angles – the swipes of spear, sword and axe and the rogue projectiles. Adrenalin would be surging and senses alive to risk and to the opportunity to land a blow – anticipating your opponent's move, where their shield might move next, gauging the gaps in their armour. No wonder people felt the gods' presence as they fought, given the intensity of their struggle and the extremity of their actions. If you were not initially at the front, the anticipation would build as you waited for the chance to step into a gap – perhaps a mixture of longing for and dreading that opportunity. This is when having your cousins and friends nearby can help; the reassurance of the familiar, people you cannot let down. Xenophon, a veteran of many clashes, gives us a pithy account of the heat of battle: 'they shoved, fought, killed and were killed'.[29]

Callimachus was one of those to die. He had led the successful right-wing, but fell before the day was out. Herodotus notes his death. Later traditions describe him pierced by so many spears that he could not fall, still hacking away at the enemies around him until his last breath. The general Stesilaus fell.[30] One author refers to Datis dying in the battle, although that is not backed up elsewhere and it contradicts Herodotus, who has him very much alive.[31] Herodotus describes the battle as lasting for a long time. We should imagine that meaning several hours overall, although estimates vary.[32] The stress and physicality of battle would be tiring. Callimachus, Miltiades and perhaps other generals and older fighters were over sixty; still fit and experienced enough to be more than handy, but old enough to feel the pressure of what they were demanding of their bodies. The bulk of the armies would be younger – between twenty and fifty. Those who had the opportunity to train seriously in athletics would be benefiting from the agility, strength and stamina that they had developed. After a while, it was clear that more Persians, Medes and Sacae were dying than Athenians. There was not much ground for them to retreat over. What were they to do? A wave of panic ran through the army. Resolution stalled. Men ceased looking for opponents ahead of them and began searching for gaps to step back into. The panic built until soon they were fleeing into the marsh:

> Here the Athenians had the victory, cutting down the fleeing Persians until they came to the sea. There they called for fire and took hold of the ships.
>
> Herodotus, 6.113.

The events in the marsh are not the glamourous side of battle. Narrow paths. Soft soil. Water. Plants. Panicked men. The greater the weight carried by those fleeing, the harder to run; the harder to get up after falling into marshland. Wet trousers. Wet corselets. Confusion. In the marsh the more lightly-armed of the Greeks could really come into their own. The heaviest hoplites might well move carefully there, but lighter hoplites and anyone else could traverse it well, hunting down the enemy. This is where hunting dogs would come in handy too – keen, agile, their barks adding to the chaos and fear. Lost, some of those fleeing hit a dead-end at a lake within the marsh. Their pursuers caught up with them, leading to a 'great slaughter'. Over 6,000 men of the Persian army were said to have been killed at Marathon. A high percentage of them will have been killed in the marsh – pierced through the back as they fled, held down drowning in the dark waters or their throats slit by a poor man's dagger. Ten years later the Persian general Artabazus would order a 'great slaughter' of Greeks in a marsh just outside Olynthus. Was this revenge for the undignified horrors of Marathon?[33]

There was no taboo in ancient warfare about cutting down the defeated. The opponent is your enemy; the less of them the better. Describing an easy massacre on a later occasion, Xenophon wondered, 'to have a crowd of enemies delivered into their hands, frightened, panic-stricken . . . how could one help regarding this as a gift from the gods? . . . so many fell within a short time'.[34] Those who fled the battle first might make it back to the ships. They were the only route to safety for Medes, Persians, Sacae and invading Greeks. Anyone who came after and made it through the watery killing-zone still had to fight at the beach. There was confusion there now as men attempted to embark. Could anyone get horses aboard in this chaos? This was the last stage of the fight. Those on the ships could see the situation well enough. The leadership faced the gruesome decision of when to pull away, knowing anyone left behind was done for. Once the Athenians had fetched fire and begun setting ships ablaze, time was up. Aeschylus' brother Cynegeirus grabbed a ship, only for an axe to sweep down desperately, chopping off his hand, leaving him to fall to his death.[35] But to everyone's surprise and to the Athenians' and Plataeans' relief, it was the defenders who had won. This short campaign and day of chaos was about to become the stuff of legend.

7

Surviving Marathon

As the ships pulled away, the Greeks on shore could exhale and begin to believe that the battle was won. Exhaustion, elation, relief – it was a lot to take on board. The smell of burning was in the air from the torched ships and grosser smells might already have been emanating from the dead. There was debris all around, and behind them on the plain battered shields (wicker and wooden), dropped weapons, bodies and the wounded. Xenophon described a battlefield some years later, capturing the distinctive horror:

> Now that the fight was at an end, a weird spectacle met the eye as one surveyed the scene of the conflict – the earth stained with blood, friend and foe lying dead side-by-side, shields smashed, spears snapped, daggers bared of their sheaths, some on the ground, some in the bodies, some yet gripped by the hand.
>
> Xenophon, *Agesilaus,* 2.14.

There was work to be done. A sacrifice would be made straightaway; the first of many giving thanks for salvation. Then there was caring for the wounded and seeing to the dead. There was another pressing concern too. Where were the Persians going and what was happening in Athens? It could not be allowed that they should win here only for Athens to fall behind them. The army was still needed to protect the city. The longer they were away, the greater the risk. Some said that the Alcmaeonids used a shield to signal to the Persians as they sailed away – a pre-arranged sign about capturing Athens.[1]

Callimachus was dead. It is reasonable to picture Miltiades taking command. It was resolved that the army would return to Athens straightaway, leaving Aristides and the rest of the Antiochis tribe to secure the battlefield. The Plataeans more than likely stayed to see to their dead. It would take the ships about a day to cover the 70-odd miles to Phalerum, the port of Athens. The army would have to move fast. Given that they had spent the day fighting and had over 25 miles to cover, they may have left at first light or rested mid-way. Herodotus avoids such trivialising details, preferring to stress that they hurried as fast as they could.

The other thing Herodotus draws attention to is the religious traditions that developed around the battle. The Athenians had been camped in the *temenos* of the sanctuary of Heracles. Back at Athens they encamped in the *temenos* of Heracles at Cynosarges.[2] There is no such thing as a coincidence in ancient thought, at least not when it comes to important events. The repetition of the god's space was a sign that something special was going on, a touch of the divine. Without directly saying so, Herodotus makes space for people to regard this as evidence of Heracles' involvement.

The army was back fast enough to see the Persians' ships arrive and leave. There would be no follow-up attack now. Perhaps that was never even intended. It has been suggested that Datis and Artaphernes simply wished to see the lie of the land around Athens for themselves – to add to their intelligence for next time.[3] No one mentions the death of Hippias at Marathon, so we must picture him with them. For a long time now he had been fervently assuring the Persians that plenty in Athens wanted him back. Not even he could make this case anymore. He was an old man. This was his last glimpse of Athens.

What of the famous run to Athens? Did anyone rush ahead of the army to bring the good news, or rather, to forestall betrayal? If we follow Herodotus, the answer is 'no'. For him, the Marathon run is the run to Sparta.[4] Stories that someone ran ahead were told in antiquity however, although apparently not until much later. Plutarch has the earliest surviving version:

> The news of the battle of Marathon Thersippus of Eroeadae brought back, as [the philosopher] Heraclides Ponticus relates; but most historians declare that it was Eucles who ran in full armour, hot from the battle, and, bursting in at the doors of the first men of State, could only say, 'Joy! We are victorious!' and straightway died . . . a self-sent messenger regarding a battle in which he himself had fought.
>
> Plutarch, *Were the Athenians More Famous in Wisdom or War?*, 3.

This comes from the same rhetorical work in which Plutarch – or, perhaps it is worth stressing, his narrator – had stated that Marathon was fought on the day the Greeks arrived, arguing for the superiority of warriors over writers, deeds over words. The runner was celebrated because he fought *and* reported, whereas someone just reporting would not have been important. By contrast, the only other ancient author who mentions this story refers to 'Philippides' making the now famous run to Athens, apparently a conflation with the man who ran to Sparta as described by Herodotus (whose manuscripts contain Philippides *and* Pheidippides in different versions).[5] In this account the runner had not fought at the battle, but was a professional messenger. It is not implausible that someone was sent ahead – able to travel faster alone. The silence of Herodotus on the matter of the run to Athens is curious but need not mean that it did not happen. All the same, we can be more confident that the story became more prominent in later years, as we will see, than we can be confident that the details of it are literally true.

With the victorious army returned the Athenians could breathe a sigh of relief. Miltiades' home-coming must have been met with joy and relief from Cimon and Elpinice, not to mention pride in his success. Elpinice's name – hope of victory – had proved a good omen. Miltiades' position would surely be different now from that of the precarious days after their first arrival from the east. Across the city, the thousands who had fought would be telling their households what had happened in the battle and how they had performed. There would be accounts for the Assembly and the Council. Just like that, the battle morphed from its brief spell as an event taking place to the beginning of its long history as something recalled and described.

The wounded

Back to the battlefield. Aristides was in command. His tribe were holding the plain, including his cousin, Callias, who had also survived. Symbolically, having men on the field confirmed a win, although in this case there would be no disputing it. On a practical level this gave them the opportunity to secure whatever the invading army had left behind and to see to the wounded and the dead – an important aspect of ancient culture.

Greek armies, particularly in this period, did not travel with much equipment for the wounded. There are few references to their care in the literature of ancient warfare, which indicates its low level on the ladder of priorities. Some care would be available. Put bluntly, social prominence would increase one's chance of survival. Those of means were more likely to have family, friends and attendants who would prioritise finding them and finding bandages, pain-relief and incantations.[6] Those lower down might be looked after, but they could not rely on it. Enemy wounded would be killed or left to die. Greeks who were very seriously wounded might be quietly put out of their misery. Some wounds cannot be survived and although this is not something that writers dwell on, euthanasia was not morally taboo.[7] Bandages to reduce blood loss were known and used. There may not have been many if any prepared in advance, but make-shift options could be rustled up from any fabric around. The few items of Greek art showing treatment typically feature bandaging scenes, such as the famous image of Achilles bandaging Patroclus' arm which was made at Athens not long before Marathon.[8] Wounds could be sewn-up, although not everyone would be willing to venture such a specialist job. The writer Theophrastus would later mock as cowards those who ostentatiously help a wounded friend rather than face the enemy. This is of course mocking hypocrisy and cowardice rather than mocking the desire to help as such; it is a scene when the enemy are still present after all. Nonetheless it is another indication of the minimal emphasis on health care.[9]

The ancient Greeks did have doctors, but they were not brought on campaign as specialists. If there were any at the battle then they would have fought too and had an equal chance of having been wounded. There is no suggestion that any stayed behind with the Antiochis tribe. Some men might have knowledge of plants to provide pain-relief or to slow blood-flow, but again, it is unlikely that much was prepared in advance; only the very fortunate would have access to it. Prayer and incantations were part of any medical treatment. These could be provided by anyone, although they would have been regarded as more effective coming from someone knowledgeable about them. It is still a widely-held belief that the right words spoken over a wound can stem blood loss.[10] Anyone with deep stab wounds, puncture wounds or limb loss would be lucky to survive. Those who had been concussed, slashed or pierced less deeply had a better chance, but there were no guarantees. There would be twists and sprains – manageable.

Of the less seriously wounded, who lived or died must have seemed remarkably unpredictable, and this is where the gods came in. They could guarantee no one's life. All Greeks knew the *Iliad*, in which gods weep as their mortal children die their fated deaths. But sometimes they could help, if they would, so prayers were worth making. The mystery of who did or did not survive moderate wounds was largely a matter of infection.[11] Blades would introduce foreign matter and bacteria into the body. Wounds were unlikely to be properly cleaned. Bandages were not sterile. A strong immune system was as good an asset as any equipment in an ancient battle. Wounded men were at risk from any comrades with diseases. Mustering an army of men from across a region inevitably leads to outbreaks, even before bad water and other risks introduce more. On long campaigns this was a particular problem. At Marathon the Athenians and Plataeans had mustered from only two communities and had not been together very long. There had been no serious outbreaks.

Epizelus son of Cuphagoras had gone blind. Herodotus reports the blinding as fact. He also records what he had heard from people who knew him regarding the cause – that he thought he was approached by a giant soldier who passed him and killed the man beside him. Epizelus had been blind since then. The unusual nature of the injury would attract interest even if there was not much anyone could do for him. Later on Epizelus featured in artistic representations of the battle and they seem to depict him fighting on after his blinding, his arm across his face, indicating the sight loss. Herodotus' account stresses that Epizelus was fighting bravely; this was not an issue of cowardice. In the modern world it is known that physical problems can have psychological causes. A case of blindness might be interpreted as trauma blindness, a symptom of post-traumatic stress disorder. Many have viewed this case in this light. Ancient fighters were protected from some of the traumas which trouble modern soldiers – they fought close to their companions, did not face heavy artillery and they grew up in a culture which celebrated battle and expected men to kill. Nonetheless, the intense violence of hand-to-hand combat is a lot to process by any standard and it is not unreasonable to think that some were deeply shaken by it. For the Athenians, Epizelus' injury appeared differently. His blindness and the figure he reported seeing were further indications of the role of the divine in the battle – something more than human at work. The depictions of him could represent him being passed by an embodiment of fear – Phobos or Deimos. Epizelus continuing to fight in the presence of Fear itself could be a visual emblem of the Athenians' resistance to the Panic that Pan unleashed. There does not seem any doubt that Epizelus was genuinely blinded. How one thinks about the cause is largely a matter of cultural interpretation.[12]

The wounded needed to get home somehow. Aristides probably saw to it that the Antiochis men began to make arrangements. This is not a topic that the Greek historians are forthcoming about. A survey of them reveals only around a dozen references to transporting the wounded, although it must frequently have needed managing.[13] Armies were not organised enough for there to be a coherent policy in advance regarding who was responsible or how they would go about it. When the wounded are mentioned, it is typically to express the extremity of a situation, when the sick and wounded were abandoned. Thucydides gives a horrifying account of Athenians left behind on the retreat from Syracuse. Plutarch relates how Agesilaus of Sparta, forced to abandon a sick favourite, told the man, 'It is hard to be compassionate and sensible at the same time'.[14] Xenophon describes an argument he had with a waggon-driver who was preparing to bury a wounded man rather than carry him. He had stopped to praise the driver for burying the dead, only for the 'dead' man to lift a leg in appeal for help![15] But these were all extreme cases in which the whole army was in jeopardy. The implied norm is that the wounded should be taken. This was certainly the case at Marathon, where the army had been victorious, in its own territory, less than

30 miles from home. Some of the wounded could walk; some could walk with assistance; some would need transport. As with receiving treatment, social status and good friends were the most reliable means of support. Plato depicts Socrates discussing this with Alcibiades and it is presented as normal that friends and kin would be the ones who might help.[16] If any preparation was done, it would have entailed setting aside pack-animals which could carry people and determining if any of the carts could be used for the same purpose. It seems likely that people would have come from Athens with further means of transport, such as extra carts or litters.[17] It would be a painful, bumpy ride, but it was better than the alternative. Once at home, female family members would be chiefly responsible for care. Affluent families might seek further help from a doctor with any chronic problems tackled by a visit to a healing sanctuary.[18]

Meanwhile wounded Persians, Medes, Sacae and Ionians were on board ship. Given the haste of the departure, no one with a very serious injury is likely to have made it; horrible for those left behind, but giving us a clearer sense of the severity of injury that those on board were dealing with. It would be the walking wounded. The same types of injuries were likely. As we have seen, similar percentages of Persians and Greeks wore armour, but the Persians' shields gave them less protection and they will have been more vulnerable to head wounds. There will have been more injuries from blunt projectiles, fewer from arrows. The situation on board ship would initially be chaotic. There was greater potential for infection in the more cramped conditions. The situation was not out of control, however. The fleet sailed to pick up their Eretrian prisoners before they headed towards Athens, and from there they sailed back to Naxos. Having the islands as stepping-stones on the way back presented opportunities for fresh water and other supplies, all of which increased the wounded's chances of survival. Islanders and Ionians would be home first; the wounded again relying on family and friends to get them where they were going or to at least notify a loved one of where they were. Did Hippias and his circle depart for Sigeum at this point or was he put through the ordeal of facing the Great King?

The spoils

The other motive for keeping men on the battlefield was to protect the booty that had been left behind. The Persian army did not travel light and even an expedition without the monarch had with it goods that could impress the Greeks. Plutarch mentions tents and utensils, valuable clothing, and all sorts of gold and silver items. Clothing and weaponry on the dead would not be off limit. Daggers, swords, spears and axes were all worth having and anything metal could be reworked. These goods would not become the property of whoever grabbed what. Some would benefit the Athenian treasury, either directly or indirectly, and others would form part of the many offerings given to the gods in thanks.

Plutarch discusses this aspect of the battle because of his biographical interest in the man left in charge. In his *Aristides*, Plutarch explores the good qualities which led to the soubriquet, The Just. Plutarch's biographical method is to compare the life of a famous Greek with the similar life of a Roman, in this case Cato the Elder. Another technique is to establish further illuminating comparisons within the *Life*. One instance of this is a comparison of two men's reactions to the battlefield at Marathon. Aristides' virtue is so well-regarded that he is left in charge, refrains from helping himself and prevents others from doing so. His cousin, Callias, however, is presented as a contrast:

> Some barbarian, it seems, rushed up to this man supposing him to be a king from his long hair and the headband that he wore, made obeisance to him, and taking him by the hand in suppliant fashion showed him a great mass of gold buried in a sort of pit. Callias, most savage and lawless of men took up the gold but the man – to prevent him betraying the matter to others – he killed. From this circumstance, they say, his descendants are called 'Pit-Wealthies', in reference to where Callias found his gold.
>
> Plutarch, *Aristides*, 5.6.

This is a little harsh on Callias. He came from an already hugely wealthy family. They were involved in mining; it is likely that their explorations around Laurium were what led to the silver boom of the 480s. That 'pit-wealth' was unlikely to have been a pit at Marathon any more than it was a pit by his house into which a wealthy Persian dropped their gold – another story that circulated.[19] So this story is unlikely to be literally true, but it has its merits. It evokes the disorder of a battlefield after a battle. It is a horrible reminder of the likely fate of anyone found alive. And it is a great example of something that we will see more of – the use of Marathon to make moral points about people and values.

The dead

The dead needed to be cared for as well as the wounded. Herodotus recorded 192 Athenians killed in the battle, a figure that is likely to be accurate as they were in the best position to record the details accurately. The names of the dead were later recorded on a burial-mound inscription, creating a long-term testament. Some 6,400 Persian dead are reported. This figure will be an amalgamation of all the ethnicities in the army, with 'Persian' acting as shorthand. It is also less likely to be accurate as there was no motivation for the Athenians to record details of the – to them – anonymous dead. It has been noted by someone with an eye for figures that the 6,400 in the *Histories* equals 100 Persians for every three Athenians; some creative guess-timating has been going on.[20] The Athenians will have been satisfied with a rough estimate, somewhere on the generous side, and we must therefore be content with the figures indicating that more Persians than Greeks were killed, without looking for a precise figure. It is to be expected that the losing side would suffer greater casualties, as flight made soldiers so much more vulnerable even without the complication of marshland and the possibility of drowning.

Most of the dead would be recognisable to friends and family. Facial wounds might make identification more difficult, but in the absence of standardised kit there would be other tell-tale signs. Failing that, there would be a list of names by tribe of those who were fighting, so roll-call would reveal the missing.[21] No figure is given for the former slaves who died. No figure is given for the Plataean dead, although if Herodotus had pursued this question further amongst the Plataeans an answer would have been available.

The dead were separated into groups that reflected the priorities of the victors. The Athenians, Plataeans and former slaves were divided into separate groups.[22] Their enemies were at some point put into a mass grave. The Athenians and Plataeans will have washed their dead and done their best to make them look decent. Whether they extended that care to the former slaves is a matter of conjecture. At home, cleaning and preparing corpses would be a job for female relatives of the dead, but in a military situation, even near home, cleaning would more than likely be done by the men on the scene in order to ensure that it was done quickly enough to prevent accelerated decomposition. It was not an insult that the former slaves were buried apart; they had died free but not yet citizens and as such their inclusion in a separate grave near the Plataeans' tomb was a given in a world that distinguished sharply between citizens and others.[23] As for the Persians, Medes, Sacae and Ionians, being stripped of valuables is the only attention they are likely to have received. We know that they were not interred immediately as their bodies were still available to be visited. The Spartans had marched to fight. They covered *c.* 140 miles in just a few days, no mean feat. They were early enough to show willing, but ultimately too late. Some said that religious restrictions delayed them; others that unrest amongst the helots did.[24]

They did not send the whole army; but then they need not have sent anyone if they were unwilling. They congratulated the Athenians and went to see the bodies out of curiosity before returning home.

The Battle of Marathon occurred at a point of transition in terms of the treatment of the war-dead. Throughout earlier generations it was the custom for most war-dead to be buried on the battlefield, with the bodies of elite figures collected, even fought for, and returned home. Vases celebrate fighting over and retrieving the dead, a practice glorified in the Homeric epics. The bodies of the dead played a prominent role in family rituals, so it was important to have a family member available for proper mourning and ongoing offerings. But the retrieval and transportation would be difficult, hence its limitation to the select few. This would change under democracy in later years. *All* bodies would be returned to Athens and honoured in communal public funerals – equality even in death.[25] Marathon fell within democracy, but the practice of returning everyone had not yet been established. In former days one might have expected Callimachus at least to have been returned to Athens, but that did not happen and nor did the return of all 192. The dead would be cremated and interred on the battlefield.

The cremation will have followed a funeral feast featuring family of the dead and prominent citizens. A pit was dug 3m deep and lined with sea-sand and greenish earth. The ashes and charred bones were placed on that surface with a wide, shallow tray in the midst of them containing ceramics and other offerings. This layer was then covered to create a large burial-mound, or soros. Even after centuries of erosion the soros is 9m above ground and *c.* 185m in circumference at the base. It must have been a striking sight in its prime. Marble slabs inscribed with the names of the dead were erected on the soros, along with an epigram reading:

> Fame, ever brilliant as she seeks out the ends of the earth
> Shall learn the valour of these men: how they died
> Fighting the Medes, and placed a crown on Athens,
> A few, accepting battle against many.[26]

Further inscriptions may have been added too. There is a tradition that the tragedian Aeschylus and poet Simonides competed for the right to have their verses used, but whether that tradition should be taken literally is another story. The form of the soros is as transitional as the rest of the treatment of the dead. An aristocratic form – funeral feast, spectacular pyre, monument raising – shared by *all* fallen citizens.[27] Marathon was an important moment for the new democracy and the treatment of the dead reflects this in the decision to honour the many in a manner formerly reserved for the few.

Because the battle had been fought and the tomb raised securely within Athenian territory, it could become an important place of commemoration. The dead were regarded as heroes; not in our sense of 'great men', but in the ancient sense of humans who fall somewhere between normal mortals and gods – supernatural beings with power that could extend beyond death, although limited to actions around their tomb. Ephebes, male Athenian youths doing their military training, would march out each year at the festival of Artemis Agrotera to lay wreaths at the soros. This would teach them what they should aspire to and reassure them that they too would find honour should they meet their end in battle.[28] The families of the dead brought offerings and so too did the people of the Marathon deme nearby. They were still bringing these offerings more than 600 years later when a visitor recorded their custom and they continued to do it for centuries after that.

8

Events after Marathon

We turn now to what happened after Marathon and to explore the *idea* of Marathon after the event. It will mean a change of pace as there is no way to cover all that came after in the same detail that we have looked at what led to Marathon, yet a swift move through history is hugely illuminating when it comes to seeing how a battle can develop a legacy and how the events that come after it shape that legacy. Arguably no battle was more significant than Marathon in shaping the Athenians' sense of themselves – part of their answer to the question *Who are the Athenians?* This in turn influenced how subsequent generations of Athenians *and* non-Athenians came to see the world. Understandably, the battle was regarded as far less significant in Persia.

Persia

As we have seen, the retreat from Greece was not a disaster. The voyage home in 490 was nothing like Mardonius' scramble following the wreck of his invasion in the North Aegean. The fleet stopped to re-supply and to confirm Persian authority in the Cyclades. Datis revisited Delos. Herodotus tells the story within a framework that reflects badly on the Persian campaign, but not upon Datis personally. A dream prompted Datis to have the ships searched. A gold-plated statue of Apollo was discovered. On finding that it had been taken from Apollo's sanctuary at Delium near the Attic coast, he took it on his own ship to Delos to be left for safe-keeping.[1] Datis is shown to do the right thing. On the other hand, the overall sense implies a dream epiphany in which Apollo expresses his displeasure; this in turn expresses criticism of the campaign. It is entirely plausible that Datis revisited Delos. He could sacrifice conspicuously once again, signalling to the wider Greek world the Persians' willingness to play nicely in the right circumstances and their long-term plans for the Aegean.

Once Datis and Artaphernes were back at court we should imagine them putting the campaign in the best light: the novelty of transporting so many by sea had worked; they had succeeded in submitting several islands, notably Naxos; Eretria had been sacked; booty had been taken from several places – valuables and people; sacrifices had been made at a major sacred site; the army had been able to make a landing on the mainland, although it was not possible to hold it at this time; the fleet had returned safely with the loss of only a handful of ships.

As we have seen, it is impossible to be sure how much the Persian high command expected from the expedition. Anyone hoping for the conquest of Greece would be sorely disappointed, but it is unlikely that many if any people had expected that at this stage. More modest hopes could be regarded as fulfilled. Darius cannot have been impressed with the loss of quite a number of troops. It seems likely that there would be disappointment that support for the Peisistratids was not forthcoming and Athens was not sacked or held. But this was no disaster; it was at worst a set-back. Most importantly, there had been no loss of territory. This was the kind of set-back that involved material gain – and that is no bad set-back at all.

Darius' reaction can also be gauged by his response to some of those involved. The captive Eretrians were brought to Susa. Execution, mutilation, or the most brutal forms of slavery were all possible outcomes. As it was, they were settled on lands not far from Susa. They could never go home, but they were free and had been done no further harm.[2] A few years later we find mention of Peisistratids still at court, so they had not entirely worn out their welcome.[3] Artaphernes remained in the Great King's favour. His uncle did not abandon him, and his son, another Artaphernes, would later be trusted with military command.[4] We do not know how Datis fared, but if he was out of favour it cannot have been far out. His family retained good standing and, like Artaphernes, his sons would gain military commands.[5]

Herodotus presents us with a furious Darius determined to take down the Athenians and conquer the whole of Greece. He issues orders for an immediate follow-up: more troops, warships, transports, horses and grain. News of revolt in Egypt strengthens his resolve to subdue Egyptians and Greeks alike. An immediate invasion is prevented only by a dispute over the succession between Darius' sons. Just as the succession issue is resolved, Darius dies. Thus, Herodotus tells us, Darius was 'robbed of his chance to punish either Egypt or the Athenians'.[6] The trouble amongst the princes provides an opportunity for Herodotus to explore a weakness of monarchy – just because rule should pass from father to son does not mean that it goes any more smoothly than other systems. The wider truth here, that a new campaign was always in the offing, seems entirely likely. Furthermore, as is often the way, the (potential) colonised were more focused on the coloniser than vice-versa; the Greeks were focused on the Persians, but the Persians had Egypt and other fronts to consider. A Greek campaign was coming, but it could wait.

Athens

The Athenians' confidence had never been higher. They knew what had happened at Eretria and Miletus. They had played a high risk game and won. The Athenians will have known that that would not be the end of the matter, but for the time being celebration and thanksgiving were in order. These would take place at domestic and state level. Families would offer sacrifices and libations, perhaps make dedications, and there were the grander spectacles of offerings and dedications on behalf of the whole community.

There was a three-fold public commemoration of the battle: the burial on the battlefield, a memorial in the city-centre and – later – a dedication at Delphi. The dead Athenians of Marathon were heroes now, part-way between mortal and god. Each passing year saw teenagers honouring those heroes at the site of their triumph, the battlefield having been altered to incorporate the soros that held their remains. This ritual renewed the battle in people's thoughts and made the fallen heroes a model of behaviour. The plaque erected on the soros proclaiming their names, their tribes and – indirectly – their achievement was an innovation that would be continued. At some point a statue of Miltiades was raised at Marathon.[7] The nature of the monument in Athens is unfortunately unknown, although it is known that it carried two epigrams, one stressing the protection of Athens, the other declaring that the Athenians had saved Greece.[8] This second epigram in particular offers valuable insight into how the Athenians perceived the events – if they had fallen, Greece would have followed. The significance of Marathon had widened from Athens to the whole mainland.

Pan entered the Marathon tradition swiftly. There was a story that this mischievous god of the flocks had appeared to Pheidippides, the runner who went to Sparta for help. On the mountain above Tegea the god called to the runner by name and asked why the Athenians ignored him. He could help them. The Athenians accepted this story. His help had duly come in spreading Panic through their enemies.[9] Herodotus tells us that after the battle the Athenians established a shrine in the side of the acropolis in Pan's honour and a festival with races. Archaeological excavation has shown that cults of Pan appear in Attica from around the time of Marathon, not only at Athens but on Mt Parnes and Mt Penteli, and at Eleusis, Daphni, Vari and Oenoe. An inscription has survived on a statue-base which reveals that Miltiades himself dedicated a statue to Pan – a personal offering from himself and his family rather than from the state.[10]

Many other deities must be thanked. A new temple was built for Artemis Eucleia, Glory, in remembrance of what she had done for the Athenians at Marathon.[11] From this time on, the Athenians would offer Artemis 500 goats a year at her festival – a fulfilment of the vow made before the battle. They had promised a goat for each invader killed and then found that they could not find enough, so great had the slaughter been. Five hundred was deemed a large enough approximation.[12] It was probably around this time that Miltiades dedicated his helmet at Olympia. This striking Corinthian helmet has survived and can be seen in the museum at the sanctuary, complete with Miltiades' name incised along the jawline.[13]

Miltiades' determination to resist the Persian advance had protected the city and its people and brought them a new respect amongst the Greeks. He asked the council if he might be awarded a crown of olive leaves in recognition of his achievement. He was told that when he had won a battle alone he might have one.[14] Athens was a democracy now; individual glory had its limits. Other men of influence from rival families must have looked at Miltiades and the Cimonids with a mixture of admiration and envious wariness.

One group whose lives were changed beyond recognition by Marathon, and yet who we hear little about, is the group of ex-slaves who fought in the battle. They had come forward on an offer of freedom suggested by Miltiades and were duly freed before the battle. They had fought side-by-side with the citizens of Athens. Though some had died, some must have survived. And now they were home, still free and members of that special group who had fought and won this crucial battle. When the new tribes were first drawn-up after the expulsion of the Peisistratids, Cleisthenes had enrolled freed slaves as citizens. This would be repeated at the end of the Peloponnesian War decades later.[15] This will be what happened with the freed slaves who fought at Marathon. New citizens – usually joining when they came of age, less frequently naturalised non-Athenians – became citizens when they were enrolled into a phratry, a sub-section of a tribe. Taking their name from an old Indo-European word meaning 'brother', the phratries were essentially the next social group up after family. They confirmed legitimate births, access to citizenship and oversaw property inheritance. Members honoured the gods together and even owned items communally for use at phratry festivals.

New members were added at the Apaturia – a three-day festival involving sacrifices to Zeus Phratrios and Athena Phratria, feasting and the presentation of prospective members. New members were deemed accepted when existing members ate the meat of sacrificed animals brought to the festival by the relatives (or other supporters) of the prospect. The Apaturia took place in Pyanopsion (roughly our October), the month following Boedromion (*c.* September), the month in which Marathon was fought.[16] After a month of waiting, perhaps with a degree of apprehension, the festival would be celebrated and the freed slaves enrolled. No doubt there will have been much revisiting of stories of the battle – of their loyalty in coming forward and of the feats that they and other members of the phratry achieved that day. Their lives would be different from that point on, as would those of their children and descendants. It was not easy to become a freed slave in Greece. Even those ostensibly freed were often made the 'property' of a god to maintain social difference. The Marathon fighters became free men and citizens in a democracy. Their bodies were their own again, or even for the first time for some. They could manage their own affairs and participate in the running of the city – a city which was on its way to becoming the most powerful in Greece.

Paros

Miltiades was in good standing at Athens and the people were in buoyant mood, revelling in a confidence born of their success. On Miltiades' suggestion, the Athenians launched their modest fleet to attack Paros, a beautiful island in the Cyclades near Naxos. With reluctance these islands had assisted the Persian fleet during the campaign. They were also relatively wealthy. Led by Miltiades, the Athenians besieged the Parians, demanding 100 talents. It did not go as planned. After nearly a month they abandoned the siege and sailed home. By now Miltiades had sustained a serious leg injury. It must have been a miserable return.

Miltiades would have to be conveyed home from the coast. He would arrive in a household relieved once again to see him, but this time without the pleasure of success and with concerns about his wound. Worse was to come. There was anger in the city about the failure of the campaign and blame was attached to its general. A trial was convened, an *eisangelia*, to be held before a large public jury or the Assembly. The case was brought by an old rival, Xanthippus. This was the opportunity the Alcmaeonids had been waiting for to rein Miltiades in. He was charged with defrauding the people – promising success, costing resources, delivering nothing. If found guilty it would cost him his life. The new political system emphasised accountability and it had no patience with failure. Miltiades' wound was not healing. He was taken to the trial but was too ill to speak. His friends defended him – these would be Cimonids or family friends, perhaps men who had been in the Chersonese with him. Cimon was still too young to speak. They defended Miltiades with reference to his service: *Things might have gone wrong on Paros, but he was no enemy of the Athenians*. They emphasised all Miltiades had achieved in the Marathon campaign and reminded the people of how he had won Lemnos and handed it to Athens.[17]

It is likely that many of the stories about Miltiades date from this time. Family stories often retold at home would now be tweaked and told publically in his defence – how he rejected Darius at the Danube, the risks he took to capture Lemnos, the loss of Metiochus, his determination at Marathon. Likewise stories were told to discredit him. A struggle would be held over the memory of Marathon. Never had it been so important to Miltiades and his circle to stress the primacy of his role. They will have celebrated his part before, especially amongst themselves, but now it was a matter of life and death that the people accept that he had been the most important driver, even as others argued the opposite. His defenders could not make things up entirely – a high percentage of the listeners had been there and had a fair idea of what had gone on – but they could present an interpretation which placed Miltiades in the most pivotal role, galvanising the people, organising, persuading less resolute generals and fighting like a hero.

His opponents would be down-playing Miltiades' part, stressing the actions of the late Callimachus and the group effort of the Athenians as a whole. Hostile versions of Miltiades' former years would re-emerge too – how he had worked with the Peisistratids, how he served with the Persians, his time as a tyrant. And then there was the Parian expedition itself. Herodotus knew some pretty damning stories about it. By his day it was said that Miltiades had refused to tell the Athenians where they were going. It was said that the desire for booty was a pretext – really he had planned the attack to take revenge on a Parian who had bad-mouthed him to Hydarnes the Persian. Hydarnes was the admiral of the Phoenician fleet who had chased Miltiades out of the Chersonese. Had this Parian told Hydarnes of Miltiades' anti-Persian sentiment on the Danube campaign? Either way, in Herodotus' world view, attacking a whole people for the purpose of getting at one man is exactly the kind of thing a tyrant would do. So too was another accusation – that Miltiades had mistreated a priestess of Demeter on Paros by holding her prisoner before following her suggestion that he should visit her sanctuary and commit sacrilege; that he had been frightened out of the sanctuary and injured his leg climbing its boundary wall. Such an attempted sacrilege would make Miltiades responsible for the failure of the expedition on a whole new level.[18] Other stories existed of course. There is a tradition that he called off the attack because a fire was seen which indicated Persian forces nearby. There was one that it was called off simply because it failed, without religious elements. And there is a tradition that Miltiades was struck by an arrow when he was near the sanctuary and that he was so concerned that this might signal Demeter's displeasure that he retreated rather than offend her further. All these stories were passed on, developed and passed on again. Some stories accuse; others defend. It is reasonable to think that their origins lie in this battle for his life.[19]

The people proved unwilling to execute Miltiades, but it was still bad news for the Cimonids. Miltiades was fined an enormous fifty talents – half of what the Athenians had expected the entire island of Paros to cough up. It will have been a bitter blow for Miltiades himself, but he was in no position to fight it. Before he could pay, he died of his wound. Gangrene had set in, sending poison coursing through his system until he succumbed. The hero of Marathon was dead within a year of his greatest triumph.

The fine was paid. How exactly is unknown. Herodotus says simply that Cimon paid it, and it is plausible that the family had the means. Most historians add bleaker details, with Miltiades dying in prison while the payment was organised. The historian Diodorus, working with an earlier history by Ephorus, knew a tradition that after Miltiades died Cimon gave himself as ransom so that the body might be returned for burial. Nepos agrees that Miltiades died in prison and has Cimon forcibly imprisoned to secure the payment, although this is unlikely to be true as this was not part of Athenian law. Nepos adds that despite Cimon's protestations, Elpinice married Callias to secure money for the fine. Elpinice certainly did marry Callias around this time and we have seen that he was wealthy; whether he paid the fine for his new wife is less sure.[20] What a bleak time for the family. Just as their position seemed secure they lost their charismatic head amidst accusations of treason.

Cimon was still young, around eighteen, too young to take a serious part in politics. Plutarch offers a glimpse of his life at this time, an image of a teenager out of control. On the one hand Cimon is praised for his nobility and truthfulness.

But on the other, it is said that his life was undistinguished except for the bad name he was earning for himself through heavy drinking and disorderly behaviour – publicly drunken nights in a small city. He was said to be less cultivated than his peers, his education having been old-fashioned. This is plausible. Having been educated outside Athens in the traditional style, he is likely to have gone without the new emphasis on science and speculative philosophy that had come into vogue in Athens. And then there were the women. He was known for his affairs and attachments. Plutarch heard of several by name – Asteria of Salamis, Mnestra, Cleitor and Isodice, who he eventually married.[21] And then there was the other woman in his life, Elpinice. Given everything that had happened during their upbringing, it is perhaps unsurprising that Cimon was close to his sister. Yet close brother-sister friendship was unusual in ancient Greek culture. Some said theirs was more than friendship. There were persistent rumours that they were lovers. Some said that they lived openly as husband and wife before her marriage to Callias.[22] The court of public opinion did not look kindly on these two young people. If Cimon was to restore their reputation he would need to do a lot to improve his image and he would need to rescue that of their father.

Political dominoes

In the year following Marathon the Cimonids were not the only family in crisis. Democratic Athens had instigated a new practice – ostracism. Once a year male citizens had an opportunity to vote for someone to be expelled from the city for ten years. They would suffer no loss of property or citizenship, but they could not enter Attica in that period. Votes were cast by scratching the target's name on a sherd – an ostracon – of pottery, hence the name. If less than 6,000 were cast, it was void; if more, the man with most was out. Its seems to have been intended to reduce factionalism and the risk of tyranny by discouraging prominent men from becoming too dominant and by removing any who did. Plutarch suggests that it purged feelings of envy without doing too much damage.[23] It gave the *demos* a means of intervening in the persisting elite rivalry.[24] It is noticeable that there was an anti-tyranny, anti-Alcmaeonid, anti-Persia vibe to the ostracisms of the 480s. The first to be ostracised was Hipparchus son of Charmus.[25] He was a Peisistratid, so he had well-established links with tyranny, yet it may have come as a surprise blow to him and his friends. He had seemed to have been forgiven for his family; he had served as archon in 496 and had fought at Marathon.

Nonetheless, he was out. Megacles was out the following year, a senior Alcmaeonid. He won the chariot-race in the 486 games at Delphi and hired Pindar to write a poem celebrating his win and chastising the Athenians: 'I rejoice at this new success; but I grieve that fine deeds are repaid with envy. It is true what they say: the abiding bloom of good fortune brings with it both good and bad.'[26] Fantastic sass.

More was to come. Xanthippus was ostracised. He had achieved a personal coup prosecuting Miltiades, but it was short-lived glory. Here was another Alcmaeonid out. Cimon, Elpinice and the other Cimonids surely relished this turnaround. Xanthippus' prominence in Athenian life was a constant reminder of Miltiades' fall. Now he was gone. Satisfying, but nonetheless leaving an air of uncertainty about the future of Athens' major players. Aristides had his turn. In 483 the Athenians ostracised the very man who had been left in charge of the battlefield at Marathon.[27] Plutarch knew a rather wonderful story in which an illiterate man asked Aristides to write 'Aristides' on an ostracon for him. As they were strangers, Aristides asked what Aristides had ever done to him. The man replied that Aristides had done nothing, but he was sick of hearing him being called 'the Just'. Aristides said nothing and scratched his name.[28] This is exactly the sort of story that might be told to critique democracy as a system that empowers the ignorant and envious. Fascinatingly, some of the Aristides ostraca survive, giving us insight into other factors at work. One of them calls him Datis' brother – an accusation of Persian sympathies, medising.[29] Aristides had associations with Aegina and may have had a link with the Alcmaeonids through Cleisthenes. Both these factors might have motivated his ostracism. We can also see that where advocating cooperation with Persia had once been simply one point-of-view amongst many, it had become a political liability.

Were the Alcmaeonids medisers? No one can be sure. Plenty of them had fought at Marathon but that does not mean that none of them would have preferred to do things a different way. They might have fancied their chances of being chosen as the new family in charge if the Persians dropped the Peisistratids. But it could simply be an accusation that was raised against them once it had become a reliable slander. This ostracism-rich period must have seen stories circulating against them, much as they had against Miltiades. It seems likely that this is a time when the shield-signal story was aired, whether or not it goes back to the time of the battle. Herodotus was close to the Alcmaeonids of his own day. He closes the account of Marathon with a rather extraordinary digression on their family history by way of bolstering his stated view that the Alcmaeonids were not guilty of the treacherous signal. Herodotus loves a digression at the best of times and typically they reflect on the main narrative in a thoughtful way. Here the narrative pace grinds unexpectedly to a near halt to discuss the family, yet he offers nothing that acquits them. Perhaps there was nothing that could be said that would really shake the doubt off. Modern scholars have enjoyed the mystery of the shield-signal: the Alcmaeonids did it and were straightforwardly guilty; there was no signal; what seemed like a signal was accident of the sun; there was a signal but it was not the Alcmaeonids who made it; the signal was for the Spartans.[30] Fundamentally we cannot be sure about the signal, but we can be sure that medising had moved from a viable position to a taboo and that the accusation of it haunted the Alcmaeonids for generations.

The weakening of the Alcmaeonids meant opportunities for others. This is the period in which Themistocles returned to prominence. His family was not famous, but he had charisma and intellect that made his voice influential. In the run up to Marathon he had been unable to convince the Athenians to focus on their fleet. This changed in the years after the battle when the mining operations in Attica hit the big time. Silver had been coming out of the ground for years, but in 483/2 a major seam was discovered. The Athenians intended to share the wealth equally between citizens until Themistocles persuaded them to ignore minimal individual benefit in favour of substantial community benefit. They would spend the silver on a fleet – 200 warships were built.[31] This was not without controversy. Massive expansion of the fleet would mean more action and more kudos for the lower classes – the men who provided the rowing power. This would be at the expense of the wealthier classes who dominated land warfare. Lower class men had always participated in land battles, but their wealthier peers were preeminent because of their access to specialist equipment and their opportunities for conspicuous engagement and leadership roles. The advancement of poorer citizens was regarded by wealthier families as a moral failure as well as a practical issue, even in a democracy.[32] Old ideas die hard. This perception of naval power may well have influenced Miltiades' alleged opposition to relying on the fleet, although it would be wrong to consider him an arch-conservative when he had moved to emancipate slaves. Both Herodotus and Plutarch say that the fleet was built with an eye to the long-rumbling conflict with Aegina, yet its moment came with a new Persian invasion. News had arrived of a huge force building. The memory of Marathon would to some extent be cheering; it was now known that the Persians could be repulsed. But all the same, the situation was ominous for the Greeks. Now we see that accusations of medism during the ostracisms had been half-hearted. All the ostracised Athenians were invited back to help with the resistance.[33]

A new invasion

Darius the Great died of natural causes in 486, leaving behind him an impressive legacy. His development of the empire's administration left it stronger and more efficient, while his building projects endured as works of colossal architectural and artistic achievement. He was succeeded by his son, Xerxes, who had been born to Atossa, making him an heir to Cyrus as well as Darius. It was a dynamic time for Persia. In terms of foreign policy, Xerxes made Egypt his priority; it was more important to recover lost territory than to make a play for new. His army put down the Egyptians' revolt, re-securing tribute and resources.[34] But eventually, a Greek campaign was on.

Herodotus presents several factors influencing Xerxes' decision. First come the personal reasons. Mardonius had failed to conquer Greece but he was still keen to be governor there, so reminded Xerxes about invading at every opportunity. The same selfish reasons motivate the Peisistratids at court. Then comes a speech from Xerxes to his council: *he will continue the custom of adding to the empire, he will take revenge on the Athenians for their attack on Sardis, and he will extend the Persian realm to include all land under God's sky bringing the guilty and the innocent alike under his sway.*[35] This is classic Herodotean tyrant talk – riding roughshod over boundaries and harming the innocent alongside the guilty as if there is no difference. Put more prosaically, the same attractions which drew Darius to attack were still there for Xerxes.

To sprint through the second invasion, some Greek states determined to cooperate defensively; others did not.[36] The Delphic oracle was characteristically ambiguous and did not encourage resistance. The Argives would not join, citing variously a recent loss of too many men, a discouraging oracle and the Spartans' refusal to put them in charge.[37] The Sicilian Greeks declined; they were facing similar threats from their own neighbour, Carthage.[38] In 481, the Greek states committed to defence formed what is now called the Hellenic League, led by the Spartans. Marathon played a part in this; it had demonstrated that it was possible for Greeks to defeat Persians in battle. There was an agreement to suspend hostilities between each other while they focused on defence. The Persian force contained a still greater variety of peoples: Persians, Medes, Sacae and Ionian Greeks featured as before, now joined by Arabians, Libyans, Lydians, Carians, Thracians and more. The fleet was made up of Phoenician and Egyptian vessels. It would be truly something to be part of an expedition like this. Whatever your feelings about empire, it was an impressive display. The empire did not homogenise its people; each contingent travelled with their own arms and dress, the combination greater than the sum of its parts. Xerxes himself led the army, assisted by Mardonius, who had been this way before. Others within the army will have been part of the earlier invasions and, as we have seen, numerous men in command were the sons of earlier combatants, notably the sons of Artaphernes and Datis. The earlier campaigns will have been in their minds, perhaps instilling a desire to do better – to right the wrong of Marathon, or perhaps more likely or at least more charitably, to add a mainland victory to their fathers' victories in the islands. Amongst the commanders was one of antiquity's female leaders, Artemisia of Halicarnassus. Xerxes did not travel lightly. In addition to his troops he brought the leisure end of his court, eunuchs, concubines and some of his children. The force advanced by Mardonius' former path – land and sea routes along the North Aegean.

On the suggestion of the Thessalians, the Hellenic League resolved to defend Greece at the pass of Tempe near Mt Olympus. Ten thousand hoplites went north. It was short-lived. The army pulled back when the Macedonians revealed the scale of the invasion and that the pass could be circumnavigated.[39] Thessaly would soon submit, led reluctantly by their leading family and the undeniable might of the invading army.[40] The Hellenic League made a second venture, this time to the pass at Thermopylae. The events of that battle are rightly famous. After an intense struggle, troops from Sparta, Thespiae, Thebes and Mycenae were wiped out. The Persian army was free to advance and revelled in the publicity coup of raising a Spartan king's head on a spike.[41] Though he did not show at Marathon, Leonidas paid dearly for continuing his brother Cleomenes' anti-Persian policy.

As the Spartans and their allies blocked the way by land, the Greek fleet prepared to meet their opponents by sea.[42] The weather was bad. Winds were high. There was a ritual show-down between the two sides, Athenians calling on Boreas the wind god and Persian Magi casting spells and making offerings to Achilles' mother, Thetis, who presided there.[43] The Persian fleet suffered significant damage. When the winds died down the fleets clashed at Artemisium to the north of Euboea. Even the stalemate that ensued counted as a success for the outnumbered Greeks. The fleets separated, with the Greeks withdrawing to Salamis near Athens.

Victory at Thermopylae gave the Persians access to Central Greece. Thebes, now surrounded, capitulated. Plataea was destroyed; those who could escape fled to the Peloponnese.[44] Attica was next in line. The size of the invasion force was now known. The Peloponnesians were unwilling to fight north of the Isthmus of Corinth. There was no point attempting another Marathon. The Athenians made a difficult decision. Like the people of Phocaea, Teos and Samos before them, they determined to abandon their city by sea rather than endure sacking and occupation.[45] The key difference was that they determined to fight in the hope of returning. The chief priestess of Athena informed the people that Athena had left, which eased the heartache and made them pack up more willingly. Women, children and men unable to fight sailed to Troezen, Aegina and Salamis. Men who could fight gathered with the fleet. With horror they saw Athens set alight, the flames rising high above the gulf.[46] The Marathon monument was amongst the items destroyed.[47] The statues of the tyrannicides, Harmodius and Aristogeiton – symbols of Athenian democracy – were removed to Susa.[48] The Greeks in Xerxes' party – Peisistratids and their circle – sacrificed on the acropolis for the first time since they (or their fathers) left for exile.[49]

The Greek fleet was hardly unified. There was talk of the Athenians setting sail to Italy for good. Eventually they were able to draw their opponents to fight in the straits of Salamis where the Persians' greater numbers and heavier ships turned advantage to liability. The Greeks won by sea and Aristides, recently returned from exile, led a ground force on Salamis which hacked down any non-Greeks who escaped drowning. It was another surprise victory for the Greeks. With the fighting season at a close, a frustrated Xerxes sailed home with the remains of the fleet. He left Mardonius in charge to sort things out with the land force. Mardonius withdrew the army from Athens to pass the winter in Thessaly.[50]

Themistocles was widely considered the architect of Salamis. Aristides was praised for his part. Like others they were of an age to have fought during both invasions – quite a claim to fame. Since Marathon, others had come of age. To return to the Cimonids, Elpinice would have left Athens with the rest of the refugees and would be waiting nearby for the outcome. Her husband Callias would be amongst those preparing to fight again. And then there was Cimon. A teen at the time of Marathon, last seen going wild in Athens, he was in his late twenties during the new invasion and it might be said that it brought out the best in him. Plutarch gives us a glimpse of him in good form just before and after the battle:

> When the Medes invaded and Themistocles was trying to persuade the people to give up their city . . . and fight the issue at sea, most men were terrified at the daring of the scheme. But Cimon was first to act and with a cheerful face led a procession of his friends through the Cerameicus up to the acropolis. He carried his horse's bridle to dedicate to the goddess, signifying that what the city needed then was not knightly prowess but men who would fight at sea. After he had dedicated his bridle, he took one of the shields which were hung up about the

> temple, prayed to the goddess, and went down to the sea. Because of his actions many began to take heart again.
>
> His physical presence was nothing to criticise. As the poet Ion says, he was tall with a thick and curly head of hair. And since he displayed brilliant and heroic qualities in the struggle [at Salamis] he quickly gained praise and good will in the city. Many flocked to him urged him to do something which would be worthy of Marathon. So when he entered politics the people gladly welcomed him and promoted him (since they were sick of Themistocles) to the highest honours and offices in the city, for the people liked him for his gentleness and honesty.
>
> Plutarch, *Cimon*, 5.

Brave, cooperative, handsome, willing to give up a class signifier in the interests of the community – it is a rather touching scene. Herodotus has little to say about Cimon, letting the story of the Cimonids fizzle out with Miltiades' disgrace, but Plutarch, ever the biographer, presents us with his subject inspiring others with his thoughtful conduct. There is another interesting factor at work here. Plutarch refers to people calling on Cimon to do something worthy of Marathon. As Miltiades' son he was right in line for this sort of challenge – to live up to his father's standard. Yet this is the sort of rhetoric that would also appeal to others. Many young men might aspire to equal their seniors' achievements. As time went on, this notion of matching Marathon would play a bigger and bigger role in the rhetoric of inspiration and accusation.

Cimon's performance at Salamis was such that he was elected general of the Oineis tribe as Miltiades had been before him. This put him in an interesting position the following year when the war roared back to life. The Persians re-occupied Athens. When the Argives told them that the Spartans were on the march, they burned the city again and moved to Boeotia, perhaps to avoid getting trapped in Attica; perhaps hoping to leave room for diplomatic solutions.[51] There would be no solution. The battle took place outside Plataea.[52]

The Battle of Plataea was a messy affair, including a great deal of uncertainty about what was happening where. The Spartans were in charge, led by the regent Pausanias. The other Peloponnesians were accustomed to follow their lead, but there were tensions with the others –Athenians (led by Aristides), Plataeans (led once again by Arimnestus), Euboeans, Aeginitans, Megarians and more. Conflict arose between the Tegeans and Athenians over who should hold the left-wing. Herodotus gives them speeches. They both cite their history of martial prowess. The Athenians conclude by arguing that even if they had never fought any battle but Marathon, Marathon would be enough to justify them taking the wing. As with other speeches we cannot be certain that this is what was said, but it is clear that by Herodotus' day it was plausible that the Athenians would use Marathon in this way – a key part of their identity, proof of their superiority. There also seems to be a sub-text advocating for Sparta and Athens to act as joint leaders of Greece. It won them the argument. The Spartans took the right-wing and placed the Athenians on the left facing the medising Greeks. Plutarch, later, includes the row but adds a more upbeat detail: the Athenians are inspired by the thought of Marathon and the proof it offered that the Persians were beatable.[53] After a drawn-out struggle the Hellenic League was victorious and saw the Persian army routed. Mardonius himself lay among the dead.

Meanwhile, across the Aegean, Spartan king Leotychides was busy with his own campaign.[54] He received a tip-off that the Ionians would act against Persia if they knew that the Hellenic League was nearby. He followed the tip, bid the fleet set sail, and took on the Persians at Mycale. They beached their ships, defeated the Persians on land and went on to destroy the Persian fleet. This battle broke the back of Persian power in Ionia. People reported seeing a herald's staff on the beach and news flew through the men of the Greeks' victory against Mardonius. It was said that the staff must have been Hermes'. How else could they know that the battles of Plataea and Mycale had been fought on the same day? Such a coincidence – and the coincidence of both battles taking place near temples of Demeter – surely proved that the gods had a hand in it.[55]

The retreat of the Persian army from Greece and Ionia was the end of the Graeco-Persian Wars. Or rather, it was the end of the Graeco-Persian Wars as such, but not the end of war with Persia. As we will see, conflict rumbled on for many years, but there would be no further invasion of the Greek mainland. No one knew that at the time. Amongst the Persians and Medes it was reasonable to assume that a follow-up assault would be organised. Amongst the Greeks it would have been sheer complacency to assume that that was the end of the matter.

Leotychides led the fleet home. The Athenians recalled their evacuees and they still had the energy to see to one of their long-term concerns. They sent ships to besiege Sestos by the Hellespont, just across from the Chersonese, and they took it as the last Persians pulled out.[56] Much to the Spartans' displeasure, the Athenians at home meanwhile had been busy fortifying the city.[57] There was still enough good will for some cooperation, however. Under the leadership of the Spartans the Hellenic League carried out joint operations to remove the Persians from further territories, at Byzantium and Cyprus. The Spartans were headed by Pausanias, who was regent for his cousin, the young king Pleistarchus son of Leonidas. Pausanias had been an effective leader throughout the invasion crisis since the death of his uncle at Thermopylae. This new phase saw him run into trouble. He seems to have been over-bearing to say the least. The allies disliked him; the Ionians could not stand him. Free sailors were punished as if they were slaves. There were rumours that he stabbed a well-born woman. The Spartans recalled him. He stood trial on a number of charges and there was talk of him trying to cut a deal with the Persians. Even after everything that had passed, Persia was still the major superpower and there was motive for ambitious men to be on the best terms that they could with them. Pausanias took shelter in Sparta's temple of Athena only for the ephors to have him walled in. He starved to death – a gruesome end for the victor of Plataea. All the same, the damage done to the Hellenic League could not be undone. The allies appealed to the Athenians to take over. The Spartans were squeezed out and Athens became the leader of a new union, the Delian League.[58]

The League's campaigns saw conflict between Greeks and Persians stretch across the Aegean and from Thrace to Egypt. Some of the men who had fought at Marathon – the *Marathonomachoi* – had senior roles, such as Aristides, who determined which members would provide ships, which would provide money and how much.[59] And it was Cimon who became the real hero of the League. He was popular amongst the allies, who he treated with characteristic honesty and mildness. He was popular at home, where those same virtues were combined with generosity – taking down fences around his orchards so the poor could help themselves and funding meals to give the less well-off more time for public life.[60] Above all his popularity stemmed from his outstanding military successes. From Thrace to Cyprus Cimon led the Greeks in successful campaigns, driving the Persian forces back into Anatolia. Athens had well and truly moved out from Sparta's shadow to become a leading Greek power, arguably *the* leading Greek power. As the architect of much of its success, Cimon's reputation was transformed. Becoming a leading military and political figure had its perils and its rewards. Amongst the latter was the opportunity to guide public perception of Miltiades and Marathon. His father had died in ignominy. Cimon would see to it that his reputation was restored.

The Persians

The invasions of Greece were already being celebrated in public art. We have from this period the earliest surviving artwork which explores these wars: Aeschylus' *Persians*. Aeschylus had fought at Marathon, where his brother

Cynegeirus had been killed, and he had fought again at Artemisium and Salamis. Despite his success as a dramatist, it was his military contribution that he was proudest of, writing his own epitaph for when the time came:

> The dead Aeschylus, son of Euphorion, the Athenian,
> this tomb covers in wheat-bearing Gela;
> the grove of Marathon can attest his valour,
> and the long-haired Mede knew it well.
>
> *Life of Aeschylus*, 11.[61]

The Persians was staged in 472, looking back to the events around Salamis eight years earlier. Years before, Phrynichus had been fined when he staged a play with a contemporary subject, *The Fall of Miletus*. Mythical subjects were the norm. But with *The Persians* Aeschylus dared something new – a trilogy (as all tragedies were) with two mythical plays and one contemporary. This time there was no need for a fine. The contemporary play dealt not with the sorrows of the Athenians' kin across the water but with their recent success and their enemies' sorrow. *The Persians* takes us from a description of Xerxes' mighty army to Xerxes on stage, distraught in rags after his defeat. By placing such an event alongside two mythical subjects, *The Persians* elevated the Graeco-Persian Wars above the everyday. Much is made of Xerxes' hubris in bridging the Hellespont and a dream sequence sees personifications of Greece and Asia freed from the yoke of Xerxes' chariot by Greece's self-respecting defiance. It is both a jingoistic 'hurrah' for the Greeks and a poignant exploration of the fragility of human endeavour.[62] Xerxes is described in terms that evoke the terror of invasion, yet he is also made ridiculous – the leader of a conquering host whose own bungles and hubris led to his defeat. It was Xerxes who had walked the streets of Athens and ordered it burnt. He was the figure who needed bringing down a peg in the Athenian imagination. This is achieved not only by presenting him despairing on stage, but by contrasting him with a more capable father. It was Darius' generals who had failed at Marathon; not Darius. Aeschylus makes Darius a figure of sombre wisdom; a ghost raised from the dead and disappointed by his son.[63]

The focus of *The Persians* is Salamis rather than Marathon, understandable perhaps given that it was the more recent event and one at which the king himself was present. The sponsor (*choregos*) was Pericles son of Xanthipus, Miltiades' prosecutor. Pericles had his own reasons for preferring a play about Salamis although it is not clear exactly how much influence the *choregos* could exert over the content of a play anyway. Marathonomachoi such as Aristides and Callias will have been in the audience, as will the sons of those men, veterans of Salamis and Plataea. Although Salamis is the main action, Marathon is its underpinning. The clashes between the Greeks and the Persians are characterised as 'Ares armed with the bow against famous spearmen', evoking the image of the spear-wielding Marathonomachoi. Xerxes' failure is described by his mother, Atossa, who remembers Marathon: Xerxes planned vengeance for those lost at Marathon but simply added to the number of Persian dead.[64] Marathon is a measure by which success and failure can be measured both in practical terms and morally. Darius lost honourably at Marathon; Xerxes was more immoral and lost more grievously.

The Persians lies at the beginning of a long process of using Marathon and the wider Graeco-Persian Wars to reflect on contemporary events and to explore human experiences – imagining Persian devastation in contrast to Greek triumph, extolling the Athenians' excellence in war, picturing hubris and pride brought low. The play operates on a hierarchy which imagines superior, masculine Greeks opposing inferior, effeminate Persians.[65] It encouraged a more oppositional view of Greek identity. It was to prove a long-lasting concept.

Drama was still a new art-form. As the century progressed, the Athenians would head an artistic revolution that developed a whole range of new literary and artistic genres which form the backbone of much of the literature and art that followed in subsequent centuries. As the Athenians developed them, they looked to Marathon as a touchstone – a common cultural reference that helped them to articulate whatever they wanted to say. Marathon occurred at just the right moment for its significance to be captured and replayed across the ages. Yet there is no one Marathon – its meanings are diverse and always open to negotiation.

9

Memories of Marathon in Fifth-Century Art and Literature

Picturing Marathon

> The following are fit topics for conversation for men reclining on a soft couch by the fire in the winter season, when after a meal they are drinking sweet wine and eating a little pulse: Who are you, and what is your family? What is your age, my friend? How old were you when the Medes invaded this land?
>
> Xenophanes of Colophon[1]

This fragment of Xenophanes sends a shiver down the spine and captures the pervasiveness of the Graeco-Persian Wars in Greek conversation and literature. He wrote this in the sixth century after the Persians had conquered Ionia. It remained a pertinent question amongst Greeks on both sides of the Aegean for decades to come, for whom the arrival of the Persians was a defining event and a shared experience despite cities playing different roles in the war. After a meal at home, with friends, with one's phratry, visiting foreign cities or the panhellenic sanctuaries, stories of the war were told, heard and passed on. These were personal, family traditions, and yet more and more they would be influenced by communal versions retold in public formats: the plays, monuments, speeches and more. Each year the festival was held at which Artemis received her thank-offerings and the dead at Marathon were honoured as heroes. In a cultural shift, Greeks began to define themselves less as peoples with various things in common, and more as people with things in common who were different, distinct, superior to their Persian foes. The Athenians had added the Graeco-Persian Wars to the key events of their identity: *Who were the Athenians?* They were the people who had fought off the Amazons under Theseus, people who had fought at Troy, and the people who had defeated the Persians at Marathon and Salamis – especially Marathon, where they had fought (almost) alone.

Cimon's victories continued, driving Persians from Caria and Lycia. After a victory at Eion in Thrace the people voted him the right to erect three statues of

Hermes with commemorative inscriptions. One celebrated his battle 'against the sons of the Mede' while another evoked the Trojan War, indirectly elevating the new wars to the level of the mythological.[2] He captured the island of Scyros and handed it to the Athenians.[3] At Eurymedon he won two victories in one day – one by sea, one by land – destroying the bulk of the Persian fleet.[4] He drove the Persians and Thracians from the Chersonese, securing that valuable peninsular for the Athenians, probably there for the first time since he was a teenager.[5] His campaigns enriched the city and that wealth went towards preparing further city walls, building public facilities and developing the site of the Academy.[6] After a bumpy start, Cimon had seen to it that the Cimonids were still a force to be reckoned with. Though still powerful, the retreating Persians were no longer as frightening to the Greeks as they had been in the 490s–80s. Cimon was a panhellenist and had seen first-hand how co-operation between Greeks led to in-roads against Persia.[7] Was it Cimon who invented the story of Miltiades telling Datis that the Greeks should rule the Medes?[8] The sentiment certainly fits.

Cimon's success was not universally well-received. Life can come at you fast. Just when he might have been expected to be celebrating his success, he was impeached. From the Chersonese he had travelled to Thasos and seized gold mines on the mainland. From there he might have attacked Macedon and seized their metal and timber-rich lands. That he had not done so was taken as a dereliction of duty. A guilty verdict would mean execution. There is a story that Elpinice tried to defend him. Though wealthy Athenian women were not supposed to leave their houses for more than a few prescribed reasons, she made her way to the house of Pericles – son of the man who had impeached her father, who now led the impeachment of her brother. She pleaded with him for Cimon's life. He is said to have smiled and told her that she was too old to be mixed up in politics. Make of that what you will. In an echo of his father's trial, the Athenians could not bring themselves to execute Cimon. He was fined an enormous fifty talents, another echo of the past.[9] With this outcome he had been more fortunate than Themistocles. The victor of Salamis also escaped execution, but had been ostracised in 472. He had been implicated in Pausanias' dealings with the Great King and seems generally to have become seen as over-bearing. He never returned.[10] Miltiades, Themistocles and Pausanias had all been cut down to size by their communities following their successes. Cimon had now suffered a similar blow but at least he was still in the game.

This mixture of success and danger meant that Cimon could not afford to be complacent. After his trial we see a concerted effort to remind the world of the contributions that he and his father had made to Athens' success. Cimon's influence can be seen in the Athenians' dedications at Delphi, dedications which projected Marathon into the panhellenic arena. From the spoils taken after the battle they erected a treasury to house their dedications and decorated it with scenes of Theseus and Heracles fighting the Amazons, an indirect reference to Athenian successes over Persia. Nearby was erected a spectacular sculpture-group created by the greatest sculptor of the age, Pheidias. The group featured Athena, Apollo and each of the heroes that the Athenian tribes were named after. They were joined by the mythical kings of Athens, Codrus and Theseus, and by Philaeus, founder of the Philaid family with whom the Cimonids were enmeshed. Amongst this august company was Miltiades himself.[11] As one commentator puts it, this was 'the mythical representatives of the Athenian polis joined together with both the great man Miltiades and his family ancestor, in the presence of the Athenian protecting goddess and the Lord of the Delphic sanctuary'.[12] The heroes conveyed the communal aspect of Marathon, but the inclusion of Miltiades acknowledged him as the architect of the victory. This was an honour that must have seemed impossible to Cimon and Elpinice back in the gloomy days around their father's death.

Had Callimachus survived the battle, things might have been different. But it was Miltiades who survived (albeit briefly) to present his version of events and his family continued to stress his importance. Callimachus was recognised for his contribution, but he would have to share the honour and he would frequently be eclipsed. His family did what they could. Callimachus had erected a statue shortly before Marathon. Someone, most likely his son, revisited it and added inscriptions announcing Callimachus' part at Marathon. The family also erected a statue on the acropolis of a winged goddess, most likely Nike – Victory. This was surely push-back, a re-urging of Callimachus' significance.[13] But who could contend with the charisma and success of Cimon? His version rang out. Marathon was the victory of *all* Athenians, but if there was one Athenian in particular, it was Miltiades.

Relations between the Athenians and Plataeans remained good. At the Great Panathenaea the Athenians included the Plataeans in their prayers as they had done ever since the first festival after Marathon.[14] In more tangible form, we find the Athenians donating booty from Marathon to pay for a new sanctuary of Athena the Warlike at Plataea. The paintings in the temple included a portrait of Arimnestus, who had led the Plataeans at both Marathon and Plataea. Other paintings drew out ideological themes related to the wars. Images of the Seven against Thebes and Odysseus slaying the Suitors were indirect ways of expressing the punishment of the medising Thebans and an end to misrule and disorder.

This framed the Graeco-Persian Wars as the upholding of hellenic values and the continuation of a historic pattern.[15]

In Athens a truly grand project was underway: the creation of the Stoa Poikile, or Painted Stoa. This costly project was instigated by Cimon's brother-in-law, Peisianax, but it has Cimon's fingerprints all over it. It is possible that Peisianax paid for it, although it seems likely that he contributed alongside money from Cimon's campaign booty.[16] Those campaigns and the paintings in the Stoa are conceptually inseparable and although he is not named anywhere in it, Cimon remained the unspoken subtext. The theme: the glory of the Greeks, the glory of the Athenians, the glory of Cimon and Miltiades – all bringing order in the face of wrongdoing.

In the heart of the city, a little to the north-east of where the temple of Hephaestus still stands, this stoa was a public space where people could meet, walk and spend time. Years later it would be the haunt of philosophers who earned the name 'Stoics' from the place where they gathered. As a stoa it was rectangular with two short walls, a long back wall and an open front of columns. The roof and stone walls made it a cool, pleasant environment. The paintings that gave it its name decorated the interior of the back wall. They were executed by some of the most famous artists of antiquity: Polygnotus, Micon and Panainus, brother of Pheidias the sculptor.[17] A fourth painting would later be added to the side wall and captured shields were displayed at the opposite end.[18] The three original paintings were a set. They featured Theseus leading the Athenians to victory over the invading Amazons, the Greek leaders gathered around the Trojan princesses at the fall of Troy, and:

> At the end of the painting are those who fought at Marathon; the Boeotians of Plataea and the Athenians are coming to blows with the barbarians. In this place neither side has the better, but the centre of the fighting shows the barbarians in flight and pushing one another into the marsh, while at the end of the painting are the Phoenician ships, and the Greeks killing the barbarians who are scrambling into them. Here is also a portrait of the hero Marathon, after whom the plain is named, of Theseus represented coming up from the Underworld, of Athena and of Heracles. The people of Marathon, according to their own account, were the first to regard Heracles as a god. Of the fighters the most conspicuous figures in the painting are Callimachus, who had been elected commander-in-chief by the Athenians, Miltiades, one of the generals, and a hero called Echetlus.
>
> Pausanias, 1.15.3.

This description was given by Pausanias, who saw the painting in the second century CE, over 500 years after it was created – a fine reminder that it was a phenomenally enduring representation of the battle. From other writers we know that Epizelus and Cynegeirus were also depicted as well as the leaders of the Persian army, Datis and Artaphernes.[19] The painting was huge, around 16m wide.[20]

The Marathon painting gives us insights into a prominent interpretation of the battle. The divine presence is very noticeable. The gods give their support, present as witnesses. The heroes actively participate. Together this expresses the idea that the Athenians and Plataeans were carrying out divine will. Amongst the humans, the Greeks' calm endurance is contrasted with the Persians' panic – or Panic, if we recall the role of Pan. And it very much is the Persians – there is no room here for admitting that Ionian Greeks were part of the attacking force; that would ruin the binary. The Persians' panic is emphasised by the attention to their flight to the marsh and the scramble at the ships. Furthermore there is Epizelus, whose courage expressed the Greeks' resistance to fear. There too is Cynegeirus, who fought beyond the very shore. Callimachus is there. That is appropriate as he was the commander, while the tradition that he fought on despite his wounds means that he too represents resilience. And then there is Miltiades, an identifiable figure portrayed in front, urging the Greeks on to the last attack.[21] In many ways the painting shows a group effort by the Athenians and Plataeans, but the handful of identifiable figures mark some out as special. There were ten generals at Marathon, but anyone looking at this painting would receive the firm impression that Miltiades made the difference.

The Marathon painting would be striking alone, yet its combination with the other two extended its meaning. As with the paintings at Plataea, the combination of subjects was chosen to deliver a message. Theseus' defeat of the Amazon invasion should be read as a forerunner to Marathon; the Athenians defending Athens (and Greece) from a foreign invader. The fall of Troy offers another clash of Greeks vs Asians, another Greek victory, this one panhellenic. This image may also have called to mind Cimon's victories in the Chersonese and at Eurymedon.[22] The fall of Troy recalls the Greeks' sense of the Trojans' law-breaking and punishment; the Amazons suggest intemperance and aggression halted. Both topics suggest the idea of wrongs being righted, justice and Greek values triumphing.[23] The enemy in all three are associated with women, and with it the Athenians' patriarchal idea of female lust for power and lack of self-control.[24] The Athenians are the opposite: manly, self-controlled, committed to freedom. We can see many of the ideas familiar from Aeschylus' *Persians* reworked here in a visual form. All three paintings chime together to tell the story of Marathon as an extension of the Athenians' heritage. A parallel is drawn between the achievements of the Athenians' ancestors and those of the modern age. From a more personal perspective, the Cimonids claimed Theseus as an ancestor. He was depicted in the Amazon painting, his sons, Acamas and Demophon, were almost certainly included in the Troy painting, and there was Miltiades beside them – a family trilogy of war on Asia.[25] The nearby Eurymedon statues extended the theme further. This is a celebration of Miltiades and Cimon, a celebration of war against Asia and a justification for the Athenians' new position as the leading Greek state.[26]

This last point is a serious one. In twenty short years, the Athenians had gone from being one power amongst many which were all less mighty than the Spartans, to the rulers of an empire. States had willingly joined the Delian League, even asking the Athenians to lead. But it was not a club you could leave. The Athenians had offered protection and reparations, but if you no longer wanted the Athenians' support, you would need protection from the Athenians. Cimon had played his part in all this. He was a panhellenist who believed in joint campaigns against Persia, but all the same, his visit to Thasos involved an argument over the Thasians' gold mines and ended in Athens seizing them. Naxos tried to leave the League and was invaded and compelled to re-join.[27] How could any of this possibly be justified? To the Athenians, Marathon and the other victories of the Graeco-Persian Wars proved their ability, their divine endorsement and their right to call the shots. Marathon stood out in this respect because it was *their* victory and because it was the battle which made later battles possible. The Stoa Poikile had a moral message, but it was also a deeply political message concerning the place of the Cimonids in Athens and the place of the Athenians amongst the Greeks.

If Cimon thought it necessary to promote his and his father's contributions, he was not wrong. Even the statues and stoa were not enough. It is unlikely that he saw it finished until years after its completion. He was ostracised in 461/60.[28] There were several factors at work. His rivalry with Pericles was a problem, and the *demos* preferred Pericles' democratic changes to Cimon's traditionalist stance.[29] As a panhellenist and a believer in the old ways it was not surprising that Cimon was fond of the Spartans and their customs; he was a philolaconian. Some even said that he was more like a Spartan than an Athenian. Things between Athens and Sparta were increasingly tense. On one occasion Cimon talked the Athenians into sending an army to help the Spartans and the Spartans mistrustfully sent them home.[30] It did not look good. The panhellenist dream of joint campaigns looked over. For some this Spartan sympathising was good enough reason to expel him. The other reason we hear of is Elpinice. She was married to Callias now and they had children, but rumours still circulated about her and Cimon. Some writers claim that this was the reason for his ostracism. It was not just authors; an actual ostracon survives on which someone scratched 'let Cimon take his sister Elpinice and get out'.[31] Who knows if there was anything more than a sibling bond between them, but clearly the rumour-mill was working overtime. Jokes were made by comedians and poets. Elpinice was an unusual Athenian woman; brought up outside Athens, partly Thracian, aristocratic in an increasingly democratic state, outspoken – all of this could play against her. Cimon's long-term reputation as a womaniser will have made it all the more plausible. More than anything, even being fond of Spartan culture was regarded amongst Athenians as an indicator that you were a bit weird about sex.[32] If there were rumours that he was too close to his sister – and there were – his love of Sparta would to some be confirmation of his guilt. All of this might have been ignored in the right circumstances, but things had come to a head. He was out, leaving his magnificent stoa behind him.

There were of course more modest ways to reference the Graeco-Persian Wars in art. It was not all stoas and temples. One art-form for which the Athenians are particularly well-known is pottery. An interesting process can be seen in the depiction of Persians in pottery, one which reflects the wider attitudes of the time. The first depictions of combat between Greeks and Persians by Athenian potters began shortly after Marathon.[33] These images tend to show duals rather than mass fighting – a tendency of the art-form. The Greek is usually shown on the left, the Persian on the right. This indicates the Greek's victory as the image is meant to be read left to right, with the advance of the left-hand figure expressing their success. All the same, the images are respectful of both parties, casting them both as serious warriors. There is interest in the equipment of both sides. Persians are shown with their characteristic wicker shields, patterned trousers and leather shoes. Their weaponry shows they mean business. Early examples depict them using spears and swords, similar to their hoplite opponents. And although their defeat is implied, they are typically shown fighting to the last – a valiant foe. This equality of enemies comes to an end in the period after the Battle of Eurymedon. While scenes of Greeks and Persians fighting continued, it became far more common to show Persians fleeing or actually defeated. There is a change in the depiction of equipment too. It becomes more common to see images of Persians with their bows prominent, stressing their difference, implying their inferiority. More frequently clothed Persians are depicted facing Greek hoplites resplendent in the nudity of the hero. And those Persian clothes become increasingly generic. Mish-mashes of generally Asian rather than specifically Persian clothing become more frequent, sometimes combined with Thracian elements. In the same vein, depictions of non-Greeks who are not Persian

Fig. 10 Combat between a Greek and a Persian. Amphora, made in Athens, *c.* 480–470 BCE. New York Metropolitan Museum of Art, 06.1021.117.

become increasingly subsumed within standardised 'Persian types' as an idea of a generic foreigner takes hold. Amazon fights become more popular. These changes reflect the increasingly xenophobic perception of Persia, based not in fear of invasion and recognition of power, but in an uneasy yet contemptuous view that characterised Persian culture as inferior, weak and effeminate.

A new era

In Persia the invasions of Greece were slipping further into insignificance. The Great King Xerxes had been murdered in 465.[34] His son and heir, Darius, was also killed. The details are vague. There was a plot at court. The captain of the king's guard was implicated, although there is a good chance that another son, Artaxerxes, instigated it. The shocking loss of the fleet at Eurymedon may have numbered Xerxes' days.[35] Artaxerxes I was the new Great King. Marathon was in the past – his grandfather's time. Salamis and Plataea were his father's time, about fifteen years ago now. There were things to think about in the west, but that was not an invasion of Greece, it was another revolt in Egypt. The Athenians sent their fleet to assist. Artaxerxes' response was one that would become familiar. It was time for money to talk. Envoys were sent to bribe the Spartans to invade Attica so that the Athenians would be forced home. As it was, the Persians succeeded in subduing Egypt without the Spartans' help, devastating the Athenian fleet in the process.[36] The talks at Sparta had fallen through and the invasion never happened, yet the fact that the talks took place demonstrates how far things had come from the Spartans' bold statement of 491 when they murdered the Persian envoys. The Spartans were coming to regard the Athenians as a menace; a greater menace than the Persians. When similar offers were made in the future, they were accepted.

The Athenians had entered a long period of conflicts. It was an ongoing effort to keep the empire in line. This included conflict with the old enemy, Aegina. There was war on and off with the Spartans – the First Peloponnesian War. There was war with the Boeotians. Cimon returned to Athens in around 451. Some said that Elpinice had a hand in arranging things with Pericles.[37] Cimon will have seen his Stoa Poikile in full glory, with the Marathon painting a part of city life. The historian Thucydides was born around this time. He was part of Cimon's extended family – he was Thucydides son of Olorus, his father carrying the family name of Cimon's maternal grandfather, King Olorus of Thrace. It is curious to think that Cimon may have met baby Thucydides or seen toddler Thucydides bumbling about.

Cimon set about arranging a five-year truce with Sparta – there were advantages to having a philolaconian about.[38] The two states would clash indirectly a few years later in the so-called Second Sacred War for Delphi, but for now hostilities were subdued.[39] The Athenians took the opportunity to look east. Cimon took a fleet to Cyprus which was still Persian-controlled; 200 Athenian ships plus allies. The fleet returned safely, but Cimon died during the campaign, either of sickness or an infected wound.[40] The latter tradition may have been told to echo Miltiades' death. Cimon was in his fifties, predeceasing a number of the Marathonomachoi. He was the greatest general of his era, a champion of panhellenic war against Persia, and the greatest advocate for Marathon's importance and his father's importance to the battle. Cimon had ensured that Miltiades was remembered as the victor of Marathon. He left behind several children and though they did not achieve the fame of himself or Miltiades, his sons were active in political life and military service. All of them will have passed on the family stories, at home and with their phratries.[41] Elpinice also kept the memories alive. Who knows if Metiochus heard of his brother's death? – the one brother the Persians' greatest Greek foe, the other living quietly with his Persian family. For the Cimonids and their friends it was the end of an era.

The situation with Persia was changing. As we have seen, Artaxerxes showed no interest in invading Greece. Around this time a truce was arranged in which the Great King committed to leave the Greek cities of Asia independent and the Athenians agreed to keep out of Persian territory. This is known as the Peace of Callias, having been negotiated by Cimon's brother-in-law. That said, it is likely that Cimon had played a role in the negotiations for all that he had spent his life fighting.[42]

Peace – or at least truce – with the Persians made it harder for the Athenians to justify their empire. This was all the more reason to bolster public works which declared the Athenians' role in defending Greece. This project was largely pushed by Pericles. New temples were built and sculptures carved to decorate them. The most famous of these was the Parthenon, which still adorns the acropolis. While the ruined temple of Athena Polias was left as a testament to the attack they had survived, Athena Parthenos' temple, begun after Marathon, was rejuvenated. Besides its splendid architecture, its ambitious decorative scheme expanded on the themes seen in *The Persians* and in the Marathon painting. Decorative blocks, *metopes*, showed mythical contests between forces of order and disorder: human Lapiths fight wild Centaurs on the south, gods fight giants on the east, on the west male Greeks fight female Amazons, and on the north were scenes from the Trojan War. Around the temple the frieze depicted the great procession of the Panathenaea – the procession that Harmodius' sister had been rejected from all those years ago. The frieze has been interpreted numerous ways. The scene with the *peplos* – Athena's dress – has been regarded as a reference to the myth of Erechtheus' daughter sacrificing herself to save the city. It has also been suggested that the young men represent those who died at Marathon – the men who had become heroes and permanent defenders of Attica. Certainly the overall effect is commemoration of the Graeco-Persian Wars and a claim to the Athenians' unique position as the protectors of Greece and its civilisation.[43]

This theme continued inside. A statue of Athena, created by Pheidias, held a shield depicting Theseus, who appeared at Marathon, fighting the Amazons. He seems to have been joined by Cecrops and Erectheus, two more kings who were said to have risen to fight at Marathon.[44] Nearby a temple of Nike was constructed. This sported a frieze depicting Greeks fighting Persians (with horses) – likely a depiction of Marathon.[45] Erected beside it, visible from the sea, was a statue of Athena 7m tall on a 2m base. She was Athena Promachos, Fighter at the Front. She was a statement of the Athenians' readiness to meet military challenges, paid for from Marathon booty.[46] This pattern continued outside Athens. Near Marathon, on the road to Rhamnous, a temple was erected to Nemesis. She had punished the Persians' hubris and would be celebrated with a fresh new temple, a testament to Marathon. The sculpture dedicated there was said to be carved from a block of marble brought by the Persians for their victory monument. Nemesis has a sense of humour.[47]

While the Athenians worked hard to organise this abundance of celebratory art, they had no intention of relaxing their hold on the islanders. They ramped up their campaigns against reluctant members and increased their export of colonists. Attempts at a mainland empire in Boeotia met with a heavy defeat at the Battle of Coronea and revolt across Euboea. Pressed, they agreed the Thirty Year Truce with the Spartans, extending the rough truce established earlier.[48] As a result of this truce, no one came to rescue Samos when it rejected the Athenians' order to hand a town over to Miletus. The Persians, contravening their agreement, offered Pericles a fortune to leave the Samian oligarchs to their own devices. Pericles rejected the offer, sailed with the fleet, took 100 adults and children hostage, dissolved the oligarchy and established a democracy. The Samians revolted as soon as Pericles left and the hostages were rescued. Of course Pericles was back in no time. He beat them in a naval battle then subjected Samos city to a nine-month siege. A huge number of Athenians were killed in a follow-up naval battle, but the Athenians ended the siege, demolished the walls, confiscated the Samian fleet, imposed a fine and took more hostages.[49] We have looked at this episode in more detail than we might have partly because it exemplifies how much the Athenians' relationship with the eastern Greeks had changed, and partly because Elpinice offered public comment on it. Her barb expresses many people's view of the Athenians' policies:

Pericles delivered the public funeral speech (*epitaphios*) after the Samos campaign. Some women crowned him with flowers like an athlete:

> Elpinice approached him and said, 'This was an amazing feat, Pericles, and deserving of wreaths. You got a lot of good citizens killed, not in a war with Phoenicians or Medes, like my brother Cimon, but destroying a city which is an ally and our kin.'
>
> As Elpinice said this Pericles listened unmoved then spoke a verse of Archilochus to her:
>
> 'Otherwise you'd not be using scent, an old crone like you.'
>
> Plutarch, *Pericles* 28.[50]

As on the previous occasion, Pericles' ridicule of Elpinice's age is no answer to her comment on public affairs. There is a lot going on in this interaction and to an extent it typifies two ways of thinking about the legacy of Marathon and the wider Persian-Greek conflict. To some, the legacy of the wars should be panhellenism, Greek self-determination and continued conflict with Persia. To others it meant that the Athenians should rule the other Greeks. Marathon could be evoked in the service of both ideas. Still, each year the battle-dead were honoured at their tomb. Prayers were still made for the Athenians and Plataeans together. There were fewer Marathonomachoi with each passing year, but no one could forget the battle. If anything there was a renewed intensity in discussing it. We will turn now to some of the ways in which it was explored.

Writing Marathon

Herodotus was a young child at the time of the Graeco-Persian Wars, born into an Ionian city that had been conquered by Lydians and then Persians. We do not know exactly when he began to write his history of the conflict, but it was well-known enough in Athens by 425 that the playwright Aristophanes expected his audience to recognise a parody of its opening.[51] The wars that had dominated the lives of Herodotus and pretty much everyone he knew prompted him to write a work of enormous depth, sophistication and vision. It was the first long historical narrative, written in determination that the great deeds of the war and why the war was fought should not be lost to time. Herodotus spoke to participants and their relatives. He provides the various explanations which he heard and occasionally offers his own. He provides an account of what happened, but also shapes the narrative to give moral warnings about the dangers of hubris and over-reach, of violating the norms and behavioural boundaries of one's community and overriding the divinely-drawn boundaries of nature.

It will already be clear how much we depend on Herodotus for knowledge of the Graeco-Persian Wars. That is not to say that the events of his adulthood did not influence how he perceived those wars. The Athenians of his adulthood were intense imperialists. While he clearly admired Athenian culture he also had his reservations. When he writes about the dangers of tyranny and the way it encourages transgression, this includes reflection on the Athenians' arguably tyrannical treatment of their erstwhile allies. This theme can be seen in the handling of the Marathon campaign as well as what followed. So while Darius is clearly presented as the baddie for wanting to expand into Europe, there are also warning signs from the Athenians. This is most apparent in the figure of Miltiades himself. It is through Herodotus that we know so much about Miltiades' life as a tyrant and his work for the tyrants who killed his father.

As Marathon approaches, Miltiades is painted in a softer light, but even then we should note how Herodotus gives him a speech urging Callimachus to fight so that victory can lead to the Athenians dominating the other Greeks. He is acting the tyrant, in Herodotus' depiction, when he instigates the attack on Paros. He has easily whipped up tyrannical urges in the Athenian people. As we have seen, Herodotus gives us a hostile interpretation of Miltiades' actions on Paros – attempting sacrilege on the prompting of a priestess he is holding captive. All of this is classic Herodotean tyrant behaviour and Miltiades dies a tyrant's death. Xerxes is a worse villain and as readers we are encouraged to support the Greeks. Nonetheless, a warning note is struck at the end of *The Histories*. Flushed with success at Sestos – that is, into Asia near where Xerxes' bridge stood – Xanthippus and the Athenians crucify their captured enemy and stone his son to death in front of him. *The Histories* looks tentatively at what the Athenians did with their success. Their earlier actions are interpreted as if their shift in behaviour was already likely – the seeds sown. It tries to warn contemporaries not to keep making the same mistakes.[52] In this way the first history reflects on the present.

Herodotus also engages with what must have been a frequent question – how did the Athenians win at Marathon? We have seen that it was commonplace to honour the gods in relation to the battle and it is entirely in-keeping with ancient society that the gods' support, punishing hubris, would be a dominant explanation. Herodotus had heard the stories. He aligns with this world-view by implying and sometimes explicitly stating divine involvement. He had even heard a story about an omen sent to Hippias – a dream about having sex with his mother, followed by his tooth falling out when he stepped onto Athenian soil. Ominous.[53] Nonetheless, Herodotus also explores the scientific analysis then in vogue. He finishes with a throw-back to Cyrus the Great observing: 'soft countries breed soft men'; maybe environment played a role.[54] There are human factors too. Darius' excessive empire-building invites disaster. The Athenians' and Plataeans' bravery is stressed, especially the bravery and determination of Miltiades. Elsewhere Herodotus mentions the effectiveness of the Greeks' equipment.[55] It is entirely plausible that veterans and their families told him that they considered this an important factor. It is equally plausible that by his day it was a view held by the wider Athenian and Greek communities. Herodotus presents the Persians making mistakes from time to time, but he never presents them as idiots, poor soldiers or cowards. On the contrary, the only person in *The Histories* who suggests that is Aristagoras, when he is attempting to persuade the mainlanders to join the Ionian Revolt. It appears as the kind of thing a blusterer would say, not a valid point-of-view. In later centuries this would become a controversial position, but to Herodotus it was not. Divine support, bravery and equipment saved the day.

By the time that Herodotus died in *c.* 425–20, the historian Thucydides had reached adulthood. He would develop this new genre by writing his *History of the Peloponnesian War*. Naturally in dealing with a later conflict he would have less to say about Marathon. Nonetheless, Marathon and the wider Graeco-Persian Wars appear in his work in illuminating ways. The first way in which they appear is to convince you to read his work. He stresses the importance of the war that he is writing about by comparing it with the Graeco-Persian Wars: that was the greatest war of the past, yet the current one involved more battles, exilings, earthquakes, eclipses, famines and plagues.[56] Thucydides is being deliberately controversial. He knows the significance of the Graeco-Persian Wars and uses the suggestion that the new war is greater to whet the reader's interest. Comparing things to Marathon became its own cultural trope, one that is still with us.

Marathon appears again when Thucydides describes the origins of the Peloponnesian War, which kicked off in 431. He takes an approach familiar from Herodotus of looking back to related events which led step-by-step to the current situation. In doing so, Marathon is included as part of an account of how the fall-out of the Graeco-Persian Wars set the Athenians and Spartans at loggerheads. Something similar occurs when he describes the fall of the tyrants, referring to Hippias, who 'in his old age came with the Medes to Marathon'.[57] These references show the importance of Marathon in tracking past and present, but they are fairly matter-of-fact. More subtle rhetorical treatments are also explored by Thucydides.

Thucydides gives us a view of how the Athenians employed Marathon and other battles of the Graeco-Persian Wars to exert moral pressure on other states. Thucydides sets the scene. The key figures in the Peloponnesian League have met at Sparta and are complaining to the Spartans about the vexing things that the Athenians have been up to, urging the Spartans to do something. They voice the opinion that the Persians lost the wars because of their own mistakes (that is, not the Athenians' excellence) and bid the Spartans avoid doing the same.[58] Some Athenian envoys happen to be there. On hearing these complaints they ask to be allowed to respond. It is worth noting that Thucydides did not have access to exactly what was said, but he is transparent in saying that his method is to convey the gist and to phrase it appropriately.[59] He reaches into the mind of the Athenian and concludes that the speaker would consider it better not to address the actual complaints, but to remind the listeners of Athens' power and to urge the old to remember and the young to learn.[60] He turns to Marathon:

> . . . To the Median War and contemporary history we must refer, although we are rather tired of continually bringing this subject forward. In our action during that war we ran great risk to obtain certain advantages: you had your share in the results, do not try to rob us of all our share in the good that the glory may do us. . . . We assert that at Marathon we were at the front and faced the barbarian single-handed.
>
> Thucydides, 1.73.

The speaker is carrying out a sleight of hand, telling the listeners that they owe their freedom to the Athenians' success at Marathon whilst insisting that he would really rather not mention it. Notice that he would prefer not to mention it because it has been said too many times! We should well believe that the Athenians lost no opportunity to beat the other Greeks with Marathon, insisting on it as the justification for their empire and whatever else they wanted. In urging 'Greek freedom' they insist on Athenian dominance. We should also note the reference to the Athenians acting 'single-handed' at Marathon. To be fair, if the Athenians had determined not to fight, there is no way that the Plataeans would have. Nonetheless, the Plataeans did show up. This talk of the Athenians fighting alone is an argument for Athenian supremacy. It is at odds with the Marathon generation's decision to join the Plataeans' name to their own in prayers, yet this claim has less to do with slighting the Plataeans than it is has with accusing the Spartans. *Where were you, the greatest land power?* this seems to say, *You let down Greece and we stepped up*. There would be a lot more talk of 'standing alone' at Marathon.[61]

Another important speech occurs once the war has started. This is Pericles' famous funeral oration, an *epitaphios*, much like the one he delivered before Elpinice accosted him. A standard form had developed for *epitaphioi*.[62] The speaker would praise the past achievements of the city, mythical and historical. They would cite their forebears' love of freedom, love of state, respect for law and brave willingness to die for those values, urging listeners to make that a model for the present. The recently dead would be praised for defending those values in the manner of their ancestors, offering consolation to the dead and motivating others to be willing to make similar sacrifices. The Graeco-Persian Wars, especially Marathon, are frequently mentioned as the middle step between the mythical past and the present. Pericles uses all these features, praising the ancestors and bidding the living emulate them. Thucydides' narrator discusses the Marathon soros when he introduces the *epitaphios*, so when Pericles then talks of the ancestors we know what he is referring to. It is an inspiring speech which became influential within Athens and in the long tradition of speech-writing which followed. Thucydides does not let us have it that easy, however. The very next section shows the lofty ideals brought low as the Athenians fall apart under the pressure of the plague. Thucydides never lets us forget that ideals are easier to talk of than to live up to.

Dramatists

Since we last saw *The Persians* on stage, drama had gone from strength to strength. While tragedy was effective at exploring conflict, direct references to Marathon and the Graeco-Persian Wars are found most frequently in comedies. Athenian comedy, represented primarily through the work of Aristophanes, is well-known for its comment on Athenian society. Aristophanes belonged to the same generation as Thucydides, born around 450, a young child around the death of Cimon and the Peace of Callias. By the time that Aristophanes' first plays were produced in the 420s, Marathon veterans would be in their eighties – there cannot have been many of them. For Aristophanes, Marathon was both a long time ago and something that people were still very exercised about. He would not remember a time before the Marathon painting was in the Stoa Poikile or when the young men had not sacrificed at Marathon each year. He lived in a world in which Marathon was a common point of reference and that is reflected in his scenes of Athenian life.

Mentioning Marathon was an efficient way of connecting to a range of associations. Much of the humour that we see in Aristophanes revolves around intergenerational tension, the sense that the worthy men of the older generation had been succeeded by an inferior set. Intergenerational strife is an evergreen topic, so it worked even once those specific older men were running out. Marathon had become a symbol of earlier generations' excellence, which went beyond the individuals concerned. Friction between generations was complicated at Athens where political changes had moved fast. Although men of the early fifth century had been busy re-shaping society, political life had changed so much since then that they now appeared old-fashioned. The association of hoplites and affluence further complicated the perception of history. Hoplite warfare had by now pushed out the unarmoured combatants and missile-throwers who once took to the field at Marathon. Moreover, it was the less affluent members of the fleet who now won more victories and kept the money pouring in. Many in the wealthier classes disapproved of these changes. This is reflected in Aristophanes' plays in which Marathon appears frequently, while Salamis never gets a mention.[63] Celebrating Marathon was a way of celebrating Athens, yet remarking on the Marathon fighters' excellence in relation to younger men's weaknesses could also serve as a way of urging a return to the ways of an earlier era. These tensions would deepen as the Peloponnesian War dragged on.[64]

Aristophanes' *Acharnanians*, produced in 425, critiques the self-serving democrats of the day, in part by accusing them of misusing the better men of the older generation. The Chorus complain that they do not get justice in court against younger men:

> Is this not a scandal? What! the water-clock is to kill the white-haired veteran, who in fierce fighting has so often covered himself with glorious sweat, whose valour at Marathon saved the country! It was we who pursued on the field of Marathon, whereas now it is wretches who pursue us to the death and crush us!
>
> Aristophanes, *Acharnanians*, 692ff.

There is humour in the hyperbolic tone with which Marathon is thrust forward. Nonetheless, there is a sincere contrast of deed (fighting in battle) against word (fighting in court) and the appeal to Marathon provides a readily understandable way of criticising the injustices of the system.

Knights was produced the following year. Again we see the injustices of politicians expressed through their mistreatment of the Marathon generation. Words and deeds are contrasted once more. While politicians talk about Marathon in their speeches, Demos – here a character – actually fought there, yet is left in need by those same politicians.[65] In the course of the play, Demos is restored to youth, sense and fortune. Marathon is once again the touchstone by which his condition is measured:

> I have turned his ugliness into beauty . . . He has once more become as he was in the days when he lived with Aristides and Miltiades.
>
> Aristophanes, *Knights* 1316ff

The Chorus, impressed, responds that Demos is 'worthy of the glory of Marathon'. This is a more optimistic use of Marathon, urging the audience to think that the better values of the past can be recreated in the present.[66]

Clouds, from 423, plays again with intergenerational contrast. It is a precursor of Monty Python jokes about how bad things were in the good old days, albeit in a far ruder form. The character Better Argument compares the Marathonomachoi with the new immodest, uneducated generation which cannot even dance properly.[67] Dance here is not a frivolous matter but a demonstration of physical ability – the agility of the soldier. As with the other references it is tongue-in-cheek, yet again it is a recognisable way of talking about moral decline.

Wasps, staged in 422, offers a more involved treatment of Marathon. The play teases older men for their great love of jury-service. Nonetheless, it makes a sincere suggestion that the older generation who fought at Marathon or forged the empire deserve something to live on. Marathon looms large in the Chorus' account of the Graeco-Persian Wars, celebrating the pursuit to the ships and squeezing out other battles so that history moves from Marathon to the Delian League campaigns.[68] Marathon is evoked again by a speaker arguing for the Athenians' right to live off tribute: no Athenians should be poor. Now that tribute is pouring in, all Athenians should eat well, drink well, be garlanded and comfortable as 'the trophies of Marathon give them the right'.[69] As in *Acharnanians*, *Wasps* suggests that the system is not serving the most deserving. In contrast to contemporary money-grabbing politicians, Marathon stands as the symbol of the deserving, as a symbol of physical, moral excellence embodied in the older generations.

Wasps won second prize. In third came a play which placed even more emphasis on Greek-Persian relations: *The Ambassadors* by Leucon. This comedy has not survived, but it appears to have featured a burlesque version of an ambassadorial visit to Athens in the run-up to Marathon. The following year Aristophanes riffed on it by referring to a 'Song of Datis', based on his representation in *The Ambassadors*.[70] The character exclaims:

> Here comes the song of Datis
> Which he used to sing while masturbating in the afternoon,
> 'Oh how happy and pleasured and bubbly I feel!'
>
> Aristophanes, *Peace*, 289–291.

It is absurd. It is rude. It ridicules the Persians generally through an out-of-control Datis. It is remarkable to see Datis on the Athenian stage almost seventy years after he had been in Greece. Plays indicate the prominence that Datis still held in Athenian culture; they also helped to maintain it.

Comedy had a long memory. Aristophanes' *Lysistrata* recalled Cleomenes being besieged on the acropolis about 100 years earlier. He does not appear as a character, but the Chorus speak as if they recall it. If they cannot do as much now against women, they say, then the trophy at Marathon should come down.[71] In a lost play, *Demes*, Aristophanes' rival Eupolis also seems to have used Marathon and Miltiades as shorthand for the good old days. It sees four generals brought back from the dead. One of them seems to have been Miltiades because at one stage someone swears, 'No, by my battle at Marathon, Not one of them will grieve my heart'. It would make sense if Miltiades were the speaker. A second speaker further contrasts past and present:

> In truth though there is much to be said, I'm at a loss for words,
> So pained am I when I see our political life. We old men didn't run the city like this.
> To start with our city's generals were
> From the greatest houses, foremost in wealth and birth.
> To them we prayed like gods; for gods they were.
> And so we were secure. But now, wherever it may be,
> We go on campaign with trash we choose as our leaders.
>
> Eupolis, *Demes, Fragment 384.*[72]

Miltiades walked the stage at a time when his grandsons would have been mature men. His victories and those of his peers were an ideal which challenged the new status quo, in the military as in politics. At times, Aristophanes' references to former times seem to be appeals for a fairer society in the present. Eupolis appears blunter in criticising not so much injustice as the prominence of a new class. The comics made jokes, but they were rarely light-hearted.

Sending up Datis and his peers was a way of ridiculing the Persians and this ridicule policed the difference between Greek and non-Greek, creating the impression that they were more different than they really were. The comics also policed masculinity with their jokes, repeating again and again scorn for men who were not of an active disposition, poor soldiers – womanly. These jokes demonstrate the intense scrutiny of men's abilities and the assumption of a hierarchy of the sexes – to be woman-like was to be ridiculous. One character, a woman joining in the policing of men, suggests that children should be tasked to sing songs in public about military heroes in order to keep cowards at home from shame.[73] Marathon above all battles taught Athenian boys and men what was expected of them; not a nuanced Marathon in which men had different opinions about whether or not the battle should be fought, but the Marathon of poetry, plays and paintings, in which all were brave, all resolute, all embracing death come what may. This was the simplified battle which called for more glories 'Else may the Marathon-plain not boast my victory trophies!'[74]

Tragedies were still going strong in Athens. *The Persians* remained something of an exception. Mythology continued as the central subject matter, yet even this scenario offered opportunities for reflections on conflict with Persia. Trojan War topics in particular lent themselves to indirect explorations of contemporary clashes. They reinforced the conceptual contrast between brave masculine Greeks and cowardly effeminate Asians.[75] Other forms of poetry continued to be popular and occasionally we get glimpses of life beyond Athens. Towards the end of the Peloponnesian War, Timotheus of Miletus visited Sparta. He performed his new poem, another retelling of Salamis from the perspective of the devastated Persians.[76] The Spartans had their own Persian War stoa, paid for by booty. Theirs did not celebrate Marathon of course – the battle they were always being reminded they had missed. Rather:

> On the pillars are white-marble figures of Persians, including Mardonius, son of Gobryas. There is also a figure of Artemisia, daughter of Lygdamis and queen of Halicarnassus … [who] distinguished herself at the naval engagement off Salamis.
>
> Pausanias, 3.11.3.

Every city had its own traditions and preferences. Around this time, however, a Sicilian Greek gave a speech at the Olympic Games urging all Greeks to put aside their differences, to remember the Graeco-Persian Wars and attack the Persians together. Although not accepted by all, Gorgias' *Olympic Oration* would reinvigorate the idea of the Graeco-Persian Wars as a stepping-stone towards the panhellenic dream of a Greek conquest of Asia.[77]

The end of the century

The beginning of the fifth century had seen the Spartans and Athenians killing Persian heralds in a statement of intent – that there would be no submission to Persia. Things looked very different as the century drew to a close. The panhellenic dream was a long way off. The Athenians suffered a catastrophic defeat attempting to conquer Sicily. Smelling blood, the Spartans formed an alliance with the Persians to ensure that the killing blow could be struck. The deal: the Persians would support the Spartans financially and Persia would collect tribute from Ionia for the first time in decades. A reinvigorated Sparta achieved victory in the Peloponnesian War in 404. The war ended with the Spartans as the major power in Greece and the Ionians as part of the Persian Empire. The more things change, the more they stay the same. Yet things were different. Although the Athenians reeled in the wake of the war and suffered the reign of the Thirty Tyrants, they nonetheless had an enriched sense of identity and self-worth that had been nourished by the years of success and cultural vibrancy since the expulsion of the tyrants and the Graeco-Persian Wars. This would sustain them and make looking to the future more possible. Marathon had helped them to see themselves in a new light and it remained part of the language of excellence and aspiration. In Athens and beyond, panhellenism was an ideal for many, a concept which looked back to the Graeco-Persian Wars and forward to new campaigns. New conflicts and decisions would come. In speeches, histories and on countless other platforms, Marathon would be fought over again as the shape of the future was determined.

10

Marathon beyond the Fifth Century

There was all to play for amongst the Greeks at the beginning of the new century. The Athenians had lost their hegemony, but the Spartans' return to the top was unpopular to say the least and there would be attempts to dethrone them. Alliances were vital and speeches and image-management were essential to those arrangements. It was widely acknowledged that how a state had behaved in the Graeco-Persian Wars a century earlier was important to claims of leadership in the present. All states were playing this game, but it is the Athenians, with their hyper-literate culture, whose texts have survived and with them their point-of-view.[1] Marathon had always been important to the Athenians, but from this point on it began to be *the* symbol of the Athenians' role in the Graeco-Persian Wars. It stressed the Athenians' commitment to freedom whilst simultaneously supporting their desire for supremacy. Rhetoric became increasingly anti-Persian, much as depictions of Xerxes became generally more negative and less subtle. Darius, who never walked the hills of Greece, was less brutally dealt with.[2] This rhetoric was influenced by the fact that after almost a century of celebrating Greek superiority, Persia's influence on the Greek world was nonetheless pervasive. Persian money continued to influence events in Greece as the Greeks fought each other. By the end of the century the landscape would be changed altogether. This chapter follows the idea of Marathon in the fourth century and beyond.

New Graeco-Persian Wars

The international situation was changing fast. Naturally that affected how Greeks perceived the Persians and how they thought about their relationship with them. Marathon remained part of people's language for describing that, but there would be changes too.

In 401, the Athenian Xenophon left a chaotic Athens to serve as a mercenary. As we have seen, earlier generations of Greeks had frequently worked in foreign armies, but that had not been common for mainlanders for some time. In Ephesus, Xenophon joined an army of Greeks from all over. They travelled east and – apparently for the first time – discovered that they had been hired to enact a coup. Their leader, Cyrus the Younger, attempted to overthrow his brother. The campaign ended when Cyrus was killed in battle. The mercenaries were stranded near Babylon, their leaders dead. Xenophon took command and the Ten Thousand Greeks fought their way home mile by torturous mile. The campaign was unusual, but what secured its lasting impact was that Xenophon, a thoughtful, original writer and a former pupil of Socrates, wrote an account of it.

This work, *Anabasis*, shows the rhetorical use of Marathon in a new context. Xenophon describes the moment when he took command and gave a speech to encourage the army. He tells them that the gods are likely to support them as they have done nothing wrong, while their enemies lied. *What is more*, he says, *your forefathers were brave, so you can be brave too – just like when the Athenians fought the Persians at Marathon. They won then, so victory is possible now. The same as Salamis; the Greeks fought, won, and raised trophies, though all seemed hopeless.*[3] We are told that the troops were heartened by this talk of former victories and they resolve to push on. For some time, non-Athenians might well have been sick of hearing about Marathon when it was so connected to the Athenians lording it over them. Now the Persians were a peril once more and Marathon could again be a symbol of panhellenism and success. The whole campaign sparked interest at home. Xenophon shaped his account to present a sort of panhellenic polis on the march. After the bitterness of the Peloponnesian War and the mess that followed, many were more than ready for this vision of unity.

News reached the Spartans in 396 that the Persians were preparing to reoccupy Ionia. The alliance that had won the Spartans the Peloponnesian War was already over. The new king, Agesilaus II, a Eurypontid, determined to strike first and ensure that conflict was kept as far east as possible. He took thirty Spartans and an army of allies. The campaign was largely successful, including victories in pitched battles. Agesilaus also improved Sparta's reputation by removing the most unpopular figures who they had left ruling Ionian cities at the end of the Peloponnesian War. But opportunity for further success ended. News arrived that the Spartans were struggling in the Corinthian War, the heir to the Peloponnesian War. The semi-panhellenic mission against Persia was over. Part of what is intriguing about this campaign is how Agesilaus chose to frame it at the outset. Marathon was not appropriate of course, but he did not associate it with *any* of the recent Graeco-Persian battles, not even Mycale. Agesilaus went right back and styled himself as a new Agamemnon leading a new Trojan War.

The Trojan War was the epitome of a successful campaign against Asia and, not incidentally, it was led by the kings of Sparta and Argos with little input from Athens. The association, though well-chosen, was not successful. Before leaving, Agesilaus had travelled to Aulis, where the Trojan expedition was said to have sailed from. He attempted to recreate Agamemnon's sacrifice, but with characteristic arrogance he had not arranged with the Boeotians if it was alright for the king of another state to turn up and sacrifice. He rejected the local priest and had his own man perform the rite. There were objections. The sacrifice was ruined in a scuffle. *No wonder the campaign fell short*, people said, *the omens were there.*[4]

Things took an interesting twist. While the Spartans had once been funded by the Persians to defeat the Athenians, money now flowed in the other direction. Pharnabazus, distant cousin and son-in-law of Artaxerxes II, could not ignore Sparta's hostility, so he re-directed the cash-flow towards Athens. The Athenians used Persian money to rebuild their city walls and bolster their fleet. Things went further. In 394 an Athenian led the Persian fleet to victory over the Spartans and the following year saw Pharnabazus cross the Aegean and lead sea-raids against the Peloponnese.[5] Not since the beginning of the fifth century had hostile Persians been on the Greek mainland. Not for the first time, conflict between the Greeks was an opportunity for the Persians. The Spartans disliked this change. In 386 the King's Peace, or the Peace of Antalcidas, was arranged. It ended the war between the Greeks with Artaxerxes II as moderator. The Peace guaranteed the autonomy of the Greek states; in effect it guaranteed the Spartans' hegemony. The price was the Ionians re-joining the Persian Empire.[6] Many saw it as a betrayal. When the Spartans were accused of medising, Agesilaus answered that they were not medising, the Persians were laconising. His answer satisfied no one.

The orators

We have seen that the fifth-century speechmakers had established a sophisticated rhetorical tradition in which Marathon was often evoked as a symbol of bravery, self-sacrifice and Athenian excellence. That tradition flourished and numerous speeches survive from the fourth century offering us insight into how the idea of Marathon continued to be deployed and adapted in new circumstances.

One orator to whom all aspiring speakers looked up was Lysias, who produced his most famous works in the early fourth century. He had not always been in Athens. He and his brother had lived in the panhellenic colony at Thurii, where

Herodotus had lived before him. They were expelled for Athenian sympathies and returned to Athens. Panhellenism remained an important ideal for him. The style of his speeches was much admired. It was so apparently simple that his listeners were swept away and found themselves trusting whatever he said. His panhellenism can be seen in many of his works. In an oration written for the Olympic Games he urged the Spartans to end the war and lead a united attack against the Persians.[7] His famous funeral speech, written for the Athenians during the Corinthian War, naturally took a less philolaconian line. Nonetheless, we see the dead praised according to the dictates of the genre in a speech that calls for an end to conflict between Greeks, with campaigns against Persia urged in its place.

Lysias' *epitaphios* includes some of the classic components of the genre. For one thing, Marathon is made the middle-ground between the present day and the age of myth. We hear about the battle against the Amazons, against Thebes and about the Athenians' support for the children of Heracles.[8] Then we arrive at Marathon. The account assumes that Darius' invasion was an act of immoral greed. He wanted *all* of Europe despite his riches. Here we can see how Persia attacking Athens has grown into the desire to conquer Greece and on to a mission to conquer Europe. The stakes have been raised. The language is interesting too; conquest here is literally 'enslavement', a chilling prospect in a slave-owning world as well as a metaphor for empire. We might notice that the Ionian Revolt goes unmentioned, so there is a sense of unprovoked aggression. The numbers are high; he talks of 500,000 Persians attacking. The Athenians think nothing of risk, only of the glory of a worthwhile death in battle. Without waiting for support, the Athenians fought alone at Marathon, glad to think that the other Greeks would thank them later.[9]

Lysias cites 500,000 men in the Persian army. This figure is intended to mean 'a huge number'. The number soars up with retelling. This serves a useful purpose and achieves a sleight of hand. Early on there was a sense of the Persians as an unstoppable military machine of indomitable fighters. Over time, in the wake of their defeats, they began to be spoken of more disparagingly. Yet it is not much of a compliment to say that the Athenians defeated an army of cowards. How can you maintain the idea of their incompetency *and* the Athenians' achievement? You stress the sheer number of incompetents. Numbers become the characteristic of the enemy, not skill or courage.

The speech tentatively mentions panhellenic cooperation at Salamis and Plataea, and then revisits Athenian supremacy. The speech mourns the dead and then makes its ultimate point – that the most profound source of mourning is

Greeks dying in conflicts against each other. In contrast with the Spartan-friendly *Olympic Oration*, the funeral speech urges panhellenic action by stressing to the Athenians that their history makes them the Spartans' equals. Marathon is key to urging that confidence. The Athenians' bravery against the odds is the essence of this retelling; it is enriched by the declaration that Marathon makes all Greeks, all Europe, beholden to the Athenians. In turn it is intended that the Athenians' confidence can lead to a unity that turns Greek aggression outwards. Marathon is carefully re-enlisted in the panhellenic cause and there is no concept of panhellenism without violence against Persia.

Plato belonged to a younger generation than Lysias, born around the beginning of the Peloponnesian War. He had grown up hearing the kinds of speeches that Lysias excelled in. He had also grown up in an Athens at constant war and lived through its defeat and the execution of his beloved teacher, Socrates. The speakers in his dialogues refer to Marathon and the wider Graeco-Persian Wars from time to time. His use of Marathon is rather different from Lysias' and serves as a good reminder that there was no universal perspective.

Plato's *Menexenus* dialogue is set in around 420 but was written after the Corinthian War ended in 386. In it, Socrates is talking to Menexenus about an upcoming *epitaphios*. Socrates remarks, a little tongue-in-cheek, that it is splendid to die in battle and so be praised so whole-heartedly. He gives a sample of what people always say:

> They praise the city; and they praise those who died in war, and all our ancestors who went before us; and they praise ourselves who are still alive, until I feel quite elevated by their laudations . . . And if, as often happens, there are any foreigners who accompany me to the speech, I become suddenly conscious of having a sort of triumph over them.
>
> Plato, *Menexenus*, 235a–b.

We get the feeling for the sort of expected rhetoric: nationalistic, even jingoistic, assuming Athenian superiority. We see the old wars acting as justification for contemporary actions. Socrates jokingly adds that he does not feel quite himself for days after he has heard such a speech. Menexenus prods Socrates, asking if he could deliver such an effective speech. *Yes*, he says, *because he has been taught by Aspasia, Pericles' mistress*. Learning from a woman is another playful joke, and we get an amusing image of Aspasia threatening to beat the speech into him. Socrates gives Menexenus his performance. He tells the story of Marathon with due rhetorical flourish: The minds of all the world were enslaved to the Persians. Darius accused the Athenians and Eretrians of attacking Sardis and sent 500,000 men, led by Datis. The Persians enslaved the Eretrians then came to Marathon assuming that they could do the same to the Athenians. No one would help, except for the Spartans, and they arrived too late. The others were too afraid. The Athenians' victory proves the courage of that generation. They were the first to defeat the Persians – the first to raise victory trophies over them. They punished Asia's pride, taught others that the Persians were not invincible and that courage conquers money and numbers.[10]

This playful treatment demonstrates how predictable Marathon rhetoric had become. The battle story has been flattened into a predictable shape. We know that the Scythians had beaten back Darius, but that is not the point. Speeches should stress the Athenians' special place as the *first*; they should be hellenocentric – *first Greeks* is what counts. Plato not only satirizes the predictability of *epitaphioi*, he seems to refer directly to Lysias' famous *epitaphos* and back to Pericles.[11] The speech is so similar to Lysias' that few will have read it without thinking of it. The nod to Pericles comes through the reference to Aspasia. A contrast is implied between Pericles and Socrates; the former a symbol of imperialism, the philosopher a symbol of virtue. Despite the similarity between the orations, Plato manages to undercut the idealisation. This is the only other place that the 500,000 figure is given; it stands out as absurdly high. While Thucydides' speakers and Lysias stressed the Athenians standing alone, Socrates gives a more panhellenic version. The Eretrians took the brunt of the invasion. The Spartans tried to help, although they did not manage it. Even before this, the reference to the Athenians' actions at Sardis deflates the image of the Persians' unbridled aggression. The narrative is complicated by these details. The Athenians are implicated, even if the Persians are wrong. Although the speech finishes with themes which we have seen since *The Persians* – unrivalled courage, hubris punished – the presentation renders the boasts slightly absurd. The typical vaunts appear bombastic and misleading.

Plato reminds us that he is not simply representing common rhetoric; he is depicting the way that boys and young men were taught to deliver it. When Menexenus is urging Socrates to give a speech, Socrates says that he is reluctant to be seen as a fool for playing 'the games of youth in old age'.[12] This is a reminder that learning to write and perform speeches of this sort had become a staple of Athenian education. Boys who were expected to participate in public life as adults – to speak in the law-courts and the Assembly – were trained to prepare speeches. The speeches that they prepared for their teachers all used Marathon in this way, appealing to the Athenians' identity. Learn how to appeal to the shared past, learn how to flatter the audience, learn how to inspire an audience with thoughts of courage, self-sacrifice and love of freedom. Learn to contrast

Greek and non-Greek. Learn the different ways of including or excluding the Spartans. Boys were taught that they should aspire to be like the Marathonomachoi, but they were also taught to make those fighters part of their vocabulary, part of their arsenal of rhetorical techniques.

If *Menexenus* playfully critiqued rhetorical tricks, Plato's *Gorgias* dialogue takes a more sombre look. *Gorgias* presents the rhetorician of the same name being quizzed by Socrates about the nature of his work. Overall the dialogue invites us to consider what rhetoric is and whether it improves society or does the opposite. Socrates' questions lead Gorgias to the point where he asserts that teaching young men rhetoric teaches them to participate in public life and thus improve society. He is soon forced to concede that no one in the present age has achieved that feat. Socrates then refers back to the good old days. Surely if rhetoric ever improved things it must have been then. *Did Themistocles, Miltiades, Cimon or Pericles ever improve anything?* This is rather awkward. Socrates goes on brutally. *Were not Themistocles and Cimon ostracised by the people just so they could stop listening to them for five minutes? What about Miltiades?* 'Miltiades, the hero of Marathon, they sentenced to be flung into the pit, and had it not been for the president, in he would have gone.'[13] This cannot be denied. In this dialogue Marathon remains a symbol of excellence, yet this is put to unusual use. Instead of signalling the Athenians' excellence, it signals their fickleness, the unreliability of democracy and the limits of rhetoric.

In 379 the Second Athenian Confederacy was founded, a union to maintain the freedoms promised in the King's Peace; one that looked a lot like the old empire.[14] The constant clashing between Athens and Sparta was not to everyone's taste. Isocrates, another student of Socrates and a skilled orator, published his greatest work, *Panegyricus*, around this time. He appeals for panhellenic unity under a joint Athenian-Spartan hegemony. He revisits familiar themes, eschewing Plato's more controversial takes. *Let us remember the battles of the old days*, he says. *The Amazons wished to conquer Greece so they focused on Athens.* Making a familiar equation, he goes on:

> When the Persians landed in Attica the Athenians did not wait for their allies, but, making the common war their private cause, they marched out with their own forces alone to meet an enemy who looked with contempt upon the whole of Greece – a mere handful against thousands upon thousands – as if they were about to risk the lives of others, not their own; the Spartans no sooner heard of the war in Attica than they put all else aside and came to our rescue, having hurried as much as if it had been their own country that was being ravaged.
>
> Isocrates, *Panegyricus*, 4.86.[15]

The speech builds to criticism of the King's Peace, contrasting it with the Peace of Callias, which had seen the Persians accept Greek independence.[16] Isocrates urges the Greeks to cease fighting and unite under joint leadership. Marathon could still serve as a symbol of panhellenism. Never mind the near-100 years of conflict that had followed. The Athenians had that one most important time defended Attica in order to defend the whole of Greece, and the Spartans had tried their best to help them. It was an idea that still had power.

Isocrates lived a long time. After many years he ceased urging the Spartans and Athenians to work together and looked to Macedon to take the lead. He wrote his *Philippus* in 346 calling on Philip II to take the united Greeks to campaign in Persia. His last major work, the *Panathenaicus* of 339, stated that his life's work had been to urge the Greeks to conquer the Persians together. That Greek unity meant conflict with Persia was a deeply entrenched idea. But before we turn to how that later manifested, we should look to the new era of historians.

New histories

Herodotus and Thucydides successfully established long historical narratives as a literary form. Others emulated them in the following years, although naturally they had their own priorities and ways of doing things. As historians their purpose was different to that of the orators, so while they too feature Marathon in their work, they were less restricted in how they discussed it.

Isocrates was said to have taught two men who went on to be famous historians. Although his work is lost, Ephorus of Cyme's history partially survives having been adapted by Diodorus of Sicily for parts of his *Library of History*. Unfortunately the section around Marathon is badly fragmented. We get two key features, which are rather different from the orator's treatments: the Persians wished to retaliate for Sardis; Datis demanded submission and was rejected by Miltiades.[17] The latter story is where we get the tradition that Datis claimed Athens through reference to the mythical past. Miltiades' reported response, hinting at Athenian conquest of Asia, is part of Ephorus' overall panhellenist theme. Diodorus features a list of medising Greeks in order to warn readers about the enemies of freedom. This too seems to reflect Ephorus' perception of the wars.[18] It is frustrating that we cannot see more of what he had to say.

The second historian, one more certainly taught by Isocrates, was Theopompus of Chios. He seems to have been unimpressed by his teacher's Athenian-friendly rhetoric. Theopompus was also a panhellenist, but more than that he was a censorious socially conservative critic of democracy. He offers a glimpse of what pro-Spartan rather than pro-Athenian panhellenism sounds like. In disappointment, he broke off his history of Greece with the Battle of Cnidus, the defeat which ended Spartan plans in Asia. Theopompus switched his panhellenic aspirations to Philip of Macedon. Theopompus' verdict on Marathon? A fragment of his *Philippica* survives that declares the Battle of Marathon did not happen as people say and nor did plenty of other things that the Athenians boast about to deceive people.[19] We so often hear the Athenian view that it is striking to hear it so forcibly rejected. It would be even more intriguing to read Theopompus' account of Marathon than Ephorus'.

Ctesias offered a more Persian-centric account. He had been a doctor at the court of Artaxerxes II for seven years. His *Persica* survives in summary form. The most notable Marathon detail is that Datis died, the Athenians refused to return the body, and this prompted Xerxes' revenge ten years later. This is likely to be sensation rather than truth, but it is another curious glimpse at less Athenian-friendly traditions.[20]

Fig. 11 Darius the Great receiving a message. There are Greek gods above him. The vase scene is thought to represent a scene from a Greek play. Made in Apulia *c.* 340–330 BCE. Naples, Museo Archeologico Nazionale, H3249.

While histories were being written, new traditions were in the making all the time. The Graeco-Persian Wars were still on stage. A spectacular vase featuring Darius is thought to represent a play set just before Marathon. Zeus, Nike, Apollo and Artemis are there too; Athena presents Hellas to them. Another play about the gods restoring order.[21] It was in the fourth century that the Athenians began claiming that they had found the bones of Theseus and returned them to Athens. It is possible that they were already saying that Cimon had found them on Scyros. It was a nationalistic claim to boost the Athenians' identity and to help them project their importance into the past.[22] The way in which this tradition developed is a reminder of how stories could emerge and be retrospectively applied to past events, mythical or historical. Marathon was a similar story-magnet.

Athens in the face of Macedon

Marathon still had currency in Athens. It was still part of the orator's tool-kit and the teacher's key topics; the Marathon painting still hung in the Stoa Poikile, and teens still trekked to the battlefield every year to make offerings to the dead heroes. Yet things continued to move on, and as the fourth century unfolded the Athenians were increasingly conscious of the growing power of their northern neighbour, Macedon. Macedon under Alexander I, known as 'the Philhellene', had been occupied by the Persians during the Graeco-Persian Wars. They were reluctant medisers. The fifth century already had stories about them aiding the Greeks.[23]

Speeches survive from this period in which the Athenians debate how to deal with the changing situation. Typically these speeches come from legal cases in which political opponents attacked each other indirectly. The speeches are replete with reference to Marathon, its old meanings re-employed for new challenges.

The greatest rivals of this period in Athens were Demosthenes and Aeschines. Both were anxious about the Macedon situation, but they differed in their approaches. In 343 Demosthenes prosecuted Aeschines for misconduct in his dealings with Philip of Macedon. He alleged that as Aeschines had opposed Philip and then changed to support peace, he must have been bribed by the king. Unusually, both prosecution and defence speeches survive.[24] Both make use of Marathon.

Demosthenes establishes the contrast between Aeschines' former and current positions by laying it on thick in his representation of Aeschines' early anti-Macedon stance:

> Who was it cried that Philip was forming a coalition of Greece and the Peloponnese while you were fast asleep? Who made those fine long speeches and read out Miltiades' decree and Themistocles' and the young men's oath?
>
> Demosthenes, *On the False Embassy*, 19.303.

The Miltiades' decree refers to the preparations before Marathon.[25] Demosthenes is showing how Aeschines had been likening the Macedonian rise to the advance of Persia – emotive arguments which urged his listeners to regard this as their own equivalent to the Graeco-Persian Wars. Only bribery could move someone from this to advocating peace, Demosthenes argues. He appeals again to the Graeco-Persian Wars: Aeschines urging peace is a disgrace – ask anyone what would have happened if the Athenians had not fought at Marathon or Salamis and they will tell you that the country would have a different name and would not be inhabited by Greeks.[26] This apocalyptic version of Marathon makes peace with Macedon appear the ultimate betrayal.

Aeschines' response was to provide a 100-year history of the events leading up to these negotiations.[27] He also praises the actions at Marathon, Salamis and Artemisium. More riskily, he does so in the context of a history of mixed successes. As well as victory at Marathon there have also been defeats. Aeschines stresses Athens' greatness with reference to its victories, but urges peace with reference to what happens when wrong decisions to go to war are made. *Yes we won at Marathon, but fighting is not always the right decision*, he argues. This does not knock the shine off Marathon, but it dares to remind people that not all battles can be Marathons. No one wanted to hear it. Demosthenes won the case.

A few years later, the Athenians and Boeotians suffered a catastrophic defeat at the hands of Macedon at the Battle of Chaeronea. Demosthenes was chosen to deliver the *epitaphios*.[28] This would be a difficult one. The defeat signalled the twilight of the Greek independent city-states. It was clear that the situation was beyond grave. As was traditional, Demosthenes praised the Athenians' ancestors. He recalls how they alone repelled the Persians by land and sea (at Marathon and Salamis), risking everything to protect all Greeks. But he keeps it brief and moves swiftly to the current war-dead. He praises their virtue and courage. He praises them with a glow usually reserved for the Marathon dead. Gently, movingly, he suggests that those who have just died defending Greece against Macedon have re-enacted the achievements of those ancestors who did the same at Marathon. As we have seen, obliquely likening the war-dead to the dead of the Graeco-Persian Wars was a standard *epitaphios* form; here the sombre tone, the tenor of the praise, and the likening of the two enemies makes the comparison more meaningful. This is one of the more profound versions of Marathon-as-consolation.

By 330, Philip was dead, and his son, Alexander III, destined to become 'the Great', had succeeded him. Demosthenes and Aeschines were still at odds over how to deal with the new reality. This time Aeschines went on the attack. He prosecuted a man called Ctesiphon for having proposed, some years earlier, that Demosthenes be awarded a victory crown.[29] Curiously, Aeschines seems to have picked up some of the arguments that Demosthenes had used when they clashed before. He stresses the excellence of the men of former times by contrast with politicians of today. This comparison is then levelled directly at Demosthenes:

> Was Themistocles, who was general when you conquered the Persian in the battle of Salamis, the better man, or Demosthenes, who the other day deserted his post? Was it Miltiades, who won the battle of Marathon, or this man? . . . By the Olympian gods, I think one should not name those men on the same day as this monster!
>
> Aeschines, *Against Ctesiphon*, 3.181–2.

After attacking Demosthenes' career, Aeschines then turns to forms of commemoration. He refers to the Marathon painting in the Stoa Poikile, not far from where they were gathered, an image still familiar to all male Athenians.

> If you were asked [who was the general at Marathon] you would all answer, 'Miltiades'. But his name is not written there. Why? Did he not ask for this reward? He did ask, but the people refused it; and instead of his name they permitted that he should be painted in the front rank, urging on his men.
>
> Aeschines, *Against Ctesiphon*, 3.186.

Aeschines stresses the communal nature of the commemoration – the group is more important than the individual. It is one thing for someone to want honours; it is another for the city to grant it. Aeschines urges the listeners to be like their ancestors not in *fighting* Marathon but in limiting the distinction given to any particular individual. It is noticeable *which* individual is brought up. As always in fourth-century discussions, Miltiades is the victor of Marathon. Cimon's campaign had achieved its end and Miltiades was firmly *the* figure pre-eminently associated with the battle. Aeschines concludes by condemning Demosthenes in the name of the dead of Marathon and Plataea; they would condemn

Demosthenes too if only they were there to do so.[30] Demosthenes retaliated with one of his most brilliant speeches. In *On the Crown* he insists that he would not dream of comparing himself to those who fought the Graeco-Persian Wars; he is a simple servant of the city. He revisits the idea he had put forward in his *epitaphios*. He praises those who fought at Chaeronea, likening it to Marathon and Salamis; the outcome was not the same, but they faced the force that threatened Greece not for themselves but to protect all humankind.[31] Demosthenes won again. Aeschines retired to Rhodes.

Other speakers played a similar game. Lycurgus, a prominent Athenian, prosecuted Leocrates around this time for having deserted the city after Chaeronea. He contrasted the days of strength when the Ionians asked the Athenians for help (i.e. the Ionian Revolt) with the tough times after Chaeronea, when it was Athens which desperately needed support (and all of its citizens to do their bit). He reminds the jurors of their time as new soldiers, ephebes; how they all swore to protect the city with their bodies and their lives. He reminds them of mythological and historical examples of people willingly making this very sacrifice. It was these examples of heroism which taught the Marathonomachoi how to be so brave as to resist all of Asia and so save themselves and Greece.[32]

Thus far the rhetoric of *Against Leocrates* is rather familiar. It then takes an interesting turn which reflects the new circumstances. The Spartans had just been near-annihilated attempting push-back against Macedon.[33] Lycurgus sympathetically includes the Spartans in his example of self-sacrifice for Greece in days gone by, indirectly reminding people of what had just happened. It is no longer necessary to downplay the Spartans' contribution to the Graeco-Persian Wars. Lycurgus quotes the Spartan poet Tyrtaeus at some length, offering one of the strongest articulations of the belief that it is excellent to die in battle for one's country and that death in battle is beautiful. This moves into a reiteration of the greatness of those who fought at Marathon and of the Spartans' less happy but nonetheless glorious deeds at Thermopylae. He cites lines written in honour of both events:

> 'Go tell the Spartans, passer-by,
> That here obedient to their laws we lie.'
>
> And to your ancestors:
>
> 'Athenians, champions of the Greeks, subdued in fight
> At Marathon the gold-carrying Medes' might.'
>
> Simonides, in Lycurgus, *Against Leocrates*, 109.[34]

The Spartans were no longer an existential threat to Athens so there was merit in this panhellenic coupling of Marathon and Thermopylae. That threat came from the Alexander and the Macedonians. Little wonder then that Lycurgus revisits Macedon's role in the Graeco-Persian Wars. What a state had done in those wars remained important for the perceived legitimacy of leadership of the Greeks, even after the Greeks had been overwhelmed militarily. Lycurgus urges his audience to consider how disgusted their forebears would be by the prospect of acquitting Leocrates of deserting Athens when they nearly stoned to death Alexander I of Macedon for demanding earth and water on Xerxes' behalf.[35] This has a very different feel from Herodotus' version of the same events. *The Histories* sees Alexander I sent to Athens after Salamis to offer terms.[36] True, Herodotus does not offer much on the Athenians' reaction to Alexander beyond them confirming to the Spartans that they will hold firm; however the representation of Alexander is largely positive, framing him as an unwilling mediser who takes risks to help the Greeks. Herodotus may present an unduly rosy picture, and it would be understandable if there had been mixed reactions to Alexander. Nonetheless, if Herodotus presents the best possible interpretation, Lycurgus is presenting the most hostile. For him, the Macedonians were straightforward medisers who disgusted the Athenians. As well as damning Leocrates, his characterisation of Macedon's actions back then reinforces his implication that the *current* Macedonians are a traditional enemy of the Athenians. The Macedonians may be off conquering Persia, but in this framing they are akin to the Persians in relation to Athens.

For the orators, Marathon reminded people of their shared identity. It could be a mark they invited people to live up to; it could be a warning that things do not always work out that way. It symbolised bravery and fighting for freedom. It symbolised Athenian and Greek opposition to Persia. And it had broadened. Now it could symbolise opposition to any enemy.

Alexander

The Athenians' continued use of Graeco-Persian War rhetoric takes on a still more complex aspect when we consider that it was competing with Macedonian claims to the same legacy. Although many Greeks would have denied that the Macedonians were Greek at all, Philip and Alexander turned Athenian propaganda on its head and cast themselves as the heirs to revenge against Persia. The Greeks had been talking about invading Persia since at least the 470s, when

Cimon and his allies promoted it.[37] But while those dreams never got far, Philip and Alexander made them happen.

Alexander and the Athenians found themselves making rival claims to who was responsible for the 'freedom' and 'autonomy' of the Greeks. Alexander's claims antagonised the Athenians, but he continued to make them, recognising how important the Graeco-Persian Wars were in asserting leadership of the Greeks. He addressed his claims to all Greeks, but tried especially to convince the Athenians, wishing to draw on them practically – to use their ships and to discourage the conflicts which had ruined earlier invasion attempts – and to draw on their symbolic importance.

Alexander began his Graeco-Persian War rhetoric before he left for Asia. Macedon's brutal destruction of Thebes was framed largely as revenge for their medising in 480. No Greeks at the time had felt the need to destroy Thebes, but framing of that sort cast a veneer over the almost unprecedented ferocity of the act.[38] Once the campaigns in Asia were underway, they were represented as retaliation for the Persian invasions. Dedications sent to Delphi and to the Athenian acropolis projected the association. More explicitly, a letter ostensibly to Darius III, but actually sent to multiple locations, declared the mission to be one of revenge:

> Your ancestors invaded Macedonia and the rest of Greece and did us great harm, although we had not wronged them prior to that; I have been appointed leader of the Greeks and invaded Asia wishing to punish you, Persians, for something you started.
>
> Arrian, 2.14.4.

This theme continued and took further material forms. After Alexander defeated Darius III at the Battle of Gaugamela in 331, Alexander contacted the Plataeans and Croton in Italy regarding symbolic gestures which evoked the Graeco-Persian Wars. Wealth captured in Persia would be used to rebuild Plataea, which had been destroyed by the Spartans and Thebans in one of the most brutal episodes of the Peloponnesian War. The Plataeans had pleaded with the Spartans to spare them in light of their service to Greece and their careful tending of the tombs of the Spartan war-dead. It was to no avail and the Plataeans fled to Athens. Now it was the Macedonians who would restore their glory; they would honour the achievements of the Graeco-Persian Wars where the Spartans and Thebans had not.[39] Another gesture came when Alexander captured Susa. Statues were discovered which had been taken from Greece during Xerxes' campaign. Alexander had many returned to Greece. The most symbolically powerful were the statues of the tyrannicides, Harmodius and Aristogeiton, which were sent to Athens.[40] This epitomised the revenge taken for the Persian invasions and cast Alexander as the defender of Athenian democracy.

It is noticeable that Marathon does not feature explicitly in Alexander's evocation of the Graeco-Persian Wars. This was likely driven by the dynamics of the battle. Darius' invasion counted as an attack that could be avenged along with Xerxes', however Marathon as a successful defensive action did not fit a revenge campaign so well as reminders of the 480 destruction. Equally, Marathon was insufficiently panhellenic to fit Alexander's needs. On a different front, mentioning Marathon could be potentially embarrassing for the Macedonians. Only a few years before, under Philip, they had raided Marathon.[41] Alongside the killing, rape, and destruction, the Macedonians had looted the Athenians' sacred trireme. The Macedonians had attacked Marathon like latter-day Persians – just what the Athenians were always saying they were.

Alexander's time was brief. Although he had sons, they did not survive to continue the dynasty. Alexanders conquests passed to prominent followers who fought and established a new set of kingdoms. Persia still existed, but the Persian Empire and the Achaemenid line was over. There were even fewer reasons now for Persians to pass on traditions about Marathon, unless perhaps to recall the days when it had been possible to take a whole army aboard ship for adventures in the far west. The details of what happened on those campaigns were not important.

So many Greeks and so much Greek culture went east in this era that it is known as the Hellenistic period. It had its historians, intellectuals such as Hieronymus of Cardia, Timaeus of Tauromenium, Duris of Samos, Agatharchides of Cnidus, Posidonius of Apamea.[42] Their works have not survived as well as Herodotus' or Thucydides'. We have only fragments and suggestions of their preoccupations and themes. They reflected on their own times and on eras gone by. The development of historiography in the wake of the Graeco-Persian and Peloponnesian Wars gave them and writers like them unprecedented information about previous generations and models and techniques which they could imitate and adapt. What has survived from this period offers a wider range of perspectives. We hear increasingly from those outside Athens and from beyond the Greek world. This partly reflects a change in literary culture – forms developed in Athens were now widespread; and in part it reflects a shift to a wider identification with Marathon. A greater range of people might now associate themselves with the Athenians/Greeks in that battle, much as a greater range of people might be associated with the Persians. More people wished to represent themselves as part of the Marathon story.

As for Greece itself, the demise of the Persian Empire would change the intensity and immediacy of references to the Graeco-Persian Wars, yet those wars continued to be an important part of Greek identity and custom. In Athens the Marathon Painting still hung in the Stoa Poikile. The teenagers still went each year to the Marathon soros, where the heroic dead were thought to be as close to the living as they ever were. There were busts of Miltiades, and from time to time coins were issued featuring him or Themistocles.[43] Athenian and non-Athenian traditions came together in a spectacular dedication at Athens by the Attalid dynasty of Pergamum, a post-Alexander kingdom in Asia Minor. This dynasty longed for their kingdom to be seen as a cultural centre, a new Athens. The kings visited Athens and sent gifts to the Athenians to foster good relations. After they defeated raiding Gauls in around 200, four statue-groups were sent for dedication on the Athenian acropolis. The statues depicted the battle of gods and giants, the battle of men and Amazons, the Battle of Marathon, and the Attalid victory over the Gauls. In doing so they elevated the importance of their victory to match mythical victories and the now near-mythical victory at Marathon. It was a way to announce the Attalids' place in the scheme of things and their place as the Athenians' friends and cultural successors.[44] As Alexander had played this game and sent his offerings to the Athenian acropolis, the Attalids dedications indirectly presented them as *his* successors too.

Polybius

The only one of the Hellenistic historians to survive beyond a few fragments is Polybius. He lived *c.* 200–118 and is known for his history of how Rome conquered the Mediterranean world. He knew about the power of empire. His early life had been dominated by the Peloponnesian Achaean League's failure to resist Rome and he witnessed Rome's destruction of Carthage first hand. Marathon is not a prominent feature of his work, but it is nonetheless instructive to see how he evokes the Graeco-Persian Wars from time to time.

Early on he pulls Thucydides' trick – he announces that his work will describe the greatest war, which is obviously great because it was larger than the Graeco-Persian Wars or the Peloponnesian War. The Graeco-Persian Wars are still what one compares events to in order to lend them suitable grandeur. Perhaps more strikingly, Polybius adds that the Romans did not gain their empire by accident;

they got it by studying those old wars and learning from them.[45] Much later in the work, Polybius raises this idea again, this time more questioning about *what* the Romans had learned. Of the destruction of Carthage he says that some admired the Romans' pragmatism, while others saw it as a symptom of the destructive craving for power which the Athenians and Spartans had shown.[46] Elsewhere Polybius had been more explicit in arguing that the Athenians had been at their best under Themistocles.[47] He compares them to sailors who cooperate in a storm but then become overconfident – surviving the storm only to wreck the ship. The Athenians worked together during the Graeco-Persian Wars, but then destroyed themselves. Themistocles serves as a good figurehead for leadership in the Graeco-Persian Wars; Miltiades would not quite do, having failed to make it much beyond the first round. With enough distance, the Graeco-Persian Wars have become a warning about what can go wrong as much as an example of cohesion in times of danger.

Interestingly, Polybius does not buy into Alexander's rhetoric about his conquest of Asia being revenge for the Persian invasions. Alexander's war, he says, was set in motion by his father's plans, and before that by the Ten Thousand's success marching through Asia and by Agesilaus' victories. These made an invasion look possible; the Graeco-Persian Wars were just a pretext to whip-up support. He sounds much like Thucydides, who had called the Athenians' talk of reprisals a pretext to do what they wanted.[48] Arrian, the best surviving historian of Alexander, would say something similar around 200 years later – burning Persepolis could hardly be considered punishment for the burning of Athens when that had been done by Persians who were so long dead.[49] The Graeco-Persian Wars remained a vital cultural reference point for articulating issues of power, empire, and statecraft – an example everyone was familiar with which could elucidate contemporary issues. Nonetheless, Polybius was too much of a realist to offer a blunt depiction of Rome as the new Persia. The comparison shifts so that variously Athens, Sparta, Carthage, Macedon, Persia and others are the face of imperial power. The Athenians are not cast as little heroes fighting a bully, but as bullied and bullies in turn.

11

Marathon under Rome

Polybius' era saw colossal changes for Rome, an average size city-state that came to dominate the Mediterranean world. They had their own history and culture and yet there was also some anxiety that came from encountering the cultural richness of other societies round-about. Many Roman intellectuals looked to the Greeks for inspiration, particularly regarding literary forms. Greek oratory, Greek historiography, Greek biography, drama, philosophy – all of this would be deeply engaged with by many of the Roman elite. If you were a Roman who was active in the courts or in politics, you had read the works of the Athenian orators and there was a good chance that you knew your Herodotus, your Thucydides and your Xenophon, and perhaps much more. In exploring Greek culture, the Romans were exposed to the extensive Greek traditions of the Graeco-Persian Wars – especially the Athenian perception of those wars. As such, Marathon and the other battles of the Graeco-Persian Wars became part of the Roman world-view, part of how they expressed themselves and how they represented their own struggles, conflicts and identity. To a great extent they adopted the perception of a struggle of civilisation and its enemies, featuring mythical conflicts such as the Trojan War and the battle with the Amazons in the first stage, the Graeco-Persian Wars of the early fifth century in the second and, thirdly, the conquests of Alexander.[1] They began to present themselves in various ways as the equivalent or heirs to the Greek conflicts of the past.

Cornelius Nepos offers us an interesting example of a Roman writer exploring Greek genres. He was born in Cisalpine Gaul *c.* 110–100. He spent most of his life in Rome, part of a vibrant scene with other intellectuals such as Cicero, Atticus and Catullus. He experimented with writing Greek forms in Latin. He wrote now-lost works of history (a Greek form) and geography (another largely Greek form). He wrote numerous biographies, a genre developed by the Greeks which emerged out of praise-speeches. Some of his biographies survive, including twenty-two *Lives of the Great Generals of Foreign Nations*. It is telling that twenty of the twenty-two non-Roman generals are Greeks. The Greeks dominated the material available to him and thus his sense of history and culture. General number one on the list? No surprise – Miltiades. Marathon signalled the beginning of non-mythical battles for which material would be readily available. Moreover, the Graeco-Persian Wars dominated Nepos' sense of history and of the 'greatness' of great generals. Miltiades, Themistocles, Aristides, Pausanias and Cimon all get biographies – five Graeco-Persian War lives within a list of twenty, which goes up to Timoleon, who died in the 330s. Interestingly, however, all is not black and white. Darius and Cyrus are picked out as the most eminent in a list of kings, while Xerxes gets special mention for the size of his army.[2] This positivity is not something that he picked up from the Greek orators, though Herodotus was not shy about the greatness of Cyrus and Darius for all that he notes their flaws.

When it came to the rhetoric of alliances and conflict, knowing how to choose the right comparisons was an important skill for any politician or general. Already when Rome had fought Macedon, the Roman general Flamininus had presented Macedon as a threat to Greece of the same scale as the earlier threat of Persia – a move right out of Demosthenes and still a powerful way to appeal to many Greeks.[3] This practice became more pronounced once the Romans were in conflict with the Parthians, a semi-nomadic people who had moved into Parthia in 247 and presented themselves as the heirs to the Achaemenids. The great orator, Cicero, well-versed in Greek oratory, thought it effective to refer to the Parthians as 'Persians' in a speech given in 57, by which time the Parthians held the former Persian heartlands.[4] After the Romans suffered a devastating defeat at the Parthians' hands at the Battle of Carrhae, the idea of the advancing Parthians as the new Persians seemed particularly apt. Presenting the conflict as a new Graeco-Persian War with themselves as the latter-day Greeks flattered the Romans by associating them with a pattern of conflicts perceived as a battle of civilisation versus barbarism (loosely defined) going back to mythology, through the Graeco-Persian Wars and Alexander to their present day. It was also a comforting model of success which was needed by those struggling without the benefit of hindsight at a point when things could go either way.

Roman identification with the Marathonomachoi and other Graeco-Persian War Greeks really took off in the imperial age. The first emperor, Augustus, really made a thing of it. When he negotiated peace with the Parthians in 21 BCE, he dedicated victory monuments styled after Graeco-Persian War monuments, complete with 'barbarian' heads to underscore the association. When conflict was back on the cards around twenty years later, he staged mock sea-battles recreating Salamis.[5] Displays with these associations continued for years. The idea was also reflected back at the Romans from outside. When Emperor Nero initiated a campaign against the Parthians, the Athenians nailed a large bronze plaque to the east end of the Parthenon honouring him as the son of a god and associating him with the Graeco-Persian War tradition. It was possible to be a proud Athenian and a loyal Roman citizen and the projection of a shared history smoothed the process. Similar monuments were erected in Asia Minor.[6] Nero himself commissioned his own version of Augustus' sea-battles to celebrate his campaign and to project his association with these well-known conflicts of the past, now including the Roman imperial past.

Meanwhile, elite Romans continued to explore Greek oratory, literature and art. Many of them studied in Athens. There were busts of Miltiades at Rome now, as well as statues at Athens, Delphi and at Marathon itself. One such bust turned up in the sixteenth century CE, inscribed bilingually. In Greek on the front side: 'Miltiades', with Latin: 'Who conquered a Persian in war in the fields of Marathon among beloved countrymen and died in the fatherland'. Followed by Greek: 'Miltiades, all the Persians and Marathon knew these, your warlike deeds/The sacred precinct of your greatness'. And on the right side:

> Warlike Miltiades, your deeds are distinguished among people.
> And if the fatherland forgets you, nevertheless all-unbound time
> announces your glory over the firm earth.[7]

Busts of this sort projected the Roman association with the Graeco-Persian War tradition. In celebrating Miltiades they also promoted patriotic values of military excellence, brotherhood between citizens and greatness achieved by active physical opposition to the enemy, specifically the Persian enemy. These are declared to be the values and actions which win a man undying glory. Cimon would surely have been satisfied with how successfully he had confirmed Miltiades' legacy as the hero of Marathon. The reference to Miltiades' death is an interesting extension of that legacy. It celebrates death in the homeland as a positive, but seems to rely on a lack of detailed knowledge of the circumstances of his death, which could potentially undermine the encouragement to give one's all for the state. His death was a story far less told than that of his victory. Marathon is 'useful', but only when used selectively.

As the threat that Parthia posed to Rome waned, the comparison of Roman conflict with the Graeco-Persian Wars seemed less appropriate. Accordingly, the Romans' emphasis on the Graeco-Persian Wars became less frequent. When Trajan launched an attack on the Parthians in 114 CE, Alexander the Great was the figure he associated himself with, without reference to the Athenians. Some

Roman authors, confident in the full swing of empire, began a push back against the Graeco-Persian War tradition and preferred to down-play the Greeks' achievements and glorify their own more directly.[8] Meanwhile, amongst Greeks living as Roman subjects the Graeco-Persian Wars were all the rage.

Greek culture under Rome

By the middle of the first century CE, Greek culture had the wind back in its sails. It had always retained importance in the Mediterranean world, but repeated conflicts and subjection to Rome were a lot to adjust to. The second half of the first century saw a return of cultural confidence and intellectual vibrancy. The period from this point onwards for the next 200 years or so is known as the Second Sophistic, a renaissance of the skills of the sophists, the speech-writers, the intellectuals of the Classical era.[9] Athens, Ephesus and Pergamum were its great centres. Many travelled to these places, amongst others, to study rhetoric in preparation for public life, however speech-writing and declamations were a prestigious cultural activity in their own right, even outside the law-court or the Senate. It will not by now be surprising to see that Marathon was a prominent feature of this cultural out-pouring.

We start with a less public work. In the first century CE, Miltiades' personal life was reinterpreted in a romantic novel. Loosely inspired by Herodotus' *Histories*, the writer imagines Miltiades as an angry father who is turned against his son by his new wife. The son, Metiochus, seems destined for marriage to Parthenope, daughter of Polycrates the tyrant of Samos. It all falls apart when Metiochus is estranged from his father and adventures ensue. The story became popular enough that Metiochus and Parthenope were depicted in the floor mosaic of a villa in Zeugma in the third century CE.[10] Marathon had its political side, but its general was a household name who could be re-imagined in a sort of fan-fiction. Metiochus the lost son was found.

Another author taking an unusual angle was Dio of Prusa, in Bithynia, sometimes known by his nickname, Dio Chrysostom – the Golden-Mouthed. He was an influential orator and philosopher who tended to idealise the Greek past. At times he appeals to his audience by reminding them of their shared Greek culture, wherever they are from.[11] He was partial to Xenophon and Plato. This influence shows up strikingly in one oration, in which he carries on where Plato left off and explores the Athenians' harsh treatment of Miltiades, Themistocles and Cimon in the face of their service to Athens. Not shy of taking the road less travelled, another oration claims to know the story of Marathon as told by a Mede: Datis was sent to submit Naxos and Eretria. After a successful campaign they were swept towards Attica where there was a brief skirmish. Xerxes led a successful follow-up campaign, killing a Spartan king and burning Athens.[12] This is not the bombastic version that was so familiar. It would not have gone down well in fourth-century Athens, although it does recall Theopompus' outspoken opposition to the usual tale. Dio's speeches rely on their audiences' familiarity with the usual narratives, but demonstrate the survival of alternative interpretations.

Plutarch

A writer of this period with profoundly enduring influence was Dio's contemporary, Plutarch of Chaeronea. Despite success as a writer in his lifetime, Plutarch chose to live mostly in his hometown, where he contributed to public life and served as a priest at Delphi. Many works from his prolific output have survived from antiquity and have been popular in virtually all ages, shaping many generations' views of Greek history and culture. Plutarch addressed numerous topics in essays, speeches and dialogues, but he is most famous for his *Parallel Lives*. These biographies paired similar Greek and Roman lives together, the better to draw out people's character traits. He comes across as an unusually humane man for his time and his works are profoundly moral, urging readers to use the biographies to help them reflect on their own lives to prompt personal and societal improvement. In politics he encourages cooperation and he repeatedly emphasises the importance of education and the management of one's emotions for personal and state success.[13] His references to the Graeco-Persian Wars are many and varied. It is instructive to consider both specific examples and to recognise the sheer range of things which he demonstrates with reference to Marathon.

In *Table Talk*, Plutarch presents examples of topics which would be normal for discussion at Greek and Roman dinner-parties. The introduction notes that questions asked should be easy while subjects should be familiar and not too grim so that those without a deep education can still participate. Contrast with Persia is established straightaway: Greeks and Romans enjoy philosophical chat after dinner, Persians do not.[14] We can conclude from these remarks that the topics which follow would be considered familiar and approachable. All sorts of topics are explored. The examples then come to a dinner held in Athens by a man called Serapion, who invited men of the Leontis tribe to celebrate with him when their tribe won a theatrical prize. It was noted that the Aeantis tribe had the privilege of never coming last and the group was challenged to consider why that was:

> Presently every one poured out something in commendation of that tribe, mentioning every matter that made for its credit and reputation. Marathon was brought in as belonging to it, and Harmodius with his associates, by birth Aphidneans, were also produced as glorious members of that tribe. The orator Glaucias proved that that tribe made up the right-wing in the battle at Marathon, from the elegies of Aeschylus, who had himself fought valiantly in the same encounter; and added that Callimachus the commander-in-chief was of that tribe, who behaved very bravely and was the principal cause, next to Miltiades with whom he agreed, that that battle was fought. To this discourse of Glaucias I added that the edict which empowered Miltiades to lead forth the Athenians was made when the Aeantis tribe was chief of the assembly, and that in the Battle of Plataea the same tribe acquired the greatest glory.
>
> Plutarch, *Table Talk*, 1.10.3

The group, rather wonderfully, decide that despite all this the real reason is probably because the tribe is named after Ajax, who could never bear to lose. We see in this light-hearted chat the ready assumption that fairly detailed knowledge of Marathon should be within a person's pool of knowledge, including who did what and who wrote about it afterwards. Being able to talk about Marathon after dinner is part of what it means to be presentable in society. It is remarkable to consider that this was written over 600 years after Xenophanes of Colophon wrote that after dinner conversation should turn to who you are, who your family are, and how old you were when the Medes came. It is a greater distance than that between now and, for example, the fall of Constantinople to the Ottomans.

Were the Athenians more Famous in War or Wisdom? is a rather different work, written as a rhetorical example. In it the speaker argues that the Athenians won their glory through physical bravery, not through its writers. We have seen already that in this work the speaker refers to a man running from the battlefield to Athens – Thersippus of Eroeadae, as one author says, although more say it was Eucles, who is named without his deme as if he would be familiar. This is the earliest surviving account of this story. The runner is said to have died after delivering his message. His effort in fighting then running to the point of death is equated to the more familiar brave actions of Cynegeirus, Callimachus and Polyzelus (another name for Epizelus) who are picked out by name. Had Eucles not fought in the battle, it is argued, no one would have considered him worthy of praise for simply reporting the events rather than taking part.[15] Elsewhere the speaker contrasts the tragedies which did Athens no good (!) with 'the shrewdness of Themistocles which provided the city with a wall, with the diligence of Pericles which adorned the acropolis, with the freedom which Miltiades bestowed, with the supremacy to which Cimon advanced her'.[16] We see here in full flow the perspective which views Miltiades, through Marathon, as a bringer of freedom. As in *Table Talk*, we also get a reminder of the classical sources which informed later writers. The speaker quotes Demosthenes, citing the practice of swearing by the memory of those who risked their lives at Marathon, not by their (less heroic therefore less important) teachers.[17] Plutarch himself is unlikely to have endorsed all of these views personally, yet his speech gives us a clear example of how Marathon continued to be used within rhetoric, particularly its role in teaching young people how to use examples when constructing arguments.

Marathon as a rhetorical device to encourage physical bravery is countered in a contrasting work of Plutarch's, *Precepts of Statecraft*. Here the speaker cautions would-be politicians against using historical examples which are inappropriate in the contemporary era. *Sure*, he says, *it is cute to see children trying on their father's shoes, but it is dangerous for politicians to urge their listeners to imitate* 'the fights at Marathon, Eurymedon, and Plataea'. Doing so will 'vainly puff-up and heighten the *demos*, [and] should be left to the schools of the sophists'.[18] This more cautious advice indirectly demonstrates how common Graeco-Persian War references were in political speeches of the era, as well as in training. The danger comes from what can befall a subject people who are constantly reminded of a proud moment of fighting against empire. The talk of its impact on people's vanity is reminiscent of Plato's Socrates joking that he feels magnificent, better than his foreign friends, after he has heard a rousing funeral oration.[19] Greek orators in this period are unlikely to have intended a genuine call-to-arms against Rome. Nonetheless they may have spoken defiantly to push-back at petty Roman interferences and to boost their own popularity by flattering the crowd.[20] The one is risky, the other immoral. *Much better*, the speaker argues, *to cite more humane events of which the people can be proud – the amnesty after the Thirty Tyrants, the fining of Phrynicus for placing a recent humanitarian disaster on stage, the celebration when Thebes was restored. These are the sorts of ancestral acts that one should celebrate and imitate.* This speech does not devalue Marathon, but presents a different point-of-view of its place in contemporary culture.

Plutarch's *On the Malice of Herodotus* is another rhetorical work, this one demonstrating forms of partiality. As the name suggests, it takes Herodotus' *Histories* as its example. *The Histories* was still widely read and was recognised as a seminal work of historiography. *Malice* sets out to show how to contradict an established narrative and how to recognise discreet or not so discreet examples of bias or 'malice'.[21] The speaker works through *The Histories* from beginning to end, but emphasises the representation of the Battles of Marathon, Thermopylae, Artemisium, Salamis and Plataea. In this sense Marathon is not picked out as unique, but the criticism of Herodotus' account offers us a valuable alternative perspective. Modelling the personal attack, the speaker implies that Herodotus is bound to be misleading on the Graeco-Persian Wars since he is from Halicarnassus, which sent men in the invasion force. He challenges accusations against the Alcmaeonids, particularly the shield-signal, saying that it is an accusation to mention something even if you then say that you do not believe it.[22] Herodotus is accused of maligning the Spartans by presenting their non-appearance as deliberate, arguing that the runner must have been sent *after* the battle.[23]

Criticism is levelled at the representation of the battle itself. The speaker argues that Marathon is made to seem less mighty than it was by the underestimation of the dead. While Herodotus referred to 6,400 Persian dead, others say that their dead appeared almost infinite. The necessary compromise on goats for Artemis is given as proof.[24] This argument fits neatly with another which is raised, although raised in relation to Plataea. Herodotus had described the Persians faring badly against the Greeks because they had less armour, less training and less skill, though they were equal in courage and strength. The speaker in *Malice* takes issue with this – *what is great or memorable about these battles if the Greeks were fighting unarmed men?*[25] Here we see a clash of ideas about the battle which reflects wider changes in the Greek and Roman perception of ethnic difference. Herodotus and Aeschylus had *both* cited the importance of different equipment. Later writers preferred to emphasise the Persians' personal inferiority.[26] Once an ethnicity-based ideology of different worth has set in, focus on equipment seems to slight the party usually deemed superior. Persian inferiority is really the *opposite* of Herodotus' position, emphasising as he does the Persians' courage and strength. In the more racist view, the Persians' strength as an army lay in numbers, not in the quality of its soldiers. Downplaying numbers and emphasising difference in equipment rather than in physical and moral worth appears a double act of bias. We need not accept this as Plutarch's own view, but it does highlight a shift in perception that had arisen over the years towards denigrating the Persians rather than respecting them as mighty (if flawed) opponents. Lastly, on Marathon, the speaker argues that the battle is diminished by reference to the Persian fleet sailing towards Athens rather that fleeing with abandon. This creates the impression that it was 'only a light skirmish with the barbarians, as the envious and ill-willed argue'.[27] Any minimisation of Marathon comes from envy, this suggests, which is of course its own rhetorical manoeuvre. Finally the speaker warns their audience to be on guard for the sorts of tricks that Herodotus has been accused of pulling, much as you must check for flies amongst flowers. *Malice* is another example of the Graeco-Persian Wars as a teaching tool. It offers insight into alternative perspectives which, taken together, suggest the gulf between ideas formed when Persia was still a threat to Greece and those at play following years of anti-Persian rhetoric and the demise of the Persian Empire.

The influence of the *Parallel Lives* on the literature of later generations and their view of antiquity can hardly be overstated. The Battle of Marathon appears on numerous occasions – we have already seen some of them – and it is used to demonstrate a variety of characteristics. In *Themistocles* (paired with *Camillus*), a young Themistocles becomes thoughtful and begins turning down invitations to parties because he is so ambitious to match Miltiades' achievement. He tells a concerned friend that 'the trophy of Miltiades will not let him sleep'. Excessive ambition is a flaw in Themistocles, but at this level it puts him on the path to greatness and ensures that he is ready for the next invasion.[28] This representation is a little at odds with how he appears in *Aristides* (paired with *Cato*). In *Aristides* he seems older at the time of Marathon, already a serious political figure. This is necessary as cooperation is a stronger theme in *Aristides*, while *Themistocles* had other priorities. Themistocles is established as Aristides' rival by the time of Marathon, in order to emphasise the virtue of cooperation – of putting enmity aside in favour of the common good. This same virtue is illustrated by the probably exaggerated story of Aristides giving up his command to Miltiades. We have already seen another important story from *Aristides* – Callias' betrayal of a prisoner and theft from the community. Again Marathon is serving as a teaching ground, contrasting Aristides' honesty in looking after the booty with Callias' treachery.[29] As discussed above, the Callias story is unlikely to be true, but the story of the two men's different behaviours on this memorable occasion highlights contrasting character traits and the contrasting impacts that those traits have on their descendants, bringing honour or shame.

In *Cimon*, Marathon is once again an inspiration; Cimon is urged to do something as great as his father's battle. Miltiades is associated primarily with bravery: Cimon is praised as being as brave as Miltiades, as intelligent as Themistocles, and more just than either of them.[30] *Cimon* (matched with *Lucullus*) goes on to deeper consideration of the Wars. The two were paired because both men fought extensively in Asia (against barbarians, as Plutarch would put it), and because they both tried to avoid conflict at home. Their love of partying is noted as a shared weakness.[31] The *Cimon* emphasises his attempts to foster good relations between Sparta and Athens and his negotiation of a peaceful transfer of allies. Concluding the biography, Plutarch remarks that no great deeds were performed by the Greeks against Persia after Cimon's death and that, on the contrary, their descent into inter-Greek wars enabled the Persians to influence them and led to the destruction of Greek power. The final line calls him 'Hellenikos hegemon', 'the leader of the Greeks'.[32] Fifth-century Athens had seen conflict between those who saw the Graeco-Persian Wars as an inspiration for war against Persia, and those who emphasised it as a justification for the Athenians to rule other Greeks. The long-view made the former of these seem the better option. While Cimon is praised for his panhellenism and campaigns against Persia, his rival Pericles, though praised for his virtues, is ultimately criticised for his divisive conduct and responsibility for the Peloponnesian War.[33] It may be recalled that Elpinice was remembered as a critical voice contrasting Pericles' wars against Greeks with Cimon's against Persians.[34] This preference for a Greece united against Persia comes through more strongly still in *Agesilaus*:

> I do not agree with Demaratus of Corinth, who said that those Greeks who did not see Alexander sitting on the throne of Darius missed a great pleasure – but rather they would probably weep when they reflected that this was left for Alexander and his Macedonians while they had thrown away the lives of Greek generals at Leuctra and Coronea and Corinth and in Arcadia.
>
> Plutarch, *Ages*. 15.[35]

A similar opinion is voiced in *Flamininus* (paired with *Philopoemen*). After the Roman general's victory removed Macedonians from Greece, Greeks praised him, commenting that although the great Greek generals could win wars, they did not always use their victories to do the right thing:

> Indeed, if one excepts the action at Marathon, the sea-fight at Salamis, Plataea, Thermopylae, and the achievements of Cimon at Eurymedon and about Cyprus, Greece has fought all her battles to bring servitude upon herself, and every one of her trophies stands as a memorial of her own calamity and disgrace, since she owed her overthrow chiefly to the baseness and contentiousness of her leaders.
>
> Plutarch, *Flamininus*, 11.

Plutarch uses Marathon in his *Lives* to demonstrate positive traits such as ambition, cooperation, honesty and bravery. Taken together, the *Lives* present Marathon as the inspiring beginning of an era of panhellenism, but one which was all too short – a moment of excellence before the self-harm set in. A view of the world without antagonism is not imagined. There will be conflict and it will either be turned outwards, towards Persia, or inwards, towards fellow Greeks. Perceiving the world through this choice, Plutarch prefers the former. Marathon is an inspiration, but it is tied to a lament for what might have been.

Self-sacrifice

To return to speech-writing, the much-prized activity of the Second Sophistic, we are fortunate in the survival of a pair of speeches written by one of the great orators of the generation after Plutarch and Dio. Polemon, a citizen of Smyrna, moved in high circles. He was a friend of Emperor Trajan and of the great philhellene emperor, Hadrian. Polemon's speeches offer further demonstration of how Marathon continued to be mined in explorations of social values. The speeches are set shortly after the battle. The premise is that the father of the man who has fought most courageously wins the honour of delivering the *epitaphios*. Two fathers battle it out. The first speaker is Cynegeirus' father, the other is Callimachus'.[36] The speeches are conspicuous for their rather grisly emphasis on the manner of the two men's deaths. Cynegeirus' father, Euphorion, repeats Herodotus' account of his hand being cut off grabbing a Persian ship; he adds that Cynegeirus grabbed the ship with his second hand only for that to be severed too. Callimachus' father counters that this is only one wound, whereas Callimachus died of many. Both speakers agree that Callimachus stayed upright after death. Euphorion attributes this to missiles supporting Callimachus; Callimachus' father claims that it was a miracle – the departing psyche ordering the body to stay put. As well as demonstrating how participants in the battle continued to be household names and subjects for rhetorical exercises, the speeches also show how Marathon continued to be used to promote military virtues. They celebrate fighting and dying for one's country, even to the extent of celebrating death by over-killing – death by more than necessary means. This was not the only occasion in which this concept was celebrated. Around this time, perhaps a little later, Justin published an epitomised version of a lost history by Pompeius Trogus. The epitome features Cynegeirus losing one hand, then the other, then fighting with his teeth until he is overwhelmed.[37] This is beyond encouraging bravery and into rather more masochistic territory.

Another figure of this period who we have encountered before is Pausanias, who wrote a travellers' guide in the 150s CE documenting the buildings and monuments which he saw on his journeys around the Greek world. His intellectual tastes and ardent patriotism are reflected in his work. It is to Pausanias that we owe the detailed description of the paintings in the Stoa Poikile in Athens. It is from him that we get the fabulous stories, still told in his time, of ghosts being heard on the battlefield. And it is from him that we get a thorough description of the tombs of the Marathon dead, including the rarely-mentioned grave of the freed slaves. This latter point has a companion piece elsewhere in the work. Of the Battle of Corinth in 146 he states that the general Diaeus 'proceeded to set free slaves, following the example of Miltiades and the Athenians before the battle of Marathon'. 146, the year that Greece became subject to Rome, is almost a cut-off point in Pausanias' *Guide*. He mentions few events related to Greece beyond that date. The free independent Greece of the past is his passion. Recognising that those days would not return, he chose to ignore contemporary events. Cities and people are judged according to what they contributed to the freedom of the Greeks.[38]

As one might expect in these circumstances, Pausanias regards Athens kindly. He treats the Athenians as the only people who never failed Greece in the face of an invader, be it the Persians, Macedonians or Gauls. On visiting Athens he shares his opinion that Marathon was the battle of which the Athenians were most proud. He commends Aeschylus for including it in the epigram intended for his tomb, where he left no word on other battles or his plays. In drawing up a list of the ten greatest benefactors to Greece, Pausanias places 'Miltiades, the victor of Marathon' first. Leonidas, Themistocles, Xanthippus and Cimon are also on the list, although not Aristides, who he condemns for charging Greeks tribute. Pausanias of Sparta is out for acting tyrannically. Xanthippus is included for his part at Mycale. Five out of the ten relate to the relatively short span of the Graeco-Persian Wars. Like Plutarch, Pausanias views that era as the glory days of unity before the disaster of the Peloponnesian War. Interestingly, despite the frequent positivity about Marathon, it is Leonidas who Pausanias picks as having surpassed all the deeds of Greeks before or after. Self-sacrifice is the ultimate demonstration of commitment. Yet even in this case, Leonidas at Thermopylae is arrayed next to Achilles at Troy and Miltiades at Marathon – battles made more glorious by the actions of one man. Pausanias visited Attica around 650 years after the Battle of Marathon. It is rather moving and certainly intriguing to think of him full of nostalgia, knowledgeable about Herodotus and Xenophon, about the new works by Plutarch, visiting the battlefield as a tourist, admiring the soros, taking notes on the inscriptions there, viewing the statue of Miltiades, and listening to the tales of the locals who had told these stories many times before, like their fathers and grandfathers before them.[39]

Herodes Atticus

When Pausanias visited Marathon he was near the home of the wealthy, influential politician and sophist, Herodes Atticus. Atticus was the son of the first Greek to be made consul *suffectus* (that is, replacement consul) at Rome and was himself the first Greek to be made a consul *ordinarius*, appointed in 143 CE. He had served as archon at Athens, as many of his family had before him. Despite this political success, it was as an intellectual and orator that he was best known. His consulship came after he had been invited by the emperor to educate the future emperors Marcus Aurelius and Lucius Verus. When he returned to live in Greece, young men travelled from all over to study with him. He funded numerous buildings, some of which still stand. These included a stadium and theatre in Athens, a theatre in Corinth, a stadium at Delphi, baths at Thermopylae, and aqueducts in Italy and near Troy. This reputation and philanthropy is relevant when we consider how he came to influence the perception of Marathon.

Herodes Atticus was from the small settlement at Marathon. He was hugely proud of its history and that of his family. He owned land where a cave-shrine for Pan was established after the battle. He claimed descent from Miltiades, via Elpinice, even naming one of his daughters after her.[40] When in Greece, he loved to spend time in his Marathon home, visiting the battlefield and taking his students there. More drastically, he seems to have had the inscriptions listing the Marathon dead removed from the soros and set-up in a sort of commemorative hall in his second home in the Peloponnese. If he was just anyone, this would not have been possible, but a man like Herodes Atticus had more than the usual sway. The inscriptions seem to have left the soros about ten years after Pausanias saw them there.[41]

As a teacher with international impact, Atticus was able to reinvigorate interest in the battle he was so fascinated by. Although references to Marathon had remained an important part of the culture of Greek and Roman rhetoric, they rise in his time, likely influenced by his encouragement and example.[42] His Marathon-mania may well have been inherited from his family. They seem to have been responsible for popularising, if not inventing, the story of Eucles the runner taking news of the victory to Athens. For them this was a family story. Since at least the second century BCE, when one shows up in an inscription, the men of Herodes Atticus' family had the names 'Eucles' or 'Herodes'.[43] At some point before 9 CE, the family erected a statue in front of the Stoa Poikile inscribed 'The new Hero Eucles, son of Herodes, of Marathon'. Plutarch, the earliest surviving source for the story, may even have been told it by Atticus' father, another Herodes Atticus who appears in *Table Talk*.[44] Plutarch refers to 'Eucles' as if the audience know very well who that is, but he adds information that he got by digging further, noting that Heracleides of Pontus said that it was Thersippus who ran. For several generations the family had been establishing their connection to the battle – their descent from Miltiades and from Eucles. Clearly they still found that there was social cache to be had from making such a claim. Atticus the orator was then able to maximise the impact of this family story through his enormous reach and reputation.

The only other ancient reference to the run comes from the writer Lucian. He came from Samosata on the Euphrates; although he wrote in Greek, Aramaic was more likely his first language. He was a witty prolific writer with a taste for the satirical. In his amusing essay *A Slip of the Tongue in Salutation*, Lucian relates a cringe-inducing moment in which he greeted someone in Greek and got the word wrong. This is the jumping-off point for numerous historic examples of greetings. He notes early on that the usual practice of greeting with 'Χαῖρε', 'Rejoice', 'Joy', began after Marathon. As he tells it:

> Philippides the dispatch-runner. Bringing the news of Marathon, he found the archons seated in suspense regarding the outcome of the battle. 'Joy, we win!' he said, and died there and then, breathing his last in the word 'Joy'.
>
> Lucian, *Laps*. 3.

Lucian does not suggest that the runner also fought in the battle; he is specific that he was a message-carrier. Lucian also leans towards the running tradition familiar from Herodotus, in which *Philippides* (or Pheidippides) runs to Sparta. Whether Lucian was the first or one in a line of people to mingle the stories is unclear. It certainly suggests that the version with Eucles was not universally accepted. Lucian will have known that tradition, but he ignores it. This is quite in-keeping with his habit of poking fun at Herodes Atticus, and is perhaps another example of him doing exactly that. Another relevant example of Lucian's sense of humour comes in his work *Tragic Zeus*. When Heracles proposes to destroy the Stoa Poikile in order to take-out a philosopher who spends time there, Zeus responds that it would be terrible to ruin 'the Stoa, along with Marathon and Miltiades and Cynegeirus' – the orators will have nothing to give their speeches about if he removes their favourite subject![45]

A writer who gives us another quite different take on Marathon is a huge admirer of Herodes Atticus: Aelian. Aelian was from Palestrina, near Rome, where he had spent much of his life enslaved before being freed and then taught

Greek and oratory. In his numerous works he exhibits the skill of applying arguments to perhaps unlikely places. In *On the Nature of Animals* he argues for evidence of divine providence in the animal kingdom. Proving that there is almost nothing that Marathon cannot add support to, Aelian demonstrates the excellent nature of dogs by reminding readers that an Athenian took a dog to Marathon as a soldier and that its performance was celebrated in the Stoa Poikile; the 'reward for the danger it had undergone [was] in being seen among the companions of Cynegeirus, Epizelus, and Callimachus'.[46]

A man even more firmly attached to Herodes Atticus' view of the world is Aelius Aristides, who had been a student of his in Athens and of Polemon's in Smyrna. Aristides' political career was cut short by chronic illness, leading him to life as a sophist. His *Panathenaicus* of 155 CE looks back to Isocrates' *Panathenaicus* from over 500 years earlier. It offers a summarised history of Classical Athens and makes a great deal of the Graeco-Persian Wars as a demonstration of Athenian excellence. He assumes that his listeners are fully aware of the details of the Battle of Marathon. He judges Marathon the greatest Athenian land-battle, alongside Salamis as its top naval victory and Mantinea its prize cavalry-battle. Much is made of the Athenians standing alone, an angle which strengthens the fourth-century BCE vibe. He describes the Great King Darius consumed with rage at the news of the defeat and collapsing to his death – a rare example of Marathon killing the king.[47] Equally indicative of his deep engagement with the intellectual life of the fourth century BCE is his third oration, *On the Four*. Here and in *A Reply to Plato*, Aristides takes issue with Plato's argument that oratory is a social evil. The four in question are Miltiades, Themistocles, Cimon and Pericles. In order to defend oratory, Aristides defends the four from the charges in Plato's *Gorgias* that they had failed to improve the Athenian people. He cites aspects of the Marathon campaign which he considered socially improving, such as the assistance provided by Pan and Heracles, the foundation of Pan's cults, Callimachus standing though dead, and the respectful treatment of the battle-dead.[48]

Aristides' orations are a fine example of how involved second-century CE intellectuals were with Classical era thinking and how deeply enmeshed Marathon and the wider Graeco-Persian Wars were in intellectual life. Aristides' *Panathenaicus* became a hugely important work. Its retelling of Classical history was used as a school resource for hundreds of years in the Byzantine Empire, where boys could read how the Athenians bravely stood alone and how Darius collapsed in rage. Philosophers continued to immerse themselves in Plato's works and they revisited Aristides' Platonic orations to consider his criticism of the great man. In the third century CE, the Neoplatonist Porphyry wrote a seven-book treatise on why Aristides was wrong about Plato. In the fourth century CE, Synesius read Aristides' work then called him an 'enemy of philosophy'. In the sixth century CE, over 1,000 years after Marathon, Olympiodorus wrote a commentary on Plato's *Gorgias* and called Aristides a 'witterer' for his criticism of Plato.[49] It is thanks to anonymous commentators on *On the Four* that we have all the alternative stories about what happened to Miltiades on Paros.

Herodotus' *Histories*, Aeschylus' tragedies, Aristophanes' comedies, and the works of the orators and philosophers were still widely read in the world of late antiquity. But despite this extraordinary continuity, of course things were different. This comes home particularly clearly in a work by Libanius from the fourth century CE. He was a Greek from Antioch who had studied in Athens in the 330s before teaching rhetoric in Constantinople and later returning to Syria. In his speech *On the Temples*, Libanius addresses Emperor Theodosius. He voices the complaint that during this emperor's reign, some have taken it upon themselves to destroy temples dedicated to non-Christian gods. He speaks rather movingly of how from the first days, humans turned to the gods for support and later learned to honour them with sanctuaries, temples and sacrifices. In later days, the emperors Valentinian and Valens outlawed sacrifice and now the temples themselves are under attack. To those who say that the world needs no temples, he replies with examples of the great things achieved by those who worshipped those gods in those ways. These include the fertility of Egypt, the conquest of Troy and Rome's rise to empire. The Battle of Marathon, he adds, was not a victory by the Athenians, but by Heracles and Pan, just as Salamis was won by the gods of Eleusis.[50] Since the day of the battle, people had attributed the Greeks' success, in part, to the gods' support. This was part and parcel of how most people saw the world, a world in which gods and heroes took an active part. Reference to the Athenians' and Plataeans' bravery, moral excellence or equipment did not diminish the assumption of divine aid. Now an unlooked-for challenge had arisen. Marathon is cited as one of the great events of history, yet it is not the Athenians' greatness which needs to be celebrated, but that of the gods themselves.

When Libanius was a young man in Athens in the 330s CE, he will have visited the Stoa Poikile and admired the paintings of the Amazon battle, the Trojan War and Marathon. He will have attended festivals and seen the temples of Artemis Eucleia, Athena Nike, the Parthenon and the huge statue of Athena Promachos which stood outside it. In 391 CE, when Libanius was an older man, Theodosius ordered all non-Christian temples to close and outlawed all 'pagan' festivals and games. Libanius is thought to have died in 393, the year the Olympic

Games ended. Within a few years, Synesios of Cyrene would write to a friend that he had visited the Stoa Poikile but found it 'no longer poikile, however, because the Proconsul took away the boards'.[51] It is at this point that Cimon's great paintings disappear from history.

It was a new era. Cultures were changing and societies reforming. There was always some continuity however. The Byzantine Empire in particular would preserve the intellectual history of ancient Greek and Roman culture. Scholars would comment on the old texts, painstakingly make copies and share them, and write new works inspired by them. There was never a time when the Battle of Marathon was forgotten. Though many works were lost over the years, there was always someone somewhere working with the old texts and giving them serious thought. And perhaps the old ways still had their power. In 500 CE Alaric the Visigoth besieged Athens with his army. Like Datis at Rhodes before him, he withdrew when confronted with Athena. High upon the acropolis, Athena Promachos claimed another victory. At least that is what the stories said.[52]

1,000 years

Those 1,000 years since the Battle of Marathon saw a curious mix of continuity and change in how the battle was perceived and remembered. It had retained a cultural relevance that few other battles could boast. It had been distilled from a battle involving a variety of peoples into a clash of Athenians and Persians. That in turn could be reconfigured to represent Greeks versus Persians, Greece versus Asia, or even Greece versus any enemy, Europeans versus Asia, civilisation versus barbarism or an easterly power like Pergamum versus the barbarian westerners from Gaul. It was a seminal event, yet its associations had proved malleable. Almost straightaway the model it offered had served as a point of nostalgic comparison, yet this too had proved an elastic concept. From striving to be like one's parent's generation or criticising the young at the expense of the old, it had stretched to include calling on people to be like their ancestors, the men in the age of free Greece.

Figures involved in the campaign had become household names. Darius was the face of the Persian side, with Datis second and Artaphernes a distant third. Amongst the Greeks, Miltiades had eclipsed the others. Callimachus was remembered to have been a commander, but was celebrated rather as one of the famous dead, alongside Cynegeirus.

Miltiades predominantly symbolised bravery and freedom. He was not recalled so much as a brilliant strategist or intellect but as a man who showed courage at a decisive moment. To a lesser extent, Cimon and Elpinice had remained famous figures. Elpinice became the (mortal) female representative of Athens in the Graeco-Persian Wars, alongside Gorgo for Sparta, Atossa for Persia and Artemisia for Ionia. The fame of the latter went some way to letting the men of Ionia off the hook.

In many instances the question of who fought had proved less important than the virtues associated with the fight – physical bravery, martial skill, endurance, willingness to die for one's community and freedom. Honesty, cooperation and the power of the divine were all taught through reference to Marathon, but so too were political tact and the fickleness of democracy. The fact that both armies were pro-empire in their own ways was typically lost beneath the more prominent principle of fighting to prevent being subject to someone else. For 1,000 years, people had been taught these values with reference to Marathon, and they had been taught how to use the battle to persuade and to inspire. Generations to come would still read the stories and the speeches. They had their own ideas about what Marathon meant.

12

Marathon after Antiquity

It would take another book to go in detail through all the ideas about Marathon over the next 1,000 years. Though we cannot look at everything, it will be worth considering some significant contributions to thinking about the battle and taking a look at some of its incarnations in the modern world. As we have seen, the Byzantine Empire kept a great deal of ancient culture alive. Many early Christian writers and philosophers were deeply engaged with ancient authors, and there was never a time when knowledge of the Graeco-Persian Wars died out. The tenth century saw the writing of the *Suda*, with its snippets about the cavalry and the Parian expedition. By the time the Byzantine Empire fell in 1453, the Renaissance was underway in Europe. That reinvigorated the study of Greek and Roman culture while Herodotus' *Histories*, with its emphasis on the rise and fall of empires, helped many Byzantine scholars make sense of what had happened.[1]

Let us start with something that reveals the winding road that is cultural memory – a Persian Romantic epic, *Wamiq u 'Adrha*, by the eleventh-century poet Unsuri. The poem, which survives in fragments, follows the story of Miltiades' son, Metiochus, and his beloved, Parthenope. The scene opens at the court of Polycrates, the tyrant well-known from Herodotus and a real-life influence on the Cimonids. Metiochus meets Parthenope – Polycrates' daughter. They seem destined for marriage but it falls apart because Miltiades has been turned against Metiochus by his new wife. The lovers are separated. Polycrates dreams that Parthenope will become Queen of Samos after many hardships. There is a good chance that this was fulfilled at the end of the poem, although that section is now tantalisingly lost.

The poem has its roots in Herodotus' *Histories* but is more closely tied to the Greek novel of the first century CE. That novel was gradually adapted and took its own journey into Persian poetry. Achaemenid and Achaemenid-related history became somewhat taboo in Persia once most people in the region adopted Islam. Nonetheless, this poem was reworked into further forms becoming a popular part of Persian culture.[2] The fame of Miltiades' lost son demonstrates ways in which some Muslim authors maintained complex involvement with the ancient cultures of the region, transforming ancient traditions into new forms.

Travellers

The first Northern Europeans who travelled to Greece in the medieval period were drawn by the crusades, not the romance of Classical Greece. The Franks occupied Greece *c.* 1200–1500, and we find the de la Roche family established in the Marathon region. Otto de la Roche, a Burgundian nobleman, had taken part in the Fourth Crusade. His son, Guy de la Roche, built a tower at Marathon in *c.* 1250. The site's proximity to the coast meant that it was still a practical place to hold. de la Roche dismantled Classical structures to build his tower. His tower has in turn been dismantled to retrieve them.[3]

Non-Greeks, particularly from France and Britain, began visiting Greece from antiquarian interest in the second half of the seventeenth century.[4] Some of them had the chance to visit the Parthenon in Athens before it was blown up by the Venetians who were attempting to oust the Ottomans in the Great Turkish War. These travellers had read about the Battle of Marathon and became the first in many centuries to visit the battlefield out of historical curiosity.

Visits increased in the eighteenth century. Richard Chandler visited Marathon in 1765. He recognised the mound there as the soros of the 192 'gallant Athenians'. He also noted the prevalence of wolves in the area.[5] Louis François Sébastien Fauvel, the French consul in Athens, visited the site in 1788 and even conducted a week-long excavation of the soros. The excavation was not deep enough to yield many results, but he extracted weaponry from the plain and sold it to museums. His map of the plain is the oldest that exists.[6]

It was by no means common for Northern Europeans to visit Greece in this period, but for those who did, a visit to Marathon was much sought-after. One visitor who brought a particularly useful set of skills with him was Lieutenant William Leake, a retired member of the British Royal Artillery. He was a founding member of the Royal Geographical Society and a Fellow of the Royal Society. He travelled all over Greece after his retirement in the early nineteenth century. Leake was able to make and publish detailed records of topography and monuments of the country. He visited Marathon in 1802 and wrote a valuable account of the Marathon marsh before it was drained. Like many before him he found bronze Persian arrowheads. Leake should be believed when he says that he discovered items of this sort, although by this time there was such a passion for collecting Marathon weapons that a shadow of doubt hangs over many of the items said to be from there. In 1836 the new Greek state took action to protect the battlefield and the soros in particular. The Minister of Education issued a ban on unofficial excavations, 'wishing this most ancient monument of Greek glory to remain untouched and untroubled'.[7]

A formal dig was permitted in 1884. The famous businessman-turned-excavator Heinrich Schliemann was given permission to investigate the soros under the supervision of the Greek archaeologist Dimitrios Philios. Schliemann did not dig deep enough to find the ashes or pots, and in disappointment concluded that it was a cenotaph from an earlier era. Although this was throwing the baby out with the bathwater, his conclusion that the soros and plain contained items from before the battle of 490 BCE was accurate. Others had thought as much before him. Captain Hauptmann Eschenburg surveyed the plain in 1884–5. It is likely that he discovered the bones of the Persians, Medes and Sacae. He located a great many skeletons heaped upon each other carelessly around a chapel near the marsh.[8] Valerios Staïs reopened the soros around 1890 and it was during this excavation that the offering trenches, layer of ashes, bone remains and a corroded spearhead were found. From this time on the mound was once again accepted (by most) as the tomb of the Marathon battle-dead. Further excavations and surveys were conducted in the twentieth century. The soros is now within a protected site and since 1975 there has been an archaeological museum at Marathon. A copy of the Aristion monument was erected near the soros and at the entrance to the site a new statue of Miltiades stands with his sword drawn and his hand up, still warding off invasion.

Ideals and associations

Visitors to Marathon over the last few hundred years were largely inspired to go by their reading of ancient literature in which the battle played such a prominent part. Since the Renaissance, Classical culture had played an ever-increasing part in education and intellectual discourse. Plutarch's *Lives* were available in Latin translation in England by the late fifteenth century; they had an enormous impact on how people perceived antiquity and upon the new literature that was written.[9] Herodotus' *Histories* were an important text during the European Reformation. Greek and Latin oratory, histories, plays, dialogues and more were essential to the education of the sons (and, occasionally, daughters) of any who could afford it, and therefore a major influence on how educated adults saw the world and expressed themselves.[10] Reports of visits to Greece and a surge in translations into modern languages at the end of the eighteenth century only increased their prominence.

The politics of the age also gave Marathon and the wider Graeco-Persian Wars a particular resonance. Philosophers such as Georg Hegel were redeveloping earlier ideas about the rise and fall of civilisations to frame Northern European states as the inheritors of civilisation, contrasting the powerful European nations of 'free individuals' with the 'oriental despotism' of Asia. The decline of the Ottoman Empire and increasing wealth and reach of European nations fed this assessment.[11] This perception only encouraged the long-standing practice of making associations between the Greeks who fought the Graeco-Persian Wars and other parties, be they the Marathonomachoi's descendants, the Attalids or the Romans. In the eighteenth century this comparison was drawn by parties across the political spectrum. British commentators within a burgeoning empire could see their country as an heir to Athens, a naval power with democratic liberal values. But, equally, revolutionaries attempting to leave that empire in the Americas or in Ireland could see themselves as fighting for freedom as ancient Athenians had before them. Revolutionary forces in France could see themselves as the Athenian heroes of new Graeco-Persian Wars, even while their British and Spanish opponents saw the France of Emperor Napoleon as the new Persia to be resisted.[12]

Lord Byron visited Marathon during his travels in Greece at the turn of the eighteenth and nineteenth centuries. In *Childe Harold*, the poem which made him a superstar, he reflected on the ephemeral nature of things and remarked on Marathon:

> Such was the scene – what now remaineth here?
> What sacred trophy marks the hallowed ground,
> Recording Freedom's smile and Asia's tear?
> The rifled urn, the violated mound
>
> Byron, *Childe Harold* (1812), Canto 2.90

We see here the association of Marathon and 'freedom' alongside a telling observation on the 'violated' soros. Byron's work raised the profile of Marathon and of modern Greece in the popular imagination. He returned to Greece during its War of Independence (1821–1832). Again he included Marathon in his poetry and this time the connection with contemporary anti-imperialist struggle was more pronounced. His great work, *Don Juan*, features a poem within a poem; a Greek poet is imagined singing about freedom. It includes:

The mountains look on Marathon –
And Marathon looks on the sea;
And musing there an hour alone,
I dream'd that Greece might still be free;
For standing on the Persians' grave,
I could not deem myself a slave . . .

The tyrant of the Chersonese
Was freedom's best and bravest friend;
That tyrant was Miltiades!
O! that the present hour would lend
Another despot of the kind!
Such chains as his were sure to bind.

Fill high the bowl with Samian wine!
On Suli's rock, and Parga's shore,
Exists the remnant of a line
Such as the Doric mothers bore;
And there, perhaps, some seed is sown,
The Heracleidan blood might own.[13]

Byron, *Don Juan* (1821), Canto 3.

The connection to the current struggle is made implicitly and then reinforced by reference to Souli. This community in north-west Greece had shown fierce opposition to the Ottomans. They defeated forces of greater numbers on numerous occasions and in one infamous incident of 1803, known as the Dance of Zalongo, a group of twenty-two Souli women threw themselves off a cliff to their deaths rather than be captured. Byron recalls this episode of modern-day self-sacrifice as an equivalent to the bravery of the past. It is interesting to see a direct reference to Miltiades mixed in. Byron draws on the Herodotean tradition of Miltiades' time as a tyrant, but here implies that a strong leader would be more useful than dangerous – perhaps a mild reference to the divisions which plagued the modern Greek resistance as they had done the ancient – an aspect so clear in Herodotus yet expunged from so much glorification of the conflict. This implied desire for a towering personality to take charge also reflects Byron's admiration for Napoleon as a revolutionary leader.[14]

The popularity of Byron's poetry fuelled an already pronounced association between the modern war and the ancient and the widespread interest in Marathon in Britain. This had been on the rise since the Battle of Waterloo of

1815, the final defeat of Napoleon by a combined allied army which ended the prospect of a French invasion of Britain. One might have thought that Plataea would be a closer comparison, but the exactness of such comparisons was never the chief concern and 'Plataea' had never become the 'magic word' that 'Marathon' was.[15] The correlation between Marathon and Waterloo was widely accepted and continued to be a common trope throughout the century in every medium from poetry to painting, plays and speeches.[16]

Byron's poem within a poem offers what seems like a traditional but was actually a very new enthusiasm amongst Greeks for their ancient history. Knowledge of antiquity was not widespread, however revolutionary leaders such as Konstantinos Oikonomos recognised the power of Classical history to inspire unity and rebellion amongst modern Greeks. He and his associates staged Aeschylus' *Persians* in opposition to Ottoman rule, its historical Graeco-Persian War themes deemed more relevant than mythical Troy stories. It was performed in Constantinople and again in smaller venues wherever possible.[17] Revolutionary leaders also recognised the potential that being seen as the heirs to Classical Greece had for mobilising the international community in their aid.[18] A manifesto was issued which cast Greece as mother to all enlightened European nations. It hit the right note. The philhellenism of the age, Byron's poetry calling for new Marathons, all fuelled the association of the ancient struggle and the contemporary. It resulted in what has been called 'the first armed intervention on humanitarian grounds in world history'.[19] Greece was confirmed as an independent state in 1832. This new importance of the ancient past is part of the context for the minister's protection of the Marathon soros four years later.

Choice and circumstance had combined to reinforce the perception of an extreme contrast between Greeks (and other Europeans) and Asians. This was by no means an inevitable way of looking at the world, but it had proved enduring. Its antagonistic and often racist perspective frequently had a detrimental effect on international relations and, from a different perspective, was an act of self-harm to European culture. As one commentator puts it:

> In doing so, the European tradition lost touch with one of its original components; oriental history and civilisation, and Jewish culture along with them, disappeared from the European tradition to which they indisputably belong.[20]

But things are always more complicated than they seem. This period also saw an increase in appreciation for Persian culture from European scholars and writers. Johann Goethe was so taken with medieval Persian poetry that he revisited his opinions about the Achaemenids and argued that they had burned the Greek temples because they thought it 'utterly reprehensible' to keep gods enclosed.[21] Abraham-Hyacinthe Anquetil-Duperron published the first editions of the *Avesta* Zoroastrian texts, which in turn contributed to decipherment of Old Persian inscriptions at Persepolis by the German scholar G. F. Grotefend by 1802. Their success was built on by the Englishman Henry Rawlinson, who transcribed Darius' Behistun Relief between 1835–46.[22] The work of these linguists opened up unprecedented knowledge of ancient Persia as described by the ancient Persians themselves. Modern Persia in this period was traumatised by exposure to the military might of Russia and Britain, which forced the country to acknowledge its technological inferiority. This created conditions in which the Persian elite was more than happy to be told by scholars such as Friedrich Schlegel that Persians and Europeans were really the same. Anquetil-Duperron had coined the term 'Aryan' to describe a linguistic grouping, based on the term 'ariya' which occurs in the *Avesta* and in Achaemenid inscriptions. Schlegel extended the idea to frame it as a racial group in opposition to Semitic peoples including Jews, Assyrians and Arabs. This was not only difference but hierarchy, with Schlegel associating 'aryan' with German 'ehre', meaning 'honour', and presenting it as a defining characteristic of European and Persian peoples.[23] While the theory of a distinct difference between Greece/Europe and Persia had many negative consequences, the development of an ideology of a superior Aryan race including both would produce its own horrors.

Youth culture

The Prussians had fought alongside the British at Waterloo, but chose not to identify it with Marathon. They had an almost century-long tradition behind them of associating their military with the Spartans, particularly in the training of cadets. This was stoked by the publication of Müller's *Die Dorier* in 1824, which further embedded the association. This difference would play out in the twentieth century, when the wars between Britain and Germany were recast by both sides as a re-run of the clash between the ancient Athenians and Spartans.[24]

In the UK, while boys in schools studied the classics as preparation for public life, so too working-class men frequently learned Classical history and literature in evening and Sunday classes and could well understand references to Marathon and to Troy.[25] Young people being home-schooled likewise explored the ancient world as part of their preparation for the modern one. Young people's interpretation of the world via Classical history can be seen in the juvenilia of those who went on to literary careers. Elizabeth Barret (later Barret Browning) had a more than ordinary intellect but was doing a fairly ordinary task when in her early teens she wrote a long poem called *The Battle of Marathon*.[26] She later explained that she created it in imitation of Pope's *Iliad*, the work which inspired her to learn ancient languages. Her introduction reveals how much the adult Hegelian world-view had influenced her perception of culture:

> Then it was that Greece began to give those immortal examples of exalted feeling, and of patriotic virtue, which have since astonished the world. ... The battle of Marathon is not, perhaps, a subject calculated to exercise the powers of the imagination, or of poetic fancy, the incidents being so limited; but it is a subject every way formed to call forth the feelings of the heart, to awake the strongest passions of the soul. Who can be indifferent, who can preserve his tranquillity, when he hears of one little city rising undaunted, and daring her innumerable enemies, in defence of her freedom – of a handful of men overthrowing the invaders, who sought to molest their rights and to destroy their liberties? ... Liberty, beneath whose fostering sun, the arts, genius, every congenial talent of the mind, spring up spontaneously.
>
> Elizabeth Barrett, *Introduction to 'The Battle of Marathon'* (*c.* 1819).

Miltiades in the young writer's poem has 'godlike' intelligence, piety and a kind heart. He leads a brilliant defeat of the army led by 'tyrant king' Darius. We can see in this work the extensive engagement with antiquity and the ideological filter which both characterise learning about the battle in the nineteenth century.

In the Brontë household of the first half of the nineteenth century, son Branwell was taught at home while the three daughters had periods of schooling and home-schooling. Learning at home included the freedom to read whatever was in the house, which provided important exposure to Classical culture and to the works of their hero, Byron. These young people experimented with working antiquity into their writing in imitation of the adult material that they read. In Charlotte Brontë's juvenilia we find a sentiment of pronounced Hegelian style in a speech given by a statesman. The statesman describes cultural 'vitality' having passed from ancient Egypt to Assyria, to the Jews, to Persia, to 'Athens and Sparta and Macedon', to Rome, then to 'the wild Goths', Mecca, the Tartars, to modern Europe and America, and finally on to his lands in the imaginary African realm of Angria.[27] Branwell joined in the creation of this world. His *History of the Young Men* imitates contemporary historiography and charts the rise of colonial settlement in West Africa. In one of the conflicts described, the colonisers attack the capital of the nearest African kingdom. Thirteen thousand Africans come to fight twelve Europeans. The Africans initially fall back, but their elite force of 700 returns to the fray:

> The battle of Marathon and the conflict at the pass of Thermopylae are not to be compared to this insomuch as there their enemies deserved not the name of men, but here 12 young soldiers had to cope with 700 furious and desperate warriors of their own nature, courageous and often tried in many dreadful wars.
>
> Branwell Brontë, *The History of the Young Men* (1830) p.34–5.[28]

Here we see a child-writer creatively responding to ideas about empire, antiquity and historiography which they have encountered in adult works. He has replicated a trick which we saw as early as Thucydides of stating a war's importance by insisting that it surpasses the Graeco-Persian Wars, that benchmark of excellence. The later tendency to disparage the Persian enemy is pronounced here; the soldiers who had conquered much of the known world are disparaged as non-men. Finally, we see the sleight of hand which is achieved by comparison with an event with an established reputation. The African soldiers are defending their home, yet it is the invaders who are characterised in the role of ancient Greeks fighting a defensive war. The aggression of colonialism is hidden under the established 'rightness' of the Marathonomachoi and the 300 Spartans with whom they are associated. It is the very youth and naivety of these child-writers which most reveals how the culture around them shaped their view of past and present.

Marathon running

Elizabeth Barrett remained engaged with antiquity into her adult life. Her marriage to the poet Robert Browning emerged from their correspondence about her translations of Aeschylus' *Prometheus Bound*. Robert Browning would go on to profoundly reshape the way that 'Marathon' registers in the popular imagination when he wrote his own Marathon poem.

Published in 1879, Browning's *Pheidippides* focuses not on the battle itself, but on the desperate runs associated with it.[29] The poem is narrated by the runner and focuses on his internal experience as he carries the message to Sparta, returns to Athens, fights in the battle, and then runs once more to Athens where he experiences his death as 'bliss'. As we have seen, Lucian had applied the name of the runner to Sparta to the runner who rushed to Athens. Browning drew on Herodotus, Plutarch and Lucian, and appears to have been the first to represent the same runner making both runs. Pheidippides tells Miltiades that Pan gave him fennel and that he will fight where the fennel grows – an extended pun on fennel's Greek name, 'marathon'. The fight itself scarcely features. The run is the great endeavour. Self-sacrifice and the beautiful death come not from battlefield glory defending freedom but a battle against the self. This new representation of what was important about Marathon was to capture the imagination of twentieth-century writers. Another significant development helped to embed it – the development of the marathon race.

The modern long-distance race was the suggestion of French scholar Michel Bréal, who mentioned it to Baron Pierre de Coubertin at the first meeting of the International Olympic Committee in 1894. The modern Olympics were the offspring of the nineteenth century's mania for sport, which had emerged through movements such as Muscular Christianity, which advocated for healthy minds in healthy bodies and an end to bloodsports and drunkenness. Conscious replication of 'hellenic excellence' fed this, so an event which replicated the physical struggle of the run after Marathon fitted in well with the new Olympic ethos.[30] The increase in leisure-time saw the 'marathon race' take off and marathons are now held frequently all over the world. In 2004, when the Olympics returned to Athens, a statue of Pheidippides was erected on the marathon route, some twelve miles outside Athens. Thanks to Browning, Pheidippides has become firmly established as '*the* Marathon runner', despite the best efforts of Herodes Atticus and his family all those years ago. Perhaps more significantly, running is now arguably the most prominent idea associated with the word 'marathon'. Endurance and struggle, yes, but by design non-violent.

The Colonels and the Shah

While countries which never experienced the Graeco-Persian Wars continued in the twentieth century to express their identities and conflicts through the prism of ancient Greece, modern Greece and Persia were participating in their own re-identification with the ancient past.

Greece suffered a Civil War from 1946–9. A coup followed in 1967, leading to a seven-year right-wing military junta by a group known as the Colonels. The Colonels' propaganda campaign involved casting leftists and communists as the new version of the country's old enemies. The regime was presented correspondingly as the new wave of a historic struggle to 'save' Greece. One manifestation of this ideological association was the annual Festival of the

Military Virtue of the Greeks.[31] A set-piece of these festivals was a huge parade featuring representations of the country's past. The US-funded army was co-opted for the purpose, as well as huge numbers of boy-scouts, actors and members of the public who were forced to participate. The parades were public, but there was special emphasis on ensuring that school-children and school-teachers attended in order to expose them to the ideology on display. For the pre-Christian world we see a familiar triptych chosen to represent Greek history: Troy, Marathon and Alexander. Later episodes followed, including the Revolutionary War of 1821–32 and the recent Civil War.[32] The nineteenth-century revolutionaries had evoked Marathon in their struggle against the Ottoman Empire and the twentieth-century leftists regarded themselves as their heirs. Through these parades, the Colonels presented themselves as the heirs to both events and cast their enemies as alien outsiders. The Marathon evoked is of course in the glorification model: Greek rather than 'Athenian', an act of complete consensus; no hint of disunity in antiquity could be admitted. As in the spectacles of Mussolini's Italy and Nazi Germany, the ancient past was flattened to create the impression of a continuous struggle leading to present re-birth. The autocratic Colonels never succeeded in persuading the majority that they were the defenders of 'Greek freedom'. The regime was deposed in 1974 when it moved for all-out war with Turkey.

Meanwhile, unrest was building in Iran, which had changed its name from 'Persia' in 1934. The 1930s was a period of intense collaboration between Germany and Iran; even the name change is thought to have come on the Germans' suggestion. The Iranian elite enthusiastically embraced the Nazi theory that the two countries were connected by their shared superior 'Aryan' heritage. The European-educated elite could thus blame Iran's ills on the influence of non-Aryan Arabs, Jews and the 'outsider' religion, Islam. After the Second World War, the new Shah, Mohammad Reza Pahlavi, renounced Germany in favour of US-UK backing, but retained a world-view in which he would bring a new era to Iran: modernising, non-Islamic, heir to the pre-Islamic Achaemenids. This peaked in the 1971 2,500-year anniversary celebrations of the Achaemenid dynasty. A simply staggering amount of money was spent on spectacles at Persepolis at which world leaders witnessed parades of Achaemenid-era soldiers and a speech at the tomb of Cyrus. This evocation of the ancient past did not include Marathon of course. The prominence of Classical Greek traditions made it impossible for educated Iranians to be ignorant of the battle, but it simply was not important within Persian imperial history and the parade was about projecting victories, strength and continuity. The celebrations were almost universally unpopular. Leftists had no wish to see the return of absolute monarchy, while Islamic conservatives were disgusted by the lionisation of a pre-Islamic era. The celebrations intended to project unity helped lead to the fall of the Shah in the Islamic Revolution of 1979. The site at Persepolis narrowly escaped destruction and the Achaemenid past became taboo.[33]

A less fraught relationship with the Achaemenid past can be seen in the traditions of the Parsi community, descendants of Zoroastrians who left Persia and moved to India between the eighth and tenth centuries CE. Because of their distinct situation, Parsi people have tended to encounter the Achaemenid-era conflicts within Eurocentric histories. This ensured that they were often more familiar with Marathon and the other battles of the Graeco-Persian Wars than many people of Iranian heritage would be, yet the Parsis' wider knowledge of their history and culture limited the significance that those battles had for them. Wealthy families in Mumbai frequently themed their tombs on Achaemenid architecture or modelled them on that of Cyrus the Great. This continued when Parsi families moved to Britain, where Achaemenid-style monuments can be seen in London. For British Parsi, the Graeco-Persian Wars are often regarded as a shared aspect of the histories of the European *and* Iranian aspects of their heritage, but without the racial overtones of Aryanism.[34]

Young people's Marathon in the twenty-first century

There is plenty to read for those inclined to find out about Marathon. Recent decades have seen superb work from scholars analysing the battle from archaeological, historical and social perspectives, bringing new shoots to an evergreen topic.[35] As the twentieth century unfolded, there was also a shift away from presentations of the battle as a struggle of civilisation versus barbarity, although aspects of that ideology are still too prevalent. Better understanding of ancient Persian culture and more focus on how antiquity has been perceived in ages since antiquity have been particularly important in understanding the battle and its afterlife in greater depth.

Marathon is still part of young people's education. While Classical history no longer dominates schooling as it once did, Marathon is well-represented in works written for children and young people. These works retell the Marathon story in their own ways. Their writers attempt to communicate a variety of values to modern young people via the Marathon tradition. In the mid-twentieth century, novelist Mary Renault wrote a children's book which retells Herodotus' history of the Graeco-Persian Wars.[36] The epiphany of Pan is ambiguously presented as possibly real, possibly exhaustion, before it is noted that this was the Judeo-Christian god who appears to people in the guise that they are open to. This Christianising of the Marathon story was not unusual in that era, but it is no longer common, in-keeping with modern mores.

The end of the millennium saw the publication of two young people's novels focused on the battle.[37] *Mission to Marathon* follows a boy called Philip who must run to Marathon to warn his family that an invasion is coming. He is encouraged by the knowledge that Pheidippides is running to Sparta. Philip and his female cousin witness the battle, anxious for their soldier brothers. The novel is informative about Greek culture generally and has a lot about managing anxiety, overcoming physical struggles and doing your best. *Athens is Saved!*, published the same year, follows slightly older characters. Cimon is in the army, though still a very young man. His peers bully him for his stutter. Miltiades is a gruff but kindly father-figure who declares that physical endurance is more important than smooth speech. Cimon and his chief tormentor put their differences behind them to fight side-by-side in the centre for the good of the community. Cimon wins the right to take news of the victory to Athens. He struggles on for the honour of his family and dies delivering the message. Both novels follow the Herodotean model closely. *Athens is Saved!* draws on the Plutarchan story of Aristides-Themistocles to model cooperation. The Marathon run tradition is important to both. *Athens is Saved!* even takes its title from Browning's poem. The novels express the virtue of physical struggle, but take running as a more relatable struggle than fighting. Neither novel demonises the Persians nor declares European supremacy; however the Persians remain an anonymous entity and the reader is invited to identify exclusively with the Greek point-of-view.

The First Marathon: The Legend of Pheidippides is an illustrated novelistic retelling of the Browning tradition.[38] It is 'an honor' for young Pheidippides to run to 'save all he loved'. He fights in the battle after returning from Sparta, then dies in Athens after running from the battlefield. Like many retellings of the story, this book offers history as etymology – why do we call marathons 'marathons'. This work takes that further than most by following up with a double-page on modern races and a double-page on the history of the running traditions. Physical exertion (to the point of death) is again valorised, with running replacing fighting. *Marathon*, a choose-your-own-adventure title, is unusual in making no mention of running.[39] The reader plays as Miltiades and must make tactical decisions about the battle. The closer the reader stays to the

Herodotean narrative, the more chance they have of succeeding. This work indirectly communicates the importance of the battle by making it the only ancient title in the series.

Boaz Yakin's *Marathon* graphic novel follows the Browning tradition of a runner who visits Sparta, fights, then dies after running to Athens.[40] Unusually, the runner is named Eucles, following Plutarch. In other respects the novel is very Herodotean. Hippias, Cleomenes and Miltiades all play prominent parts. Aimed at a slightly older audience, there is greater emphasis on retelling the story as a collision between tyranny, democracy and empire. Another nod to Plutarch has Eucles make peace with a childhood bully. This is one of few works which include a female character. Eucles' wife makes a parallel run through the city to bring an offering to Pan – the god most prominent in modern retellings. The reader is left to decide for themselves whether Eucles really saw the god or whether he is simply exhausted. Athens repels the Persian fleet with the Telesilla trick of disguising everyone as soldiers. While running is very much the focus, this work also includes detailed depictions of violence, including scenes of over-killing which suggest the Callimachus tradition. It seems likely that the topic and style were influenced by Miller's *300*, yet the material is handled more subtly.

Frank Miller's *300* follow-up, *Xerxes: The Fall of the House of Darius and the Rise of Alexander*, followed Yakin's *Marathon*.[41] This graphic novel and its film adaptation introduced Marathon to a massive audience. The novel contrasts hyper-masculine Greeks with monstrous non-Greeks. Hyper-masculinity is reinforced by a contrast between an extremely feminine Miltiades, who begs for death when the Persians approach Athens, and a macho Themistocles, who shows endurance through another demonstration of the Telesilla trick (possibly borrowed from Yakin). Darius is killed by Aeskylos; he dies warning Xerxes to leave the Greeks alone. Hubristic effeminate Xerxes ignores him. Their dynasty is destroyed by an avenging hyper-masculine Alexander. The film (which had an 18 certificate, but attracted younger audiences) replaced Alexander's campaigns with a Salamis narrative. Miltiades is absent altogether. The contrast of masculinities is between Xerxes and Themistocles. The former is susceptible to an Amazon-like Artemisia, the latter resists her. In an example of the sexual violence that pervades so much modern media, Gorgo and Artemisia are both raped; in *300* Gorgo endures it as a mirror of Leonidas' self-sacrifice; Artemisia's rape symbolises the conquest of Ionia. Novel and film alike are extreme versions of the racist, sexist interpretation of the conflict.

History book *The Ancient Greeks* is written for a much younger audience than *Xerxes*; however it is another example of traditional ideas alive in modern publishing.[42] While the tone is light-hearted, the double-page on the Graeco-Persian Wars places a now unusual focus on Persian hubris. Darius is pictured saying 'These Greeks think they're so great? See how they do against my mighty army!' above the information that the Greeks won. Xerxes follows, admiring his bridge. It is curiously reminiscent of Aeschylus' *Persians* and would perhaps sit better if Persians had appeared in any further context than this and the Alexander double-page; there is no *Ancient Persians* in the series.

From Greek artist-writers, we have the graphic novel *Democracy*. It offers a detailed retelling of the fall of the Peisistratids and rise of democracy. Marathon acts as the finale which proves that democracy will work.[43] For younger children there is *The Battle of Marathon*.[44] This history book makes space for information about Persia as well as Athens. Darius is depicted not as a ridiculous figure, but as one who finds the Greeks too talkative and democracy inefficient. In contrast to many works, there is an attempt to show a balanced view of what each society looks like from the outside. Images of Athenians protesting show the purpose of democracy and link the events of 490 to political participation in the modern age.

Afterword

For an event that lasted only a short time, the Battle of Marathon has a long history. It has found relevance in every generation that followed, albeit greater or lesser significance according to place and time. The word 'marathon' is likely more widely-known and used than in any previous era. The impact of the modern race has been such that 'marathon' can now be used even more figuratively of anything that takes a long time, determination and endurance. It is probably fair to say that this would not offend the values of the battle's participants.

Some young people learn about Marathon as part of the study of ancient history, however the marathon sporting event is now so ubiquitous that modern retellings of the battle are often history-as-etymology – answering *Why do we say that?* This has enabled the battle to retain greater prominence in modern culture and education that it might otherwise have had. The battle is no longer an event frequently evoked by politicians or philosophers, so there is no reason for young people to be taught to recognise the term in order to equip them to understand contemporary political discourse.

Modern retellings continue the long history of using the battle to communicate values. Particularly owing to *300*, Thermopylae is a more widely-recognised ancient battle and the go-to event for lionising militaristic self-sacrifice. The very deaths wrought by the failure at Thermopylae are taken as proof of commitment, which the successful defence at Marathon does not offer so starkly. Miltiades survived. Callimachus and Cynegeirus once offered death-in-battle for Marathon, but they are not the household names they once were. The celebration of the Spartans' deaths arguably fosters an essentially sado-masochistic outlook, although their famed refusal to give up their weapons has perhaps driven its popularity in certain circles more than the appeal of death in the service of the community. Nonetheless, the 'beautiful death' ideology is still at work in many modern retellings of the Battle of Marathon. It has been reapplied from death-in-battle to death by running-induced exhaustion. Eucles/Pheidippides became the more acceptable face of dying-in-the-moment-of-glory – dying through exertion, but not speared-through or mutilated, like Callimachus and Cynegeirus. Herodes Atticus and his circle promoted this, and thanks to Browning and the sporting tradition Pheidippides is now the main face of dying for achievement. For many years such celebrations perpetuated militaristic self-sacrifice. The running tradition encourages the idea of doing your absolute best for yourself and your community while supressing the celebration of violence, which is perhaps no longer as palatable as it once was.

The gods have a very reduced role in modern retellings. For centuries, Marathon was regarded as a demonstration of the gods' active role in human lives. We saw how the Athenians made thank-offerings to Artemis and other gods for many centuries. We saw how Libanius presented Marathon in defence of the Greek gods in the twilight years of their worship. A shift took place over time which meant that even into the twentieth century, the battle could be regarded (albeit not universally) as an example of the Judeo-Christian god's interventions. Pan has been the best survivor. The picturesque story of his appearance in the mountains is the most common divine inclusion in modern retellings. It is frequently unclear how he actually helps; he may be a psychological symptom of exhaustion, but the appearance of the goat-headed god on a mountain-path seems to appeal to modern ideas of the Greek milieu. The battle is often still regarded as a moral matter; the punishment of hubris remains a common subtext (occasionally still explicit), however the association between hubris-punished and the divine is now much vaguer. Fifth-century Athenians would have been surprised that Heracles is more associated with the battle than Theseus, but then modern readers expect to find Heracles helping people while they expect Theseus to be in the labyrinth.

We have seen that the political situation was complex in the Marathon era. There were many reasons why Greeks might work with the Persians. It became a taboo position, but for a long time it was simply one of a variety of options. This aspect of Marathon has frequently been simplified in the years after the battle, but it is important to remember it if we mean to view the situation clearly.

For the Cimonids, the survival of the family depended on the outcome of the battle. Equally we have seen how the celebration of the battle became part of the family's survival in a volatile climate. At the same time, the family demonstrate the fluidity of things in that era. Miltiades became a hero of democracy, yet he had practiced tyranny; he was an aristocrat, yet he freed slaves. The family could have stayed in the east. One son did and became a hero of Persian poetry. As it was, they chose Athens. Cimon became the champion of panhellenic action against Persia. Fluid circumstances prompt interesting choices.

Many have been inspired by the panhellenism that came with Marathon, though many have been cautioned by its aggressive focus. We have also seen that this battle to resist empire could be used to justify imperialism, ancient and modern. We have seen it used to support antagonistic, even racist perceptions of the world. Talk of Marathon 'saving' civilisation relates to both aspects of that world-view and it would arguably be better if that died out. Marathon was important to ancient Athens, and ancient Athens has been important to world culture since then. It can be disturbing to think that things might have been different. On the other hand, we do not know what would have happened or what would have been different. History is not like toppling dominoes, in which one thing leads inevitably to another.

Marathon has a role in the story of early democracy. The Athenians' brave defence of their city and its independence has rightly been celebrated. The story of Marathon does not have to be told in a divisive way. It can also be recalled that the Persians brought democracy to many Greeks in this era and that there were many admirable aspects to their own system of governance and wider culture. Equally it can be recalled that there is also a long history of critiquing democracy via Marathon. The Athenians who so earnestly defended themselves were enthusiastic about taking freedom from others and the trial of Miltiades can be seen as accountability in action, or as the fickleness of the crowd. It is not a clear-cut moral tale. While the story of Marathon has justified imperialism, it has also encouraged a great many people defending their homes and countries, often in times of grave peril. That too is part of its history.

Marathon is also a story about how events are remembered. It prompted a new form of communal commemoration that has been much imitated. Even so, communal memory often sidelined some participants; the former slaves, the non-hoplites, the non-Athenians. Marathon shows us how we shape our past, or how people might use the past to manipulate us. It has been used to persuade. It has been used to teach generations of young people the techniques of persuasion. It confronts us with the question of what stories about the past modern identities are based on; what values we attach to them; what values we pass on through them. Perhaps we should recall Plutarch's observation that it is all very well and good celebrating Marathon, but sometimes we might do well to recall the peaceful achievements of the past. But since we often like the peril and extremity of battle, we should perhaps consider what the healthiest ways are to tell such a story. The twenty-first century has already found many options. Darius, Datis and Artaphernes; Miltiades, Cimon, Elpinice and Callimachus – they are not huge household names, but they are still known all over the world. They walked the earth in an era that captured the imaginations of the generations that followed. Their struggle connects us across time, be it to the Barrett Brownings or Byzantine scholars, Plato or Plutarch, Xenophon or Hollywood. That endurance and connectivity is something special. Long may it continue.

Notes

1 Athenians at a Turning Point

1 Hdt. 6.34–8. The family tree is complex. It is possible that Miltiades the Founder was Cimon's half-brother rather than half-uncle, but on balance, uncle seems more likely.

2 Wade-Gery (1951) p.214; Forsdyke (2005) pp.122–4, by contrast suspects the family retro-fitted this story. Cimon's victory, Hdt. 6.103.

3 Cimon's murder, Hdt. 6.103, with 6.39. Thuc. 6.54–6 with Aristotle, *Ath.Pol.* 18.

4 Thuc. 6.59; *Ath.Pol.*19.

5 Hdt. 5.62–3.

6 Thuc. 6.59. Sealey (1976) p.17, suggests this motive.

7 Hdt. 5.65.

8 Hdt. 5.66–72; *Ath.Pol.* 20–2.

9 Cleomenes was Isagoras' guest-friend, meaning that Cleomenes probably stayed with Isagoras in Athens. Hostile rumours circulated that Isagoras' wife had an affair with Cleomenes – shameful in and of itself and more so for the implication that Isagoras may have allowed it as part of the 'cost' of support. See Hdt. 6.70. Cleomenes was the elder half-brother of the more famous King Leonidas, who fought at Thermopylae.

10 There is extensive literature on the fascinating topic of Athenian democracy. See for eg. Osborne (1996) ch.9; with Forsdyke (2005) Ch.3.

11 Hdt. 5.74–7; Paus. 1.28.2, M.L. 15. See Osborne (1996) p.295.

12 Kuhrt (1988) pp.87–99, explores the gesture, although West (2011) pp.9–21, notes how unlikely it is that the Athenians ever fulfilled their promise.

13 Hdt. 6.38. Nephew or, possibly, great-nephew.

14 The plate, attributed to Paseas, is housed in the Ashmolean Museum, Oxford (AN1879.175). Its style shows that it was created between 520–510 BCE, making Miltiades' departure in *c.* 516 the ideal occasion – a convincing theory suggested by Wade-Gery (1951).

15 Hammond (1956) p.120 n.3.

16 Hdt. 4.83–144.

17 Hdt. 4.137.

18 Hdt. 5.25–7.

19 Thuc. 6.59.

20 Half-brother Hegesistratus. The Athenians had fought the Mytileneans for Sigeum before Peisistratus re-established control and installed his son by an Argive woman to rule it, Hdt. 5.94–5.
21 Hdt. 6. 136–40, with Nepos, *Milt.* 1–3; Diod.Sic. 10.19.6. There has been speculation on the date of this campaign, some placing it earlier, however shortly before his return to Athens in 493 makes the most sense. See Evans (1963).
22 Miltiades charged, Hdt. 6.104; council, Hdt. 6.38.
23 Gruen (1970).
24 Thuc. 1.70.
25 See Morgan (2016) pp.106–24.
26 Florence Museo Archeologico 3845, Morgan (2016) pp.121–2.
27 Humans basing gods on their own experiences, see Xenophanes of Colophon: 'But if cattle or lions had hands, so as to paint with their hands and produce works of art as men do, they would paint their gods and give them bodies in form like their own – horses like horses, cattle like cattle' (cited by Diog Laer. 3.16). On atheism, see Whitmarsh (2016).
28 Euripides, *Phoenician Women* 1577–8.
29 van Wees (2004) pp.16; 118–21; 136; Nevin (2017).
30 van Wees (2004) p.50, estimates that about 1/10 Greeks wore a cuirass.
31 For an even-handed discussion of the 'hoplite controversy', see Kagan & Viggiano (2013). Krentz (2010) pp.146–52, discusses running, with the running-in-armour competition at p.150.
32 van Wees (2004); Konijnendijk (2012) p.5, 8, 10; Kagan & Viggiano (2013).
33 Cawkwell (1989); van Wees (2000); (2004); Krentz (2010) pp.51, 54, 57, 59–60; Kagan & Viggiano (2013).
34 See Kagan & Viggiano (2013).

2 The Greek World

1 See Morgan (2016) ch.1; Hall (1997); Walbank (2002) pp.239–56, on variety within Greekness. On colonisation, Osborne (1996) pp.104–29.
2 See Hall (2000) ch.6.
3 Hdt. 1.171; Hale (1997).
4 The reforms at Sparta took place gradually rather than being one individual's work. The main developments took place over the seventh century, although alterations continued. On Spartan society, see Powell (2017).
5 Morgan (2016) ch.5.
6 Hdt. 3.39–60.
7 Plut. *On the Bravery of Women*, 4; Paus. 2.27.7–8 with 2.20.8; contrast Hdt. 6.76–83.

8 Hdt. 7.133. Sealey (1976) pp.13–20.

9 Hdt. 5.75.

10 Hdt. 6.84.

11 Hdt. 5.49–51. See Georges (2000) p.38, with ch.4.

12 Hdt. 6.48–50; 6.73.

13 Hdt. 6.75.

14 Hdt. 6.61–70.

15 Htd. 6.65.

16 Hdt. 6.74–84. Cleomenes' daughter, Gorgo, was Leonidas' wife, uncle-niece incest being accepted throughout the ancient Greek world.

17 See Buck (1979); Schachter (1981–).

18 Heracles, see e.g. *Iliad* 19.98–9, although he became associated with Argos. Sophocles' *Oedipus Rex* and *Antigone* and Aeschylus' *Seven Against Thebes* offer these myths; also see Euripides' *Phoenician Women* and *Suppliant Women*, and *Odyssey* 11.271–80, with Apollod. *Bibl.* 3.5.7–3.6.

19 See Hdt. 6.108, with Thuc. 3.68. These events took place *c.* 519/18–509/8 BCE. Aeolic Greek has many affinities with Attic, so Athenians and Plataeans had little adjusting to do to converse smoothly, see Hall (1997) p.156.

20 'The Versailles of Ionia', a great expression from Georges (2000) p.22.

21 Hall (1997) esp. ch.3. With Hdt. 1.146.

22 See Burgess (2014) ch.5.

23 See Burgess (2014) ch.4; Gresseth (1975).

24 Hecataeus of Miletus wrote in the sixth-century BCE about non-Greeks and their myths; see Thomas (2000) on Herodotus' context, with Morgan (2016) pp.189–206. Ionian architecture, Osborne (1996) pp.262–80.

25 On Ionian identity at Athens, Hall (1997) pp.51–6. Sigeum, Hdt. 5.94–5; Hippias' move, 5.56; Lampsacus, Thuc. 6.59.

26 See e.g. Hdt. 8.138; Ovid, *Met.* 11.95–220.

27 Hdt. 1.14–28 for the Lydian conquest. Georges (2000) p.8: 'Everything we know about archaic Lydia points to an increasingly close cultural, political, and economic union between Lydians and Ionians.' See Georges, p.22 for Greek tyrants styling themselves after Lydian kings, with Kuhrt (1995) pp.567–72 on Lydia generally.

28 Hdt. 1.92. Croesus' family is a fine demonstration of the cosmopolitan nature of the area. His father married two women, a Carian and a Greek (whose son was called Pantaleon). Of Croesus' sisters, one married King Astyages of Media; the other married Melas, tyrant of Ephesus.

29 Dedications by Croesus, Hdt. 1.50–2; 1.92; by his father and grandfather, Hdt. 1.25. These dedications made a profound impression on the Greeks by their colossal value and craftsmanship.

30 Hdt. 1.46–56; 1.71; 1.90–92.

31 Hdt. 1.71–72; 1.76.

32 Hdt. 1.75-77, 1.83; Polyaenus, 7.8.

33 Hdt. 1.79–85. Herodotus tells us (1.86–90; 1.207) that after preparing to execute him, Cyrus spared Croesus' life and made him an adviser. The 'Myson amphora' (Louvre, G197) depicts Croesus upon the pyre following that tradition, although it is unlikely that the Persians would even plan to execute someone that way given their religious belief about the purity of fire. Ctesias (7, epit. 30; 33) heard that Croesus was given land near Ecbatana and survived Cyrus. It was once thought that the Nabonidus Chronicle from Babylon (*col. II, ll. 15–18*) referred to Croesus' death; however it is now regarded as doubtful that this (damaged) text refers to Lydia. Croesus' family seem to have survived. Herodotus describes his grandson as the wealthiest man after the Great King (Hdt. 7.27). See Shapur Shahbazi (1993).

34 Cyrus tempts the Greeks, Hdt. 1.76; rebukes them, 1.141.

35 Hdt. 1.154–61; Sekunda (2008) p.68.

36 Hdt. 1.162–171.

37 On coinage, Osborne (1996) pp.250–59.

38 See eg. Osborne (1996) p.320; Harrison (2011) pp.38–44; Morgan (2016) p.80–1, who notes that some may have been slaves. For Democedes, see Hdt. 3.129–37 and below p.62.

39 Georges (2000) p.5 and 8 with n.36.

40 Georges (2000) p.11 with n.46.

3 Persia

1 Kuhrt (1995) pp.647–8; Briant (2002); Harrison (2011); Llewellyn-Jones (2013); Stolper (2017).

2 Kuhrt (1995) pp.652–6.

3 Hdt. 7.61.

4 Zia-Ebrahimi (2011) p.463.

5 Kuhrt (1995) pp.649–52; Cook (1983) pp.44–5.

6 See Mitchell (2020) on Cyrus. Hdt. 1.123–3.11; with the Cyrus Cylinder, British Museum 90920 (https://www.britishmuseum.org/collection/object/W_1880-0617-1941). Cyrus' dual-heritage, discussed by Herodotus (1.108–122) is also referenced in a biblical dream sequence: 'behold another beast . . . like to a bear . . . raised up on one side . . . "Arise, devour much flesh"' (Daniel, 7.5).

7 Hdt. 2.1–3.26, with Lloyd (1982); Sommer (2001).

8 A Zoroastrian text, the Older Avesta was transmitted orally for many years before being written down in the Sasanian period (224–661 CE) when Zoroastrianism became the state religion. There is no historical or archaeological context for its use;

it is dated on linguistic grounds. The relationship of older texts to later Zoroastrianism is improperly understood.

9 Garrison (2011); with Potts (2011) pp.812–13.

10 Colburn (2011) p.88, citing F. M. Henkelman, 'The other gods who are: studies in Elamite-Iranian acculturation based on the Persepolis Fortification tablets', *Achaemenid History 14* (Leiden, 2008) pp.427–52.

11 Potts (2011) p.817–18, with Strabo, 15.3.14.

12 Hdt. 1.131–2.

13 Potts (2011) pp.815–17.

14 Hdt. 1.136; Plato, *Alcibiades* 122a.

15 Harrison (2011) p.82. He notes how well Greek sources capture the tone of Persian inscriptions (e.g. Hdt. 5.105; 7.8).

16 Stronach (2011) pp.475–88. Tuplin (2017).

17 Hdt. 1.135; Xen. *Cyro*. 1.3.3

18 Stronach (2011).

19 Stronach (2011) p.478, n.3.

20 Stronach (2011) p.481.

21 Sekunda (2008) p.71; Konijnendijk (2012) p.5 n.26.

22 Sekunda (2008) p.73, with Charles (2012) p.261 n.15.

23 Figure 5. See Delaporte (1910) image 403; Sekunda (2008) p.69.

24 Hdt. 9.63.

25 Hdt. 7.61.

26 Hdt. 1.135; Charles (2012) pp.262–3.

27 Charles (2012) p. 260, with Hdt. 9.22.

28 Konijnendijk (2012) p.5, with Greek figures from van Wees (2004) p.50 n. 10: *c*. 1/10 Greeks had a metal cuirass, *c*. 1/3 greaves.

29 Stronach (2011) p.484. On the Immortals, Hdt. 7.41.

30 Herakleides of Kyme (689), *BNJ*.

31 Konijnendijk (2012) p.6.

32 Sekunda (2008) p.81.

33 Sekunda (2008) p.76.

34 Colburn (2013).

35 Hdt. 3.61–70.

36 On Smerdis, see Kuhrt (1995) pp.664–5, with Cook (1983) pp.49–53, who notes that while Ctesias has Cambyses die from an injury at home in Babylon, the Demotic Chronicle coincides more with Herodotus and records him dying on the journey. Darius' Behistun inscription insists that Cambyses died by 'own death', which seems to be an insistence on accidental or natural death rather than murder.

37 Hdt. 3.139, with Cook (1983) p.46; Herodotus has Darius' father in Persia, but the Behistun inscription places him in Parthia and is to be preferred. See Hdt. 7.2 for

marriage to Gobryas' daughter. Some conflate this Gobryas with the Gobryas who was satrap of Babylon under Cyrus and Cambyses; the dates make it unlikely that they are the same person, however the shared name makes kinship likely.

38 Herodotus has Aspathines named as a conspirator, but Darius does not mention him in his account of the coup, naming Ardumaniš instead, King and Thompson (1907) column 4.86.

39 Hdt. 3.80–7, with Cook (1983) p.55.

40 e.g. Cook (1983) p.53.

41 King and Thompson (1907); Cook (1983) p.55; Kuhrt (1995) pp.665–6.

42 Hdt. 3.139–49; 5.25–7.

43 King and Thompson (1907) column 5.74.

44 Kuhrt (1995) pp.665–6; Cook (1983) pp. 55–7; 67.

45 Cited by Harrison (2011) p.63, who discusses the conflicts and contradictions that exist in the study of women in Achaemenid Persia, pp.63–72. For her encouragement to invade, see below, p.62.

46 Hdt. 7.69.

47 Hdt. 6.43–5 (for which also see pp.61–2 below); PF 688, a5 for indications that his marriage was earlier.

48 Deaths of Phratagune's sons, Hdt. 7.224; Artabanus warns Darius, Hdt. 4.83, Xerxes, 7.10–18, 7.46–53; his sons at Thermopylae, 7.66; 7.75; 8.26.

49 This seems to be how he is recalled in Aristophanes' *Peace* (lines 289–92), in which a character sings 'like Datis' in inaccurate Greek while masturbating. See Molitor (1986) and below, p.132.

50 For example, described in the Lindian Chronicle as dedicating to Athena, see below, p.58. and by Herodotus as dedicating to Apollo, below pp.67 and 97. On Datis in PF, Q 1809, Lewis (1980).

4 Revolt in Ionia

1 See Georges (2000) pp.5–10. This contradicts the view put forward by, for instance, Hart (1982) p.85, who places greater emphasis on the expense of tribute.

2 Hdt. 5.25–7.

3 Georges (2000) pp.21–2.

4 Hdt. 5.30+

5 Georges (2000) p.15.

6 Hdt. 5.96.

7 Hdt. 5.97. *Iliad*, 5.62, a reference to the ships that took Paris to Sparta, beginning the Trojans' troubles.

8 Hdt. 5.100–2.

9 Ramage (1978) p.8, with Harrison (2011) pp.47–9 on reactions from scholars.
10 Aristagoras: Hdt. 5.126; Histaeus, 6.5. On leg wounds as a tyranny motif, see Nevin (2017) pp.61–2.
11 Hdt. 5.117–20.
12 Lindian Chronicle (532) *BNJ*; Higbie (2003); Nevin (2017) p.28. Datis in PF, Q 1809; Lewis (1980).
13 Hdt. 6.6–17.
14 Tuplin (2017).
15 Hdt. 6.19.
16 Hdt. 6.19; Strabo, 11.11.4.
17 Hdt. 6.21.
18 *Iliad* 19.301.
19 Hdt. 6.22–3.
20 Hdt. 5.105.
21 Hdt. 6.44–5.
22 Doctor and Atossa, Hdt. 3.133–5; Figs, Deinon of Kolophon (690) *BNJ*, cited by Harrison (2011) p.142 n.38; p.66 discusses issues with interpreting Persian motives.
23 Revenge, Hdt. 5.73 & 5.105, with above note; Darius wishes to submit all the Greeks, Hdt. 6.94; Balcer (1989) p.128 notes the convergence of conquests.
24 Silver, noted by Georges (2000) p.15; Attica as a base for future conquest, Sealey (1976) p.17; Hippias as Greek enforcer, Doenges (1998) p.4. Dio, *Orations* 11.148–9, has a fictional Mede minimise the plan, saying that the mission was only to take Naxos and attack Eretria.

5 The Plain of Marathon

1 Hdt. 6.102.
2 Hdt. 1.61–2, with *Ath.Pol.* 15.2.
3 Hdt. 5.63–76.
4 Hdt. 6.48–9.
5 Diod.Sic. 10.27. Georges (1994) pp.66–8, considers Datis' argument a genuine diplomatic position and notes how similar it is to that made by Xerxes to the Argives in 481 (Hdt. 7.150). Flower (2000) pp.85–6 with n.76, like Georges considers the propaganda genuine but the response a later invention.
6 Hdt. 7.133.
7 Sealey (1976) pp.13–20. Hdt. 6.48–50; 73.
8 Hdt. 6.48–9.
9 Hdt. 6.94.

10 Ancient troop numbers are always approximate. It is impossible to be sure how many were sent, although from the start it has been said that the Athenians were outnumbered. Herodotus gives no troop numbers, but elsewhere cites 200 men per ship (Hdt. 7.184). Roughly 600 ships with *c.* 50 troops and *c.* 150 crew would mean *c.* 30,000 soldiers, *c.* 90,000 crew, some of whom might be used for light military service. Balcer (1989) p.130 is amongst those who suspects that only *c.* 30-50 per cent of the 600 ships were actually triremes, which suits Plato's reference to 300 triremes plus transports (*Men.* 240a). That would mean *c.* 15,000 soldiers, 45,000 crew, although Plato's hyperbolic maths makes that 500,000 troops, in satirical imitation of Lysias 2.2 (see below pp.141–3.) The numbers go up drastically over time. Nepos' 200,000 troops (*Milt.* 4.1) is clearly too many.
Hignett (1963) p.59 suggests 20,000 Persian troops based on the number of dead; Hammond (1968) pp.32–3 thought this too low, preferring 25,000 fighters and *c.* 90,000 support. Billows (2010) p.199 concurs, with *c.* 100,000 men, including 25,000 infantry and several thousand cavalry. Doenges (1998) p.6 argues that this number 'boggles the mind', preferring a fighting force of '12,000 to 15,000 with minimal logistic support'. Twelve thousand would be risky given that the Persians knew the Athenians had an army and might be joined by allies. Krentz (2010) pp.91–2, 209, gives an overview of theories and prefers 18,000–24,000 troops plus crews.

11 Hdt. 6.96–9, with Plut. *Mal.Hdt.* 36.

12 Hdt. 6.97–8; 6.118, with Nevin (2017) p.59; 45–6.

13 The fall of Eretria, Hdt. 6.100–1, with Plato, *Laws* 698d. A handful of Eretrians did well out of medising. Xenophon met a family near Pergamum descended from an Eretrian who had been given the rule of four cities by Xerxes for his willingness to promote the Persian cause, Xen. *Hell.* 3.1.6 and *Ana.* 7.8.8. Destruction of Eretria, Krause (1972); Reber (1980).

14 The death of Minos' son, Apollod. *Bibl.* 3.15.7; Paus. 1.27.10; Theseus defeats the Marathonian Bull, Strabo, 9.1.22. For detailed discussions of Marathon's topography, see Pritchett (1965) pp. 87–8; Vanderpool (1966) pp.93–106; Hammond (1968) pp.14–26; van der Veer (1982) pp.290–321.

15 Heracles' *temenos*, Hdt. 6.108, 6.116; Kron (1999) pp.65–8, discusses Oxford Ashmolean Museum 1911.615, which appears to show heroes emerging. Also see Lucian, *Gods in Council*, 7. Athena's sanctuary, *Schol.* Pi. *Ol.* 13.56; excavation revealed a boundary marker naming Athena and female statuettes round-about, see van der Veer (1982) esp. p.295 n.15. *Odyssey* 7.80.

16 Paus. 1.32.7.

17 Hdt. 1.169; 6.22–3.

18 Miltiades' reintroduction, Hdt. 6.103–4. *Ath.Pol.* 27.3, names Laciadae as the family's deme, which makes Oineis their tribe.

19 Hdt. 6.105–6, with Nepos, *Milt*, 5.

20 Herodotus does not give an account of the debate in Athens, although there must have been one; Nepos, *Milt*, 5 gives an account although implausibly only the generals participate; see Hamel (1998), pp.164–7. Miltiades' decree: Paus. 1.32.3, with 7.15.7 and 10.20.2; Dem. 19.303; Aristotle, *Rhetoric* 3.10.7. Notopoulos (1941) pp.352–4; Hammond (1968) p.34; Krentz (2010) p.103 n.4.

21 Oath, Rhodes and Osborne (2003) no.88; vow to Artemis, Xen. *Ana*. 3.2.11–12. It is possible that this promise was made on the battlefield, but battlefield sacrifices are rarely elaborate and the Lycaeon's proximity to the temple of Artemis Agrotera strengthens the likelihood that departure was the appropriate moment.

6 The Fight

1 Marathon, Theseus, Codrus, Neleus, and Echetlus (Plut. *Thes*. 35; Paus. 1.15.3; 10.10.1–2), Cecrops (from the shield of Athena Parthenos, see Harrison (1972) pp.367–8), giant (Hdt. 6.117), Heracles (Hdt. 6.116–7; Paus., 1.15.3), Hera, Demeter and Core, Athena (Hdt. 6.111; Paus. 1.15.3; 1.28; Polemon 1.35; 2.41; 2.62), Hecate (Plutarch, *Mal.Hdt*. 26), Apollo, Artemis, Pan (Tod, 1948) p.14; Hdt. 6.105); Hippias' omen (Hdt. 6.107). See Nevin (2017) pp.81–4.

2 Athenians' camp, Hdt. 6.108; 6.116 (for the Herakleion, see Van der Veer (1982) pp.295–7); Stakes, Nepos. *Milt*. 5, with Hammond (1968) pp.38–40. On numbers, Herodotus gives no figure, but most ancient authors cite 9,000 Athenians and 1,000 Plataeans (Nepos, *Miltiades*, 5; Paus. 10.20.2; and Pseudo-Plut. *Parallela Minora* 1, *Mor*. 305B; Justin, 2.9, makes it 10,000 Athenians, 1,000 Plataeans). Hammond (1968) pp.33–4, 10,000 the minimum; Krentz (2010) p.102 & 105, suggests 16,000 including the poor, rising to 22,000 at the maximum, including Plataeans and (theoretically) 4,000 Athenians who might come from Euboea.

3 e.g. Plutarch makes this claim in *De glor. Ath*. 8, however his speaker is making a rhetorical flourish contrasting decisive military action with writers dilly-dallying. See below, pp.160–1.

4 See Bicknell (1970) pp.427–42, contrasting Hdt. Hdt. 6.103; 6.109–11 and *Ath.Pol*. 22.3.

5 See Jameson (1991) and Parker (2000); (2004).

6 Notopoulos (1941) p.353.

7 See Evans' discussion of the 'cavalry problem' (1993) pp.279–307. Nepos, *Milt*. 4–5; for images of the battle see ch. 9; ghost horses, Paus. 1.32; captured horses, Aelius Aristides, *Panathenaicus*, 106–8.

8 Munro (1899); Billows, (2010) p.210. Nepos, *Milt*. 4.1; 5.4–5.

9 Priam's journey, *Iliad* 24.471; Ernst Curtius suggested as long ago as 1857–67, in his *Griechische Geschichte,* that the cavalry re-embarked; Munro (1899) pp.189–90, took it further with the division of forces theory. Burns (1984) pp.88–9. Text of the Suda, from Evans (1993) p.295.
10 Krentz (2010) pp.139–43; 218–19.
11 Hdt. 1.63 and 6.78.
12 Evans (1993) supposes a maximum of 200 horses, stressing the difficulty of bringing more.
13 Aelian, *On the Nature of Animals*, 7.38, and see below, pp. 86 and 169.
14 Hdt. 6.109–110. They had met at least at Ephesus and Labraunda; Konijnendijk (2012) p.7 stresses the Greeks' disconcerting record. Billows (2010) p.210 considers the real debate was whether to meet this half here or the other half heading to Athens.
15 Attack to pre-empt medising, Sealey (1978) p.191. Intelligence failure, Luginbill (2014).
16 Persians attacked: Munro (1899) p.196, 'the impending arrival of the Spartans forced the Persians to make the attempt'; Evans (1993) pp.287, 300–1, 'logic points the finger at the Persians: somehow, Datis and Artaphrenes initiated the battle'; Doenges (1998) p.12, Datis attacked 'not because he feared the arrival of the Spartans but because further delay was useless'.
Greeks attacked when cavalry left: Burn (1984) p.247; Cawkwell (2005) p.89; Billows (2010) p.210.
17 Hammond (1968) pp.18–9 has the sea at the Persians' back; most others place the sea on the Persians' left. van der Veer (1982) pp.310–9 analyses options in detail.
18 Plut. *Aristides*, 5.
19 This remains contentious. The following items offer insight into the discussion, although they are by no means exhaustive. Wheeler (1991) p.134 talks of 'a fully developed Athenian phalanx [which] faced the Persians at Marathon'; Lazenby (1991) p.98 argues that phalanx depth was significant from at least Marathon onwards, arguing for similarity to later classical battles; Krentz (2010) p.60 (with Krentz (2002) pp.35–7), considers Marathon an early example of the exclusive hoplite phalanx; however he includes some light-armed fighters, p.151. van Wees (2004) p.180 places more emphasis on the traditions of the fallen slaves as demonstration that light-armed and non-armoured men were there, with the exclusive hoplite phalanx coming later. See also above, p.18.
20 Jameson's memorable phrase (1991) p.221.
21 Anderson (1991) p.21.
22 There has been near-endless discussion of this charge. To give a sample: Hammond (1968) p.29 has them in heavy armour doing the full mile 'at the double'. Hanson (1991) p.63 n.2 has them in heavy armour managing only a short distance; Krentz

(2010) pp.146–52 has them in lighter armour running the full mile; van Wees (2004) pp.171–2 and 186–7 pictures lighter armour over a shorter distance.

23 Doenges (1998) p.1; Hammond (1968) p.28; 57.

24 van Wees (2004) p.180; Krentz (2010) p.158 prefers to follow the gist of Herodotus' battle and picture a messy, disorderly coming together of the wings.

25 Xen. *Cyropedia*, 2.3.9–11.

26 Isocrates, *Panegyricus*, 86.

27 Lazenby (1991) pp.71–3; Anderson (1991).

28 Hdt. 9.62–3.

29 Xen. *Hell.* 4.3.19, describing the Battle of Coronea in 394.

30 Ht. 6.114, with p.165 below.

31 Ctesias, *Persica* 22; contradicting Hdt. 6.118–9, with below, p.145.

32 Two extremes: Hanson (1991) p.63 n.2 imagines battles decided within an hour; Krentz (2010) pp.156–7, estimates at least six hours.

33 Pursuit to the ships, Paus. 1.15.3; ignorance of the paths, Paus. 1.32. The executions at Olynthus, Hdt. 8.127; Hammond (1968) p.30, suggests copy-cat revenge.

34 Xen. *Hell.* 4.4.12, describing a massacre of Corinthians by the Spartans.

35 Cynegeirus' death, Hdt. 6.114 with below, p.165. Aeschylus' presence is reported in the *Life of Aeschylus* and Plutarch, *Greek Questions*, 1.10.3. See van Wees (2004) p.222 on the social acceptance of killing in a rout, with Nevin (2017) ch.4 on potential complications. Callimachus' death is often placed on the beach; however it is Herodotus' usual practice to mention notable deaths at the end of the narrative, so that is not evidence that he died at that time, especially when the Athenians' frieze depicting the battle indicates that his death was earlier, see Harrison (1972) pp.353–78.

7 Surviving Marathon

1 Hdt. 6.115. See below, pp.105–6.

2 Hdt. 6.116.

3 Doenges (1998) pp.15–6.

4 Hdt. 6.105–6, with above, p.72, and below, pp. 160 and 167–8.

5 Lucian, *Laps*, 3. See below, p.168.

6 Noted in van Wees (2004) p.146. Lazenby (1991) p.102 makes a similar observation and notes how few references there are in ancient literature to care for the wounded.

7 There are no references to, for example, killing a man whose bowels had been irreparably cut open, but there are some references to armies killing their wounded rather than leaving them to enemy non-Greeks: some of Xenophon's men asked him to kill them rather than let the Persians get them (Xen. *Ana.* 4.5.16); later Greeks

killed their wounded rather than leave them to the Gauls (Paus. 10.23.7). These examples are cited in Hall Sternberg (1999) p.201.

8 A red-figure kylix made *c.* 500, now in Berlin Antikenmuseen (F 2278), Beazley ref. 200108.

9 Theophrastus, *Characters* 25.5–6. van Wees (2004) p.148 notes this rather brutal mockery. Lazenby (1991) p.102 notes Xenophon's reference (Xen. *Hell.* 4.5.15) to some injured Spartans being assisted – another rare mention of aiding the wounded, this time without mockery.

10 Renehan (1992) discusses the example of *Odyssey* 19.455–8, in which Odysseus' uncles use bandages and magic words to stem the bleeding after a hunting accident.

11 Internal bleeding was another killer. See van Wees (2004) p.148, where the handful of cases cited in ancient medical treaties (*Epidemics*) are discussed: nine died of their wounds, two survived thanks to treatment, one survived for six years after the doctor failed to remove an arrow.

12 Hdt. 6.117, with below, p.119. Wheeler (2004) discusses psychological factors. Also see van Wees (2004) p.151 and Crowley (2012), albeit on a later period. See Harrison (1972) pp.367–9 for the figure as Phobos.

13 Hall Sternberg (1999) p.191.

14 The retreat from Syracuse, Thuc. 7.75; Agesilaus: Plut. *Sayings of the Spartans* 3.17; *Agesilaus* 13.

15 Xen. *Ana.* 5.8.6–11, cited by Hall Sternberg (1999) at p.199.

16 Plato, *Alcibiades* 1.115b, cited by Hall Sternberg (1999) p.198.

17 See Hall Sternberg (1999) p.192.

18 See above n.11.

19 The family's mining is noted by Pliny, *Natural History* 33.113, who had it from Theophrastus. The story of the Persian in Callias' abandoned house come from the *Suda*, 1.

20 Hdt. 6.117. 192 ÷ 3 = 64 x 100 = 6,400, demonstrated by Avery (1973) p.757.

21 See Vaughn (1991).

22 Paus. 1.32.

23 Notopoulos (1941) and below, pp.100–1.

24 Hdt. 6.120. Religious restrictions (Hdt. 6.106) are not implausible and were accepted by later writers such as Strabo, 9.1.22. Security concerns: Plato, *Laws* 698e, with M.L. 22. Plut. *Mal.Hdt.* 26 takes a different view, see below, p.162.

25 On war-dead, see Kucewicz (2020), with Martin (2020) for the dead in ancient Greece.

26 Trans. Pierre McKay, inscription *SEG* LVI (2006) 113–4, no. 430. See esp. Spyropoulos (2009).

Thuc. 2.34; Paus. 1.32.3 (with 1.29.4). Hammond (1968) pp.15–9; Whitley (1994); with Jacoby (1945) on epigrams, esp. pp.160–1; 175–6.

27 Whitley (1994). At p.213 he writes: 'It is a monument that looks both forward to the full democracy of the late fifth-century, and backward to the world of the Archaic aristocracy.' It is likely that the pit and mound were adapted from an earlier tomb.
28 Ephebes: *IG ii* 1.47I. See Kearns (1989); Kron (1999) on heroes. Paus. 1.32.4.

8 Events after Marathon

1 Hdt. 6.118.
2 Hdt. 6.119.
3 Hdt. 7.6.
4 Hdt. 7.74, Xerxes has him commanding the Lydians and Mysians.
5 Hdt. 7.88.
6 Hdt. 7.1–3; with Plato, *Laws*, 3.698e.
7 Paus. 1.32.3–4.
8 Jacoby (1945) esp. pp.17–18.
9 Hdt. 6.105. Manuscripts of *The Histories* give his name as both 'Pheidippides' and 'Philippides'. Paus. 1.28.4; see below, see above, p.91, and below, pp.119, 167, 169–70, 182, 185–6, 190.
10 It reads, 'Me, the goat-footed Pan, the Arcadian, who is against the Medes, and for the Athenians, Miltiades put up', *Anth. Pal.* 16232. See Athanassaki (2016) p.218; Mastrapas (2013) esp. p.113 on this inscription, and for a wider discussion of Pan and the relationship between Athens and Arcadia.
11 Paus. 1.14.5.
12 Xen. *Ana.* 3.11.12.
13 Olympia Museum B 2600. The inscription (*IG I3*1472) reads 'Miltiades dedicated [this] to Zeus'.
14 Plut. *Cim.* 8.
15 Post-reforms, Aristotle, *Politics*, 1275 b 37; Peloponnesian War, Diod.Sic. 13.97.1.
16 Parke (1977) pp.88–92. And see Notopoulos (1941) pp.352–4.
17 Hdt. 6.136; Plato, *Gorgias*, 515c–517a.
18 Hdt. 6.132–6; Hydarnes as Phoenician admiral, Hdt. 7.135.
19 See Nevin (2017) pp.49–65, with n.80–7.
20 Dies in prison, Diod.Sic. 10.30.1; Nepos, *Milt.* 7; dies in prison, fine paid by Callias, Nepos, *Cimon*, 1; Plut. *Cim.* 4.3–7.
21 Plut. *Cim.* 4.
22 Plut. *Cim*, 4; Nepos, *Cimon*, 1.
23 Plut. *Arist.* 7.
24 Forsdyke (2005) Ch. 3 and 4.
25 *Ath.Pol.* 22, cites the ostracism of Hipparchus as its first use.

26 Pindar, *Pythian Ode 7, For Megacles of Athens Four-Horse Chariot Race 486 B.C.*
27 Xanthippus: *Ath.Pol.* 22.6 with 28.2; M.L. 22; Aristides: *Ath.Pol.* 22.7.
28 Plut. *Arist.* 7. Plutarch is contrasting Aristides' cooperative spirit with its opposite.
29 M.L 21: 42. Raubitschek (1957); Lang (1990) pp.35–40.
30 For an overview of these competing views, see Gillis (1979) pp.45–58.
31 Hdt. 7.144; *Ath.Pol.* 22.7.
32 Voiced clearly in Plato, *Laws*, 4.706–7.
33 *Ath.Pol.* 22.8.
34 Hdt. 7.7.
35 Hdt. 7.5–7.9.
36 Hdt. 7.134–2.
37 Hdt. 7.148–52. Parker (1985) p.298, calls the tradition an 'apologetic fiction'.
38 Hdt. 7.153–67.
39 Hdt. 7.173.
40 Hdt. 7.128–30; 7.172.
41 Hdt. 7.175–7; 7.184–7; 7.201–39. The Mycenaeans insisted that their modest cohort of 80 stayed until the very end too, Paus. 10.20.2.
42 Hdt. 7. 178–96; 8.1–22. With Plut. *Mal. Hdt.* 34; *Them.* 8.
43 Hdt. 7.189 and 7.191, see Nevin (2017) pp.84-6.
44 Hdt. 7.50.
45 Hdt. 8.40–1, with 1.169 and 6.22–3.
46 Hdt. 7.51–6
47 Jacoby (1945) p. 178.
48 Arrian, 3.16; 7.19.
49 Hdt. 8.54. Nevin (2017) pp.23–7.
50 Salamis, Hdt. 8.56–96; retreat, Hdt. 8.97–108; 113–20.
51 Hdt. 9.12–13.
52 Hdt. 9.19–70.
53 Above note, with Plut. *Arist.* 12 and 16. Flower (2000) pp.78–80, notes the panhellenic tone of the implication of Athens and Sparta as equals.
54 Hdt. 9.90–107.
55 Hdt. 9.100–1. See Nevin (2017) pp.86–99 on the religious traditions around Plataea.
56 Thuc. 1.89.
57 Thuc. 1.89–93.
58 Hdt. 8.3.2; Thuc. 94–5; 1.128–34 (Pausanias), Thuc. 1. 95–6 (Delian League); Arist. *Ath.Pol.* 23.2; Nepos, *Pausanias*, 2–5; Plut. *Arist.* 23; *Cim.* 6 (the stabbing); *Them.* 22–3. Also see Diod.Sic. 11.50, a debate at Sparta in 475 on whether to challenge the Athenians over their new hegemony.
59 Thuc. 5.18; *Ath.Pol.* 23.5; Plut. *Arist.* 24.
60 *Ath.Pol.* 27.3; Nepos, *Cimon*, 4; Plut. *Cim.* 10.

61 With Paus. 1.14.5, and below, p.166.
62 Bridges (2015) pp.30–5; Harrison (2000b) p.51ff; 135 n.1, for an overview of both perspectives.
63 On the contrast between Xerxes' might and his failings, Bridges (2015) pp.22–35; contrast between Darius and Xerxes, pp.26–30. Also Castriota (1992) p.85; Martin (2020) pp.67–75.
64 Aesch. *Persians*, lines 81–5 & 473–7.
65 See esp. Hall (1989) pp.56–100; (2006) pp.184–224.

9 Memories of Marathon in Fifth-Century Art and Literature

1 Xenophanes of Kolophon (450) *BNJ*.
2 Plut. *Cim.* 7.
3 Thuc. 1.98–9; Plut. *Cim.* 7–8; *Theseus* 36, and below, p.. See Nevin (2017) pp.66–9, with Zaccarini (2015) pp.174–98.
4 Thuc. 1.100; Plut. *Cim.* 12–13; (somewhat confused) Diod.Sic. 11.60.6–11.61.7.
5 Plut. *Cim.* 14.
6 Plut. *Cim.* 13.
7 See esp. Flower (2000) pp.77–89.
8 Flower (2000) pp.85–6 argues so. See above p.66.
9 Thuc. 1.100; Plut. *Cim.* 14–15 makes light of the trial in wishing to maintain a sense of Cimon's popularity; Plut. *Pericles* 10 gives a better sense of the peril; *Ath.Pol.* 27.1
10 Thuc. 1.135–8; Diod. Sic. 11.54–9; Nepos, *Themistocles*, 8; Plut. *Them.* 22–3.
11 Paus. 10.10.1–2; 10.11.5.
12 Gehrke (2009) p.89. Gensheimer (2017) on the treasury. Arafat (2013) pp.82–4, places less emphasis on the Marathon connection but also notes the remarkable combination of immortals, heroes and Miltiades. At Olympia, Miltiades' dedication of an ivory horn was displayed alongside a sword said to belong to the mythical Pelops, an extraordinary honour (Paus. 6.19.6).
13 *I.G.* I^2 609. Jacoby (1945) p.158, with n.8 and p.176 n.80. For the statue, Raubitschek (1999) pp.18–20.
14 Hdt. 6.111.
15 Paus. 9.4.1–2. Castriota (1992) pp.63–76. Plut. *Arist.* 20.3 associates this temple with Plataea; the theme of the paintings would be equally appropriate.
16 Castriota (1992) p.76.
17 Pliny, *Nat. Hist.* 35.34; Plut. *Cim.* 4. See Stansbury-O'Donnell (2005) for more on the painters.
18 The fourth painting depicted the moments before the Battle of Oinoe between the Athenians and Spartans. Paus. 1.15.2–3 does not say whether it was created at the

same time; it has been the source of much discussion as it does not fit the rest of the scheme. Stansbury-O'Donnell (2005) pp.78–81 demonstrates the likelihood that it was added later. Castriota (1992) p.78, drawing on Francis and Vickers (1985), offers an alternative explanation.

19 Pliny, *Nat. Hist.* 35.34; Aelian, *On Animals* 7.38.
20 Stansbury-O'Donnell (2005) p.77.
21 Harrison (1972) p.356 discusses the evidence for his pose, including Aeschines, *Against Ctesiphon* 3.186, who notes that the Athenians allowed an image of the communal struggle of the Athenians, with Miltiades shown at the front urging the army on.
22 Castriota (1992) p.77. Stansbury-O'Donnell (2005) p.78, suggests rather that the Amazons evoked Cimon's victory on Scyros, Troy the one at Eion.
23 Castriota (1992) pp.76–133.
24 Castriota (1992) pp.82–9.
25 Flower (2000) p.89 with n.88.
26 Francis and Vickers (1985) p.105 and 112; Castriota (1992) pp.80–1; Stansbury-O'Donnell (2005) p.78; Nevin (2017) pp.64–5.
27 Thuc. 1.98–9; Diod. Sic. 11.70.
28 Plut. *Cim.* 17; *Pericles*, 9; Stansbury-O'Donnell (2005) pp.81–2 estimates that the paintings were nearing completion or just about finished at the time of the ostracism.
29 *Ath.Pol.*28; Plut. *Cim.* 15; 17, *Pericles* 9. Forsdyke (2005) pp.167–9; Raubitschek (1991a).
30 Thuc. 1.102; Diod. Sic. 11.64; Plut. *Cim*, 17.
31 Kerameikos O 6874; Siewert (2002) T 1/67. Zaccarini (2011) p.296 notes that Philochoros (of Athens (328) *BNJ* F30) claimed that Hyperbolos was the only man ostracised for immorality, while Andocides (4.33) claimed immorality was the only reason Cimon was expelled. Nepos (*Cimon*, 1) preserves an apologetic tradition that they were legally married being only half-siblings, however it is more likely they were unmarried full siblings. Plutarch (*Cim.* 15) preserves one of the teasing poems written about Cimon, a verse by Eupolis: 'He was not such a scoundrel as they go/Only too lazy and fond of drinking/And often he would spend nights in Sparta/And leave Elpinice to sleep alone'. There was also a rumour that Elpinice had an affair with the painter Polygnotos and that he included her face in Stoa Pokile as the princess Laodice (Plut. *Cim.* 4); clearly she was the target of a great deal of malicious comment.
32 Zaccarini (2011) p.297. At p.303 he notes that Elpinice's unusual freedom was 'at best felt as disturbing to the Athenian male-dominated society'.
33 See for example the red-figure cup in the Ashmolean Museum, Oxford, 1911.615, one of the earliest depictions. On the trends pottery, see Miller (1995), with Fairey (2011), esp.168–9.

34 Diod.Sic. 11.69.

35 Flower (2000) p.77.

36 Thuc. 1.104; 1.109-10; Diod.Sic. 11.71, 74–5, 77.

37 Plut. *Cim.* 17–18; *Pericles* 9. Plutarch's chronology of these events is shaky. It may be that Cimon's ten years were up and there was no need for negotiations, but the timing is uncertain. It tells its own story that some thought Elpinice could and would do something like this.

38 Thuc. 1.112 mentions the truce; Andocides 3.3–4; Diod.Sic. 1.86.1; Plut. *Cim.* 18 explicitly credit Cimon.

39 Thuc. 1.112, see Nevin (2017) pp.166–8.

40 Thuc. 1.112; Diod.Sic. 12.4.6 (illness); Nepos *Cimon* 3.4 (illness); Plut. *Cim.* 18–19 (some say illness, some say infected wound).

41 Cimon's sons were Lacedaemonius, Thessalus, Oulios, Miltiades, Cimon and Peisianax. Pericles was said to have disliked them as having 'something alien' about them and to have then gone out of his way to thwart them. This extended to sending too few troops out with Lacedaemonius to Corcrya so that he would be shamed by the inevitable failure, Plut. *Pericles*, 29, with Thuc. 1.50. Connor (1967) and Flower (2000) p.78 on the panhellenic tone of Cimon's name choices.

42 Diod.Sic. 12.4.4–6. Some have doubted the reality of this agreement as Thucydides does not mention it explicitly; however Thuc. 8.56.4 and 8.58.2 imply that an agreement of this type had been reached. See Samons II (1998) for a detailed discussion.

43 See esp. Boardman and Finn (1985) pp.250–1 on the frieze as the Marathonomachoi; Connelly (2014) on Erechtheus' daughter.

44 Harrison (1966).

45 Harrison (1972).

46 Another work by Pheidias: *IG* I^3 435; Demosthenes 19.272; Paus. 1.28.2.

47 Paus. 1.33.2–3. Arafat (2013) p.80.

48 Thuc. 1.23; 1.35; 1.140.2; 1.144–5; 7.18.2.

49 Plut. *Pericles*, 24–8. Plutarch remarks that Duris of Samos wrote an account of this episode detailing torture and crucifixion of the Samians by the Athenians. Plutarch suggests that this is an exaggeration, yet the circulation of such an account indicates the reputation that the Athenians were earning. The Peloponnesian League allowed this to happen. An inscription (M.L. 56) suggests that the Spartans initially voted for war to stop it, but the Corinthians dissuaded them (Thuc. 1.40).

50 Archilochus, *Fragment 205*, trans. West. Scott-Kilvert translates it more loosely but perhaps expressing the meaning more clearly: 'Why lavish perfume on a head that's grey?'

51 Aristoph. *Ach.* 515ff: Hdt. 1.1–5. Dion. Hal. *Thuc.* 5 tells us that Herodotus was born 'a little before the Graeco-Persian Wars.'

52 Hdt. 6.109; 9.120–2. Harrison (2000a) explores *The Histories*' morality. On the ending, see Boedeker (1988) with Nevin (2017) p.62.

53 Hdt. 6.107.

54 Hdt. 9.122; Thomas (2000). Herodotus gives this as Cyrus' direct speech.

55 Hdt. 9.62–3.

56 Thuc. 1.1 and 1.23.

57 Thuc. 1.18; 6.59 (part of 6.53–9).

58 Thuc. 1.69.

59 Thuc. 1.22. 1.20–2 features Thucydides' discussion of his method.

60 Thuc. 1.72.

61 Konstantinopoulos (2013) esp. p.63 on the accusation implied. And see below, pp.139–44.

62 Thuc. 2.34–46. Pericles' notorious remark in this speech that a woman's greatest glory is to not be spoken of (2.46) accords well with his reported remarks to Elpinice; on the other hand he does not seem to have applied this principle to his own life, having replaced his wife with the extraordinary Aspasia, a widely spoken-of Milesian courtesan. The plague is described movingly at 2.47–55.
There is a great deal of scholarship on the nature of epitaphioi. See esp. Walters (1980); Loraux (1986) notes at pp.69–72 that the Trojan War was not a favoured subject for epitaphioi as the Athenians had played such a small part at Troy; Thomas (1989) esp. pp.84–93 and 196–237; Volonaki (2013) pp.165–8, including remarks on this speech and Marathon. Also see Ch.10.

63 Carey (2013) pp.127–9.

64 Gehrke (2009) pp. 88–91; Carey (2013). van Wees (2004) pp.195–7; Pritchard (1998); (2010).

65 Aristoph. *Knights* 781–3.

66 Carey (2013) pp. 140–2.

67 Aristoph. *Clouds*, 961–1000.

68 Aristoph. *Wasps*, 1060–101, esp. 1087–8, with Carey (2013) pp.128; 135.

69 Aristoph. *Wasps*, 711. Carey (2013) pp.139–40.

70 See Molitor (1986); Raubitschek (1991a).

71 Aristoph. *Lysistrata*, 273–85.

72 Eupolis, *frag. 106*, see Carey (2013) pp.140–1, with n.38.

73 Aristoph. *Clouds* 658ff; *Assemblywomen*, 675–90.

74 Aristoph. *Lysistrata*, 285.

75 Hall (1989) pp.56–100; (2006) pp.184–224; Flower (2000) p.90; Nippel (2002) pp.290–304.

76 Timotheus, *The Persians*, Flower (2000) pp.90–1.

77 Philostratus, *Lives of the Sophists* 1.9. Flower (2000) pp.66, 92–3. Some place the speech in 392, but 408 is more likely – Gorgias would have been about 100 in 392. Volonaki (2013) p.168 with n.9.

10 Marathon beyond the Fifth Century

1 Marincola (2007) p.106, 108, 114.

2 See above note, with Gehrke (2009), pp.88–93; Castriota (1992) p.79 with n.95; Xerxes: Bridges (2015) pp.99–112.

3 Xen. *Ana.* 3.2.11–13. See Lane Fox (2004).

4 Xen. *Hell.* 3.4.3; Xen. *Ages.* 1–2.17; Plut. *Ages.* 6–18. Nevin (2017) pp.151–6; 162; with Tuplin (1993).

5 Athens' walls and the King's Peace, Diod.Sic. 15.9.5, 15.19.4, with 15.9.3–5, 15.19.1 for the Spartans' regrets; Battle of Cnidus, Xen. *Hell.* 4.3.10–12; Plut. *Ages.* 17; raids, Xen. *Hell.* 4.8.1–10; Plut. *Ages.* 23.

6 King's Peace, see Cawkwell (1973). Agesilaus' retort, Plut. *Ages.* 23.

7 In 388. Lysias 33, with Diod.Sic. 14.109 and Dion. Hal. *Lysias* 29.

8 Lysias, 2.4–16.

9 Lysias, 2.20–6. Volonaki (2013) pp.169–73; at p.173 this speech is called 'the best example of the "Greek patriotism" reading of Marathon'.

10 Plato, *Menexenus*, 240a–d.

11 Volonaki (2013) pp.173–5.

12 Plato, *Menexenus*, 236c.

13 Plato, *Gorgias*, 515c–517a.

14 On the Second Athenian Confederacy, see Diod. Sic. 28.1–30.1f, with Cawkwell (1973).

15 Amazons: Isoc. *Paneg.* 4.68. Castriota (1992) p.80; Flower (2000) pp.93–5.

16 Isoc. *Paneg.* esp. 4.118–20.

17 Diod.Sic. 10. 27, with Hekataios (264) *BNJ*. Flower (2000) p.85 n.76.

18 Diod.Sic. 11.3.1; Hdt. 7.150; Ephoros (70) *BNJ*; Marincola (2007) pp.110–23, with Hau (2016) pp.248–58 on Ephorus' moral purpose.

19 Theopompos of Chios (115) *BNJ* F153. See von Fritz (1941); Marincola (2007) p.107, 109–10; Hau (2016) pp.258–70.

20 Bigwood (1978) pp.24–5; Marincola (2007) pp.107–9; Morgan (2016) ch.4.

21 Naples, Museo Archeologico Nazionale: H3249, Beazley 9036829; Llewellyn-Jones (2012) pp.331–40.

22 Diod.Sic. 11.60.2; Plut. *Thes.* 36.1; *Cim.* 8. See Zacharinni (2015), with Nevin (2017) pp.66–9.

23 Hdt. 7.173. Also see 5.18–21, 8.136 and 8.140–4, and 9.44–9 for other instances of the Macedonians' anti-Persian or pro-Athenian actions.

24 Dem. 19. *On the False Embassy*. See Efstathiou (2013).

25 See above, p.72.

26 Dem. 19.312.

27 Aeschin. 2.

28 Asked to speak: Dem. 18.285; Plut. *Dem.* 21.2. The speech is Dem. 60. See Volonaki (2013) pp.175–7, Kremmydas (2013) p.210.

29 Aeschin. 3. Efstathiou (2013) pp.190–3.

30 Aeschin. 3.259.

31 Dem, 18. 206–10.

32 Lycurgus 1. Ionian Revolt-post-Chaeronea, 1.42; ephebes, 1.76–7; oath of Plataea, 1.80–1; Codrus' self-sacrifice, 1.84–8 (a myth which recalls ephebic service, see Steinbock, 2011); the gods aid a man willing to sacrifice himself for his father, 1.95–6; these examples and *Iliad* 15.494 inspiring the Marathonomachoi, 1.104; Tyrtaeus, 1.107.

33 Under King Agis III. See Diod.Sic. 17.48.1–2; 17.62.6–63.4; 17.73.5–6.

34 Jacoby (1945) esp. p.160 with n.17.

35 Lycurgus, 1.71.

36 Hdt. 8.136; 8.140a–b, with above n.23.

37 See above p.112 and 115–24.

38 Arrian, 1.9.7, presents it as the gods' revenge for medising, drawing on Alexander's propaganda, which he had likely read in works by Callisthenes, Ptolemy or Aristobulus. See Kremmydas (2013) pp.201–4.

39 Plut. *Alex.* 34.1–2, with Plut. *Arist.* 11 and 21.2; Kremmydas (2013) p.205; Nevin (2017) pp.88–92, with n.40. For the fall of Plataea, see Thuc. 3.52–67, esp. 3.58.4, with Nevin (2017) pp.99–101. Croton was sent spoils because an athlete of that city had equipped a ship at his own expense to fight at Salamis when all the other Greeks in Italy declined.

40 Arrian, 3.16.7–8.

41 Dem. 4.34; Kremmydas (2013) pp.207–8.

42 See Hau (2016) pp.124–68, on these authors.

43 Gerkhe (2009) p.93.

44 Paus. 1.25.2, with Polybius 16.25–6. See Pollitt, (1986) pp.90–5, with Gehrke, (2009) pp.93–4; Spawforth (1994) p.235. There is some debate over whether Attalus I or II dedicated the statues; Pollitt favours Attalus I. This is the same dynasty that produced the phenomenal Pergamum altar, now in the Berlin Staatliche Museum.

45 Polybius, 1.63.

46 Polybius, 36.9.

47 Polybius, 6.43–44.

48 Polybius, 3.6; Thuc. 1.92.

49 Arrian, 3.18.11–12. Also see Plut. *Alex.* 38; Diod.Sic. 17.72; Curtius 5.7 for their comments.

11 Marathon under Rome

1 Marincola (2007) p.105 refers neatly to the Romans' vision of the Graeco-Persian Wars as 'the centre piece of a glorious triptych'.

2 Nepos, *On Kings*, 1.2–3.
3 Spawforth (1994) p.242, with n.39.
4 Cicero, *On his House*, 60, cited by Spawforth (1994) p.240.
5 *Res.Gest.* 23; Cassius Dio 55.10.7; Ovid *Ars Amat.* 1.171–2, see Spawforth (1994) pp.237–41.
6 See Spawforth (1994) pp.234–7; pp.246–7.
7 *IG* 14.1185 (=*SEG* 13.479), https://edh-www.adw.uni-heidelberg.de/edh/inschrift/HD022711
8 Spawforth (1994) pp.243-44.
9 See esp. Swain (1996) pp.17–42; 65–100.
10 See Hägg and Utas (2003), with Utas (1995). Metiochus, Hdt. 6.41; Polycrates' daughter, Hdt. 3.124. Mosaic, see Stoneman (2012) p.11.
11 Dio Chrysostom, e.g. 43.3; 44.10.
12 Dio, 73; 11, esp. 11.145; 11.147–49. See Swain (1996) pp.187–241; Bowie (2013) pp.243–4.
13 See Marincola (2012); with Duff (1999).
14 Plutarch, *Table Talk*, 1.1.1–5.
15 Plut. *De.glor.Ath.* 3; with Athanassaki (2016) and below, pp.167–8.
16 Plut. *De.glor.Ath.* 5.
17 Plut. *De.glor.Ath.* 8, citing Dem. 18.208.
18 Plut. *Precepts of Statecraft*, 17.
19 Plato, *Menexenus*, 235a–b, see above, pp.141–3.
20 Spawforth (1994) pp.245–6.
21 Plut. *Mal.Hdt.* 1–9.
22 Hdt from Halicarnassus: Plut. *Mal.Hdt.* 35; 43. Alcmaeonids: *Mal.Hdt.* 27, with 16 and 70. See above, pp.87 and 105–6.
23 Plut. *Mal.Hdt.* 26, citing Diyllus of Athens.
24 Plut. *Mal.Hdt.* 26; with Xen. *Ana.* 3.2.12, see above, pp.72 and 100.
25 Plut. *Mal.Hdt.* 43; Hdt. 7.62.
26 van Wees (2004) p.181 with n.50 notes the onset of resentment in attributing victories to equipment; Konijnendijk (2012) esp. p.6 notes how Herodotus' and Aeschylus' explanation gave way to an opposite view, which emphasised personal difference.
27 Plut. *Mal.Hdt.* 27.
28 Plut. *Them.* 3.
29 Plut. *Arist.* 5.
30 Plut. *Cim.* 4–5.
31 Plut. *Cim.* 3, and see the *synkrisis*, the comparison, of both *Lives*.
32 Plut. *Cim.* 19.
33 Plut. *Pericles,* 21; 29–31; *synkrisis* 3: 'the Peloponnesian War was a ground of great complaint against Pericles. For it is said to have been brought on by his contention

that no concession should be made to Sparta . . . the courteous and gentle conduct of Fabius towards Minucius contrasts forcibly with the factious opposition of Pericles to Cimon and Thucydides, who were both good and true men.'

34 Plut. *Cim.* 28, see above, p.125.

35 See with this Plut. *Alex.* 37 and 56.

36 See Reader and Chvála-Smith (1996), with Harrison (1972) pp.358–60, and Philostratus, *Lives of the Sophists*, 533.

37 Justin, *Phillipic Histories*, 2.9.

38 Stoa, Paus. 1.15; ghosts and graves, 1.32; slaves freed at Corinth, 7.15.7, with 10.20.2, noted by Notopulos (1941). See Habicht (1985) esp. pp.95–116.

39 Most proud of Marathon and Aeschylus' epigram, Paus. 1.14.5; list of benefactors, 8.52; Leonidas, 1.13.5; the battlefield, 1.32. For Pausanias' extensive knowledge of Greek writers, see Habicht (1985) pp.97–8.

40 Philostratus, *Lives of the Sophists*, 2.

41 Bowie (2013) pp.251–2; Athanassaki (2016) pp.221–7. It is possible that the inscriptions and fragments found at his home were copies, but there is a good chance that they are the originals.

42 See Bowie (2013).

43 Athanassaki (2016) esp. p.221 shows how the family established the connection.

44 Plut. *Table Talk*, 8.4; 9.14, Athanassaki (2016) p.217, with p226, citing the suggestion first made by Ewan Bowie.

45 Lucian, *Tragic Zeus*, 31. In *Teacher of Rhetors*, 18, Lucian pokes fun by having a teacher advise would-be speech-makers to bring up Marathon and Cynegeirus as often as possible, and 'always have Athos being sailed through, the Hellespont crossed on foot, and the sunlight cut-off by Median missiles . . .'. See Athanassaki (2016) pp. 215–19; 226–7; Bowie (2013) pp.248–50.

46 Aelian, *On the Nature of Animals*, 7.38. Plutarch, *Cato*, 5, has his own dog story: Xanthippus gave an honourable burial to the dog that swam beside his ship when the Athenians abandoned their city. Plutarch is making the point that Cato did wrong in selling his slaves when they became elderly, much as it is cruel to reject a donkey or a dog once they need care.

47 Aelius Aristides, *1, Panath.* 104–10; 347; 126 and 167; 114.

48 Aelius Aristides, *3, On the Four.* See Bowie (2013) pp.247–8, with Trapp (2020) for a discussion of Aelius Aristides' work within the context of his times.

49 Trapp (2020).

50 Libanius, *Oration* 30 *To Theodosius. For the Temples,* 31–2.

51 Synesios of Cyrene, *Epistle* 35, see Stansbury-O'Donnell (2005) p.74, with n.7.

52 A story from the Greek historian Zosimus 5.6.2, written shortly after the event. See Gerkhe (2009) p.94.

12 Marathon after Antiquity

1 Zali (2015); de Bakker (2015).
2 See above, p.158. Hägg and Utas (2003), with Utas (1995).
3 Vanderpool (1966) pp.93–106.
4 See Constantine (2011), with Pollard (2020).
5 Chandler (1776) pp. 165–6. Constantine (2011) ch.9; Krentz (2010) p.111 notes the atmospheric remark about wolves.
6 1792, Paris, Bibliothèque Nationale, Collection Barbier, no. 1341. See Galanakis (2013), with Krentz (2010) pp.114–15, 122–3.
7 Leake (1829); with Hammond (1968) pp.21–6. Galanakis (2013) for more collectors and the unreliability of some attributions.
8 Vanderpool (1966) p.101 n.15.
9 Africa (2011) p.252.
10 Herodotus: Ellis (2015); education plus, see e.g. Sachs (2010) pp.1–46; Vasunia (2005).
11 See e.g. Nippel (2002) pp.304–10; Hall (2006) ch. 7.
12 Rood (2007); Rood (2016); Smith (2016).
13 Byron, *Don Juan*, Canto 3. 86, 95 and 96.
14 On Byron's admiration for 'Promethean' Napoleon, Bloom (1960).
15 A phrase from Byron, *The Plain of Marathon*. In a further example of how such comparisons worked both ways, Byron had called for 'a new Thermopylae' and new Miltiades, but saw nothing to celebrate in Waterloo.
16 Rood (2007) expands on this.
17 Van Steen (2007); with (2013); Hall (2006) p.223.
18 St Clair (2008) ch. 2; Heraclides and Dialla (2015) ch. 6.
19 St Clair (2008) p.105.
20 Gehrke (2009) pp.94–5, with Hegel, lectures given in the 1820s–30s collected as *Philosophy of History* (1970) pp.314ff.
21 Goethe (2019) p.362.
22 Walker (1987) pp.48–52.
23 Zia-Ebrahimi (2011).
24 Roche (2012); Hardwick (2013) pp.285–7, drawing on Elizabeth Vandiver (2010).
25 See Hall and Stead (2020).
26 *The Battle of Marathon: a poem written in early youth*, limited publication in 1820 and 1991. On her education, see Hurst (2006) pp.2–10, 31, 189–90.
27 Brontë (1835) in Alexander (1991) vol 2.2. pp.305–6.
28 Brontë (2010) with Nevin, http://www.omc.obta.al.uw.edu.pl/myth-survey/item/989
29 Cunliffe (1909); Gehrke (2009) pp.96–7; Athanassaki (2016) pp. 227–8.
30 Gehrke (2009) pp.96–7.

31 See Van Steen (2015).

32 Van Steen (2015) pp.281-2. The other features were Constantine the Great, the 961 CE re-conquest of Crete, and the 1940 repulse of the Italian invasion.

33 Zia-Ebrahimi (2011), (2016) Ch.8; Grigor (2005).

34 Llewellyn Morgan, *On Common Ground: Thoughts on Competition over Central Asian Origins, with reference to the British in India, the Parsis, and Modern Japan*, Maynooth University (online) 25.11.2020; Stewart (2010).

35 See the bibliography, with Lianeri (2007); Rhodes (2013).

36 Renault (1964); Nevin: http://www.omc.obta.al.uw.edu.pl/myth-survey/item/994

37 Trease (1997); Nevin: http://www.omc.obta.al.uw.edu.pl/myth-survey/item/872; Ross (1997); Nevin: http://www.omc.obta.al.uw.edu.pl/myth-survey/item/870

38 Reynolds (2006); Nevin: http://www.omc.obta.al.uw.edu.pl/myth-survey/item/869

39 Smailes (2011); Nevin: http://www.omc.obta.al.uw.edu.pl/myth-survey/item/871

40 Yakin (2012); Nevin: http://www.omc.obta.al.uw.edu.pl/myth-survey/item/335

41 Miller, *300* (1998; film, 2006); *Xerxes* (2018; film 2014). With Easton (2019).

42 Greenberg (2017); Nevin: http://www.omc.obta.al.uw.edu.pl/myth-survey/item/342

43 Papadatos (2015); Santos: http://www.omc.obta.al.uw.edu.pl/myth-survey/item/704

44 Mandilaras (2017); Volioti: http://www.omc.obta.al.uw.edu.pl/myth-survey/item/644

Bibliography

Africa, Thomas. *A Historian's Palette: Studies in Greek and Roman History*. Regina Books, 2011.

Alexander, Christine A. *An Edition of the Early Writings of Charlotte Brontë: Volume II, Part 1 and 2: The Rise of Angria 1833–1835*. Blackwell, 1991.

Anderson, J. K. 'Hoplite Weapons and Offensive Arms."' *Hoplites: The Classical Greek Battle Experience*, ed. V. D. Hanson, Routledge, 1991, pp.15–37.

Arafat, K. W. 'Marathon in Art'. *Marathon – 2,500 Years: Proceedings of the Marathon Conference 2010*, ed. C. Carey and M. Edwards, BICS 124, 2013, pp.79–90.

Athanassaki, Lucia. 'Who Was Eucles? Plutarch and His Sources on the Legendary Marathon-Runner (*De Gloria Atheniensium* 347CD).' *A Versatile Gentleman: Consistency in Plutarch's Writing.* ed. J. Opsomer et al., Leuven University Press, 2016, pp.213–28.

Avery, H. C. 'The Number of Persian Dead at Marathon.' *Historia*, 22.4, 1973, p.757.

Balcer, J. M. 'The Persian Wars against Greece: A Reassessment.' *Historia*, 38.2, 1989, pp.127–43.

Bicknell, P. 'The Command Structure and Generals of the Marathon Campaign.' *L'Antiquité Classique*, 39, 1970, pp.427–42.

Bigwood, J. M. 'Ctesias as Historian of the Persian Wars.' *Phoenix*, 32.1, 1978, pp.19–41.

Billows, R. A. *Marathon: How One Battle Changed Western Civilization*. Duckworth, 2010.

Bloom, Harold. 'Napoleon and Prometheus: The Romantic Myth of Organic Energy.' *Yale French Studies*, 26, 1960, pp.79–82.

Boardman, John and Finn, David. *The Parthenon and Its Sculptures*. Thames and Hudson, 1985.

Boedeker, Deborah. 'Protesilaos and the End of Herodotus' *Histories*.' *Classical Antiquity*, 7.1, 1988, pp.30–48.

Bowie, Ewan. 'Marathon in the Greek Culture of the Second Century AD.' *Marathon – 2,500 Years: Proceedings of the Marathon Conference 2010*, ed. C. Carey and M. Edwards, *BICS* 124, 2013, pp.241–54.

Briant, Pierre. 'History and Ideology: The Greeks and "Persian Decadence."' *Greeks and Barbarians*, ed. Thomas Harrison, Edinburgh University Press, 2002, pp.193–210.

Bridges, Emma. *Imagining Xerxes: Ancient Perspectives on a Persian King*. Bloomsbury, 2015.

Brontë, P. B, *The History of the Young Men*, ed. William Baker et al., Juvenilia Press, 2010.

Buck, R. J. *A History of Boeotia*. University of Alberta, 1979.

Burgess, Jonathan. *Homer*. Bloomsbury, 2014.

Burn, A. R. *Persia and the Greeks: The Defence of the West, c. 546–478 BC*. 2nd ed. Duckworth, 1984.

Carey, Christopher. 'Marathon and the Construction of the Comic Past.' *Marathon – 2,500 Years: Proceedings of the Marathon Conference 2010*, ed. C. Carey and M. Edwards, *BICS* 124, 2013, pp.123–42.

Castriota, D. *Myth, Ethos, and Actuality: Official Art in Fifth-Century B.C. Athens*. University of Wisconsin Press, 1992.

Cawkwell, G. L. 'The Foundation of the Second Athenian Confederacy'. *Classical Quarterly*, 23.1, 1973, pp.47–60.

Cawkwell, G. L. 'Orthodoxy and Hoplites.' *Classical Quarterly*, 39.2, 1989, pp.375–89.

Cawkwell, G. L. *The Greek Wars: The Failure of Persia*. Oxford University Press, 2005.

Chandler, Richard. *Travels in Greece*. 1776.

Charles, M. B. 'Herodotus, Body Armour and Achaemenid Infantry.' *Historia*, 61.3, 2012, pp.257–69.

Colburn, H. P. 'Orientalism, Postcolonialism, and the Achaemenid Empire: Meditations on Bruce Lincoln's "Religion, Empire, and Torture."' *BICS* 54.2, 2011, pp.87–103.

Colburn, H. P. 'Connectivity and Communication in the Achaemenid Empire.' *Journal of the Economic and Social History of the Orient*, 56.1, 2013, pp.29–52.

Connelly, J. B. *The Parthenon Enigma*. Alfred Knopf, 2014.

Connor, W. R. 'Two Notes on Cimon.' *TAPhA*, 98, 1967, pp.67–75.

Constantine, David. *In the Footsteps of the Gods: Travellers to Greece and the Quest for the Hellenic Ideal*. Bloomsbury, 2011.

Cook, John. *The Persian Empire*. Dent and Sons, 1983.

Crowley, Jason. *The Psychology of the Athenian Hoplite: The Culture of Combat in Classical Athens*. Cambridge University Press, 2012.

Cunliffe, J. W. 'Browning and the Marathon Race.' *PMLA*, 24, 1909, pp.154–63.

Davies, J. K. *Democracy and Classical Greece*. 2nd ed., Fontana Press, 1978.

de Bakker, Mathieu. 'Explaining the End of an Empire: The Use of Ancient Greek Religious Views in Late Byzantine Historiography.' *Histos Supplement*, 4, 2015, pp.127–71.

Delaporte, Louis-Joseph. *Catalogue Des Cylindres Orientaux et Des Cachets Assyro-Babyloniens, Perses et Syrocappadociens de La Bibliothèque Nationale, l'Académie Des Inscriptions et Belles-Lettres*. 1910.

Delbruck, H. *Geschichte Der Kriegskunst*. 1920.

Doenges, Norman, A. 'The Campaign and Battle of Marathon.' *Historia*, 47.1, 1998, pp.1–17.

Duff, Timothy E. *Plutarch's Lives: Exploring Virtue and Vice*. Oxford University Press, 1999.

Easton, Seán. 'The Dueling Greek Golden Ages of *300: Rise of an Empire* (2014).' *Screening the Golden Ages of the Classical Tradition*, ed. Meredith Safran, Edinburgh University Press, 2019, pp.101–18.

Efstathiou, Athanasios. 'The Historical Example of Marathon as Used in the Speeches *On the False Embassy, On the Crown*, and *Against Ctesiphon* by Demosthenes and

Aeschines.' *Marathon – 2,500 Years: Proceedings of the Marathon Conference 2010*, ed. C. Carey and M. Edwards, *BICS* 124, 2013, pp.181–98.

Ellis, Anthony. 'Herodotus Magister Vitae, or: Herodotus and God in the Protestant Reformation.' *Histos Supplement*, 4, 2015, pp.173–245.

Evans, J. A. S. 'Note on Miltiades' Capture of Lemnos.' *Classical Philology*, 58.3, 1963, pp.168–70.

Evans, J. A. S. 'Herodotus and the Battle of Marathon.' *Historia*, 42.3, 1993, pp.279–307.

Fairbanks, Arthur, *The First Philosophers of Greece*. Trubner, 1898.

Fairey, Emily. 'Persians in Frank Miller's *300* and Greek Vase Painting.' *Classics and Comics*, ed. George Kovacs and C. W. Marshall, Oxford University Press, 2011, pp. 159–72.

Flower, M. A. 'From Simonides to Isocrates: The Fifth-Century Origins of Fourth-Century Panhellenism.' *Classical Antiquity*, 19.1, 2000, pp.65–101.

Forsdyke, Sara. *Exile, Ostracism, and Democracy: The Politics of Expulsion in Ancient Greece*. Princeton University Press, 2005.

Francis, E. D., and Vickers, Michael. 'The Oenoe Painting in the Stoa Poikile and Herodotus' Account of Marathon.' *ABSA*, 80, 1985, pp.99–113.

Funke, Peter. 'Marathon and the Construction of the Persian Wars in Post-Antique Times.' *Marathon – 2,500 Years: Proceedings of the Marathon Conference 2010*, ed. C. Carey and M. Edwards, *BICS* 124, 2013, pp.267–74.

Galanakis, Yannis. 'Re-Thinking Marathon: Two 'memorabilia' from the Battle of Marathon at the Pitt-Rivers.' *Rethinking Pitt-Rivers: Analysing the Activities of a Nineteenth-Century Collector*, 2013, available at: http://web.prm.ox.ac.uk/rpr/index.php/object-biography-index/1-prmcollection/648-marathon-spearheads.html

Garrison, Mark. 'By the Favor of Ahuramazda: Kingship and the Divine in the Early Achaemenid Period.' *More Than Men, Less Than Gods: Studies on Royal Cult and Imperial Worship*, ed. P. P. Iossif et al., 2011, pp.15–104.

Gehrke, Hans-Joachim. 'From Athenian Identity to European Ethnicity. The Cultural Biography of the Myth of Marathon.' *Ethnic Constructs in Antiquity: The Role of Power and Tradition*, Amsterdam University Press, 2009, pp.85–100.

Gensheimer, Maryl. 'Metaphors for Marathon in the Sculptural Program of the Athenian Treasury at Delphi.' *Hesperia*, 86.1, 2017, pp.1–42.

Georges, Pericles. *Barbarian Asia and the Greek Experience*. Johns Hopkins University Press, 1994.

Georges, Pericles. 'Persian Ionia under Darius: The Revolt Reconsidered.' *Historia*, 49.1, 2000, pp.1–39.

Gillis, Daniel. *Collaboration with the Persians*. Franz Steiner, 1979.

Greenberg, Isabel. *The Ancient Greeks*. Francis Lincoln, 2017.

Gresseth, Gerald. 'The Gilgamesh Epic and Homer.' *Classical Journal*, 70, 1975, pp.1–18.

Grigor, Talinn. 'Preserving the Antique Modern: Persepolis '71.' *Future Anterior: Journal of Historic Preservation, History, Theory, and Criticism*, 2.1, 2005, pp.22–9.

Gruen, Erich. 'Stesimbrotus on Miltiades and Themistocles.' *Classical Antiquity*, 3, 1970, pp.91–8.

Habicht, Christian. *Pausanias' Guide to Ancient Greece*. University of California Press, 1985.

Hägg, Tomas, and Utas, Bo, eds. *The Virgin and Her Lover: Fragments Ancient Greek Novel and a Persian Epic Poem*. Brill, 2003.

Hale, John. 'Not Patriots, Not Farmers, Not Amateurs: Greek Soldiers of Fortune and the Origins of Hoplite Warfare.' *Men of Bronze: Hoplite Warfare in Ancient Greece*, ed. Donald Kagan and Gregory Viggiano, Princeton University Press, 2013, pp.176–93.

Hall, Edith. *Inventing the Barbarian: Greek Self-Definition through Tragedy*. Oxford University Press, 1989.

Hall, Edith. *The Theatrical Cast of Athens: Interactions Between Ancient Greek Drama and Society*. Oxford University Press, 2006.

Hall, Edith, and Henry Stead. *A People's History of Classics and Graeco-Roman Antiquity in Britain and Ireland 1689 to 1939*. Routledge, 2020.

Hall, Jonathan M. *Ethnic Identity in Greek Antiquity*. Cambridge University Press, 1997.

Hall Sternberg, Rachel. 'The Transport of Sick and Wounded Soldiers in Classical Greece.' *Phoenix*, 53.3, 1999, pp.191–205.

Hamel, D. *Athenian Generals: Military Authority in the Classical Period*. Brill, 1998.

Hammond, N. G. L. 'The Philaids and the Chersonese.' *Classical Quarterly*, 6, 1956, pp.113–29.

Hammond, N. G. L. 'The Campaign and Battle of Marathon.' *Journal of Hellenic Studies*, 88, 1968, pp.13–57.

Hanson, V. D. 'Hoplite Technology in Phalanx Battle.' *Hoplites. The Classical Battle Experience*, ed. V. D. Hanson, Routledge, 1991, pp.63–84.

Hardwick, Lorna. 'Moving Targets, Modern Contests: Marathon and Cultural Memory.' *Marathon – 2,500 Years: Proceedings of the Marathon Conference 2010*, ed. C. Carey and M. Edwards, *BICS* 124, 2013, pp.275–88.

Harrison, Evelyn. 'The Composition of the Amazonomachy on the Shield of Athena Parthenos.' *Hesperia*, 35.2, 1966, pp.107–33.

Harrison, Evelyn. 'The South Frieze of the Nike Temple and the Marathon Painting in the Painted Stoa.' *American Journal of Archaeology*, 76.4, 1972, pp.353–78.

Harrison, Thomas. *Divinity and History: The Religion of Herodotus*. Clarendon Press, 2000a.

Harrison, Thomas. *The Emptiness of Asia: Aeschylus' 'Persians' and the History of the 5th Century BC*. Duckworth, 2000b.

Harrison, Thomas. *Writing Ancient Persia*. Bloomsbury, 2011.

Hart, J. *Herodotus and Greek History*. Croom Helm, 1982.

Hau, Lisa, I. *Moral History from Herodotus to Diodorus Siculus*. Edinburgh University Press, 2016.

Heraclides, Alexis, and Ada Dialla. *Humanitarian Intervention in the Long Nineteenth Century: Setting the Precedent*. Manchester University Press, 2015.

Higbie, Caroline. *The Lindian Chronicle and the Greek Creation of Their Past*. Oxford University Press, 2003.

Hignett, C. *Xerxes' Invasion of Greece*. Clarendon Press, 1963.

Hurst, Isobel. *Victorian Women Writers and the Classics: The Feminine of Homer*. Oxford University Press, 2006.

Jacoby, Felix. 'Some Athenian Epigrams from the Persian Wars.' *Hesperia*, 14.3, 1945, pp.157–211.

Jameson, M. H. 'Sacrifice before Battle.' *Hoplites: The Classical Greek Battle Experience*, ed. V. D. Hanson, Routledge, 1991, pp.197–227.

Kagan, Donald, and Gregory Viggiano, eds. *Men of Bronze: Hoplite Warfare in Ancient Greece*. Princeton University Press, 2013.

Kearns, Emily. *The Heroes of Attica*. University of London, *BICS* 57, 1989.

King, L. W., and R. C. Thompson. *The Sculptures and Inscription of Darius the Great on the Rock of Behistûn in Persia*. British Museum Press, 1907.

Konijnendijk, Roel. '"Neither the Less Valorous nor the Weaker": Persian Military Might and the Battle of Plataia.' *Historia*, 61.1, 2012, pp.1–17.

Konstantinopoulos, V. L. 'The Persian Wars and Political Conflicts in Athens.' *Marathon – 2,500 Years: Proceedings of the Marathon Conference 2010*, ed. C. Carey and M. Edwards, *BICS* 124, 2013, pp.63–8.

Krause, C. *Eretria Ausgrabungen Und Forschungen IV. Das Westtor Ergebnisse Der Ausgrabungen 1964–1968*. Francke Verlag, 1972.

Kremmydas, Christos. 'Alexander the Great, Athens, and the Rhetoric of the Persian Wars.' *Marathon – 2,500 Years: Proceedings of the Marathon Conference 2010*, ed. C. Carey and M. Edwards, *BICS* 124, 2013, pp.199–212.

Krentz, Peter. 'Fighting by the Rules: The Invention of the Hoplite Agon.' *Hesperia*, 71.1, 2002, pp.23–39.

Krentz, Peter. *The Battle of Marathon*. Yale University Press, 2010.

Kron, U. 'Patriotic Heroes.' *Ancient Greek Hero Cult: Proceedings of the Fifth International Seminar on Ancient Greek Cult, 21–23 April 1995*, ed. R. Hägg, 1999, pp.61–83.

Kucewicz, Cezary. *The Treatment of the War Dead in Archaic Athens: An Ancestral Custom*. Bloomsbury, 2020.

Kuhrt, Amelie. 'Earth and Water.' *Achaemenid History: Method and Theory*, ed. A. Kuhrt and H. Sancisi-Weerdenburg, Nederlands Instituut voor het Nabije Oosten, 1988, pp.87–99.

Kuhrt, Amelie. *The Ancient Near East, c. 3000–330, Vol.2*. Routledge, 1995.

Lane Fox, Robin, ed. *The Long March: Xenophon and the Ten Thousand*. Yale University Press, 2004.

Lazenby, John. 'The Killing Zone.' *Hoplites: The Classical Greek Battle Experience*, ed. V. D. Hanson, Routledge, 1991, pp.87–109.

Leake, William. *The Demi of Attica I*. 1829.

Lewis, David. 'Datis the Mede.' *Journal of Hellenic Studies*, 100, 1980, pp.194–5.

Lianeri, Alexandra. 'The Persian Wars as the "Origin" of Historiography: Ancient and Modern Orientalism in George Grote's *History of Greece*.' *Cultural Responses to the Persian Wars: Antiquity to the Third Millennium*, ed. E. Bridges et al., Oxford University Press, 2007, pp.331–54.

Llewellyn-Jones, Lloyd. 'The Great Kings of the Fourth-Century and the Greek Memory of the Persian Past.' *Greek Notions of the Past in the Archaic and Classical Eras: History without Historians*, ed. John Marincola et al., Edinburgh University Press, 2012, pp.317–46.

Llewellyn-Jones, Lloyd. *King and Court in Ancient Persia 559–331 BCE: Debates and Documents in Ancient History*. Edinburgh University Press, 2013.

Lloyd, A. B. 'The Inscription of Udjahorresnet: A Collaborator's Testament.' *Journal of Egyptian Archaeology*, 68, 1982, pp.166–80.

Loraux, N. *The Invention of Athens: The Funeral Oration in the Classical City*. Trans. A. Sheridan, 1986.

Luginbill, Robert D. 'A Most Disastrous Success.' *L'Antiquité Classique*, 83, 2014, pp.1–14.

Mandilaras, Philippos. *The Battle of Marathon*. Papadopoulos Publishing, 2017.

Marincola, John. 'The Persian Wars in Fourth-Century Oratory and Historiography.' *Cultural Responses to the Persian Wars: Antiquity to the Third Millennium*, ed. E. Bridges et al., 2007, pp.105–25.

Marincola, John. 'The Fairest Victor. Plutarch, Aristides, and the Persian Wars.' *Histos*, 6, 2012, pp.91–113.

Martin, Bridget. *Harmful Interaction between the Living and the Dead in Greek Tragedy*. Liverpool University Press, 2020.

Mastrapas, Antonis. 'The Battle of Marathon and the Introduction of Pan's Worship to Athens: The Political Dimension of a Legend through Written Evidence and Archaeological Finds.' *Marathon – 2,500 Years: Proceedings of the Marathon Conference 2010*, ed. C. Carey and M. Edwards, BICS 124, 2013, pp.111–22.

Miller, Frank. *300*. Dark Horse, 1998.

Miller, Frank. *Xerxes: The Fall of the House of Darius and the Rise of Alexander*. Dark Horse, 2018.

Miller, Margaret C. 'Persians in the Greek Imagination.' *Mediterranean Archaeology*, 19/20, 2007, pp.109–23.

Miller, Margaret C. 'Persians: The Oriental Other.' *Notes in the History of Art*, 15.1, *Representations of the 'other' in Athenian Art c. 510–400 B.C.*, 1995, pp.39–44.

Mitchell, L. G. '"What Age Were You When the Mede Came?" Cyrus the Great and Western Anatolia.' *Achaemenid Anatolia: Persian Presence and Impact in the Western Satrapies 546–330 BC. Proceedings of an International Symposium at the Swedish Research Institute in Istanbul, 7–8 September 2017*, ed. A. P. Dahlén, Uppsala University, 2020, pp.197–216.

Molitor, M. V. 'The Song of Datis.' *Mnemosyne*, 39.1, 1986, pp.128–31.

Morgan, Janett. *Greek Perspectives on the Achaemenid Empire: Persia Through the Looking Glass*. Edinburgh University Press, 2016.

Munro, J. A. R. 'Some Observations on the Persian Wars.' *Journal of Hellenic Studies*, 19, 1899, pp.294–333.

Nevin, Sonya. *Military Leaders and Sacred Space in Classical Greek Warfare: Temples, Sanctuaries, and Conflict in Antiquity*. Bloomsbury, 2017.

Nippel, Wilfried. 'The Construction of the "Other."' *Greeks and Barbarians*, ed. Thomas Harrison, Edinburgh University Press, 2002, pp.278–310.

Notopoulos, J. A. 'The Slaves at the Battle of Marathon.' *American Journal of Philology*, 62.3, 1941, pp.352–4.

Osborne, Robin. *Greece in the Making, 1200–479 B.C.* Routledge, 1996.

Papadatos, Alecos, and Abraham Kawa. *Democracy*. Bloomsbury, 2015.

Parian, Saber Amiri. 'A New Edition of the Elamite Version of the Behistun Inscription (II).' *Cuneiform Digital Library Bulletin*, 2020.1, 2020.

Parian, Saber Amiri. 'A New Edition of the Elamite Version of the Behistun Inscription (I).' *Cuneiform Digital Library Bulletin*, 2017.3, 2017.

Parke, H. W. *The Festivals of the Athenians*. Thames and Hudson, 1977.

Parker, Robert. 'Greek States and Greek Oracles.' *Crux: Essays Presented to G.E.M. de Ste Croix on His 75th Birthday*, ed. P. Cartledge and F. D. Harvey, Duckworth, 1985, pp.298–326.

Parker, Robert. 'Sacrifice and Battle.' *War and Violence in Ancient Greece*, ed. Hans van Wees, Duckworth, 2000, pp.299–314.

Parker, Robert. 'One Man's Piety: The Religious Dimension of the *Anabasis*.' *The Long March: Xenophon and the Ten Thousand*, ed. Robin Lane Fox, Yale University Press, 2004, pp.131–53.

Pollard, Lucy. *The Quest for Classical Greece: Early Modern Travel to the Greek World*. Bloomsbury, 2020.

Pollitt, J. J. *Art in the Hellenistic Age*. Cambridge University Press, 1986.

Potts, Daniel. 'Iran.' *The Oxford Handbook of the Archaeology of Ritual and Religion*, Oxford University Press, 2011, pp.811–25.

Powell, Anton. *A Companion to Sparta: Two Volumes*. Wiley-Blackwell, 2017.

Pritchard, David. 'The Symbiosis between Democracy and War: The Case of Ancient Athens.' *War, Democracy and Culture in Classical Athens*, ed. D. Pritchard, Cambridge University Press, 2010, pp.1–62.

Pritchard, David. '"The Fractured Imaginary": Popular Thinking on Military Matters in Fifth-Century Athens.' *Ancient History*, 28.1, 1998, pp.38–61.

Pritchett, W. K. *Studies in Ancient Greek Topography: Part 1*. California University Press, 1965.

Ramage, Andrew. 'Lydian Houses and Architectural Terracottas.' *Archaeological Exploration of Sardis*, Harvard University Press, 1978.

Raubitschek, A. E. 'Das Datislied.' *The School of Hellas: Essays on Greek History, Archaeology and Literature*, ed. Dirk Obbink and Paul Vander-Waerdt, Oxford University Press, 1991a, pp.146–55.

Raubitschek, A. E. 'Ostracism: The Athenian Ostraka.' *The School of Hellas: Essays on Greek History, Archaeology and Literature*, ed. D. Obbink and P. A. Vander Waerdt, Oxford University Press, 1991b.

Raubitschek, A. E. *Dedications from the Athenian Acropolis: A Catalogue of the Inscriptions of the Sixth and Fifth Centuries B.C.* Ares, 1999.

Reader, W. W., and A. J. Chvála-Smith, eds. *The Severed Hand and the Upright Corpse: The Declamations of Marcus Antonius Polemo*. Scholars Press, 1996.

Reber, K. *Eretria Ausgrabungen Und Forschungen X. Die Klassischen Und Hellenistischen Wohnhauser Im Westquartier*. Francke Verlag, 1980.

Renault, Mary. *Lion in the Gateway: The Heroic Battles of the Greeks and Persians at Marathon, Salamis and Thermopylae*. Hillside Education, 1964; 2013.

Renehan, Robert. 'The Staunching of Odysseus' Blood: The Healing Power of Magic.' *American Journal of Philology*, 113.1, 1992, pp.1–4.

Reynolds, Susan. *The First Marathon: The Legend of Pheidippides*. Albert Whitman, 2006.

Rhodes, P. J. 'The Battle of Marathon and Modern Scholarship.' *Marathon – 2,500 Years: Proceeding of the Marathon Conference 2010*, ed. C. Carey and M. Edwards, *BICS* 124, 2013, pp.3–22.

Rhodes, P. J., and Osborne, R., eds. *Greek Historical Inscriptions: 404–323* BC. Oxford University Press, 2003.

Roche, Helen. 'Go Tell the Prussians: The Spartan Paradigm in Prussian Military Thought during the Long Nineteenth Century.' *New Voices in Classical Reception Studies*, 7, 2012, pp.25–39.

Rood, Timothy. 'From Marathon to Waterloo: Byron, Battle-Monuments and the Persian Wars.' *Cultural Responses to the Persian Wars: Antiquity to the Third Millennium*, ed. E. Bridges et al., Oxford University Press, 2007, pp.267–98.

Rood, Timothy. '"Je Viens Comme Thémistocle": Napoleon and National Identity after Waterloo.' *Graeco-Roman Antiquity and the Idea of Nationalism in the 19th Century: Case Studies*, ed. Thorsten Fögen and Richard Warren, De Gruyter, 2016.

Ross, Stewart. *Athens Is Saved!* Readzone, 1997.

Sachs, Jonathan. *Romantic Antiquity: Rome in the British Imagination, 1789–1832*. Oxford University Press, 2010.

Samons II, Loren J. 'Kimon, Kallias and Peace with Persia.' *Historia*, 47.2, 1998, pp.129–40.

Sealey, Raphael. *A History of the Greek City-States 700–338* BC. 1978.

Sealey, Raphael. 'The Pit and the Well: The Persian Heralds of 491 BC.' *Classical Journal*, 72.1, 1976, pp.13–20.

Sekunda, Nicholas. 'The Might of the Persian Empire.' *The Ancient World at War*, ed. Philip de Souza, Thames and Hudson, 2008, pp.67–86.

Shapur Shahbazi, A. 'Croesus.' *Encyclopaedia Iranica*, VI/4, 1993, pp.401–2, available at: http://www.iranicaonline.org/articles/croesus

Siewert, Peter, ed. *Ostrakismos Testimonien 1. Die Zeugnisse Antiker Autoren Der Inschriften Und Ostraka Über Das Athenische Scherbengericht Aus Vorhellenistischer Zeit (487–322)*. Franz Steiner Verlag, 2002.

Smailes, Gary. *Marathon*. Franklin Watts, 2011.

Smith, A. D. 'Classical Ideals and the Formation of Modern Nations in Europe.' *Graeco-Roman Antiquity and the Idea of Nationalism in the 19th Century: Case Studies*, ed. Thorsten Fögen and Richard Warren, De Gruyter, 2016, pp.19–44.

Sommer, B. D. 'The Babylonian Akitu Festival: Rectifying the King or Renewing the Cosmos?' *Journal of the Ancient Near Eastern Society*, 27, 2001, pp.81–95.

Spawforth, Antony. 'Symbol of Unity? The Persian-Wars Tradition in the Roman Empire.' *Greek Historiography*, ed. S. Hornblower, Clarendon Press, 1994, pp.233–47.

Spyropoulos, George. *Η Στήλη Των Πεσόντων Στη Μάχη Του Μαραθώνα Από Την Έπαυλη Του Ηρώδη Αττικού Στην Εύα Κυνουρίας*. 2009.

St Clair, William. *That Greece Might Still Be Free: The Philhellenes in the War of Independence*. Open Book Publishers, 2008.

Stansbury-O'Donnell, M. D. 'The Painting Programme in the Stoa Poikile.' *Periklean Athens and Its Legacy: Problems and Perspectives*, ed. J. Barringer and J. Hurwit, University of Texas Press, 2005, pp.73–87.

Steinbock, Bernd. 'A Lesson in Patriotism: Lycurgus' Against Leocrates, the Ideology of the Ephebeia, and Athenian Social Memory.' *Classical Antiquity*, 30.2, 2011, pp.279–317.

Stewart, Sarah. 'The Zoroastrian Burial Ground at Brookwood Cemetery.' *The Middle East in London*, Sept., 2010, pp.6–7.

Stolper, Matthew W. 'The Oriental Institute and the Persepolis Fortification Archive.' *Die Verwaltung Im Achämenidenreich – Imperiale Muster Und Strukturen. Administration in the Achaemenid Empire – Tracing the Imperial Signature.* ed. Bruno Jacobs et al., Harrassowitz Verlag, 2017, pp.37–59.

Stoneman, Richard. 'Persian Aspects of the Romance Tradition.' *Alexander Romance in Persia and the East*, ed. R. Stoneman et al., Barkhuis, 2012, pp.3–17.

Stronach, David. 'Court Dress and Riding Dress at Persepolis: New Approaches to Old Questions.' *Elam and Persia*, ed. J. Ivarez-Mon and M. Garrison, Eisenbrauns, 2011, pp.475–88.

Swain, Simon. *Hellenism and Empire: Language, Classicism, and Power in the Greek World, AD 50–250*. Clarendon Press, 1996.

Thomas, Rosalind. *Oral Tradition and the Written Record in Classical Athens*. Cambridge University Press, 1989.

Thomas, Rosalind. *Herodotus in Context: Ethnography, Science and the Art of Persuasion*. Cambridge University Press, 2000.

Tod, M. N. *Greek Historical Inscriptions. Volume 2*. Clarendon Press, 1948.

Trapp, M. B. 'With All Due Respect to Plato: The Platonic Orations of Aelius Aristides.' *TAPhA*, 150.1, 2020, pp.85–113.

Trease, Geoffrey. *Mission to Marathon*. A & C Black, 1997.

Tuplin, C. J. *The Failings of Empire: A Reading of Xenophon's Hellenica 2.3.11-7.5.27*. Franz Steiner, 1993.

Tuplin, C. J. 'War and Peace in Achaemenid Imperial Ideology.' *Electrum*, 24, 2017, pp.31–54.

Utas, Bo. 'The Ardent Lover and the Virgin – a Greek Romance in Muslim Lands.' *Acta Orientalia Academiae Scientiarum Hungaricae*, 48.1, 1995, pp.229–39.

van der Veer, J. A. G. 'The Battle of Marathon: A Topographical Survey.' *Mnemosyne*, 35.3, 1982, pp.290–321.

Van Steen, Gonda. 'Enacting History and Patriotic Myth: Aeschylus' *Persians* on the Eve of the Greek War of Independence.' *Cultural Responses to the Persian Wars: Antiquity to the Third Millennium*, ed. E. Bridges et al., Oxford University Press, 2007, pp.299–330.

Van Steen, Gonda. 'All the King's Patriots? The "Persians" within the Walls of Nineteenth-Century Athens.' *BICS* 126, 2013, pp.79–96.

Van Steen, Gonda. 'Parading War and Victory under the Greek Military Dictatorship. The Hist(o)rionics of 1967–74.' *War as Spectacle: Ancient and Modern Perspectives on the Display of Armed Combat*, ed. Anastasia Bakogianni and V. M. Hope, Bloomsbury, 2015, pp.271–90.

van Wees, Hans. 'The Development of the Hoplite Phalanx: Iconography and Reality in the Seventh Century.' *War and Violence in Ancient Greece*, ed. Hans van Wees, Duckworth, 2000, pp.125–66.

van Wees, Hans. *Greek Warfare: Myths and Realities*. Duckworth, 2004.

Vanderpool, E. 'A Monument to the Battle of Marathon.' *Hesperia*, 35.2, 1966, pp.93–106.

Vasunia, Phiroze. 'Greek, Latin and the Indian Civil Service.' *Cambridge Classical Journal*, 51, 2005, pp.35–71.

Vaughn, Pamela. 'The Identification and Retrieval of the Hoplite Battle-Dead.' *Hoplites: The Classical Greek Battle Experience*, ed. V. D. Hanson, Routledge, 1991, pp.38–62.

Volonaki, Eleni. 'The Battle of Marathon in Funeral Speeches.' *Marathon – 2,500 Years: Proceedings of the Marathon Conference 2010*, ed. C. Carey and M. Edwards, *BICS* 124, 2013, pp.165–80.

von Fritz, Kurt. 'The Historian Theopompus.' *The American Historical Review*, 46.4, 1941, pp.765–87.

von Goethe, J. W. *West-Eastern Divan: The Complete, Annotated New Translation, Including Goethe's 'Notes and Essays' and the Unpublished Poems*. Trans. E. Ormsby, Gingko, 2019.

Wade-Gery, H. T. 'Miltiades.' *Journal of Hellenic Studies*, 71, 1951, pp.212–21.

Walbank, F.W. 'The Problem of Greek Nationality.' *Greeks and Barbarians*, ed. Thomas Harrison, Edinburgh University Press, 2002, pp.234–56.

Walker, C. B. F. *Cuneiform*. 10th ed., British Museum Press, 1986.

Walters, K. R. '"We Fought Alone at Marathon": Historical Falsification in the Attic Funeral Oration.' *Rheinisches Museum Für Philologie*, 124, 1981, pp.204–11.

West, Stephanie. 'A Diplomatic Fiasco: The First Athenian Embassy to Sardis (Hdt. 5.73).' *Rheinisches Museum Für Philologie*, 154.1, 2011, pp. 9–21.

Wheeler, E. L. 'The General as Hoplite.' *Hoplites: The Classical Greek Battle Experience*, ed. V. D. Hanson, Routledge, 1991, pp.121–70.

Wheeler, Graham. 'Battlefield Epiphanies in Ancient Greece: A Survey.' *Digressus*, 4, 2004, pp.1–14.

Whitley, James. 'The Monuments That Stood before Marathon: Tomb Cult and Hero Cult in Archaic Attica.' *American Journal of Archaeology*, 98.2, 1994, pp.213–30.

Whitmarsh, Timothy. *Battling the Gods: Atheism in the Ancient World*. Vintage, 2016.
Yakin, Boaz. *Marathon*. First Second, 2012.
Zaccarini, Matteo. 'The Case of Cimon: The Evolution of the Meaning of Philolaconism in Athens.' *Όρμος – Ricerche Di Storia Antica*, 3, 2011, pp.287–304.
Zaccarini, Matteo. 'The Return of Theseus to Athens: A Case Study in Layered Tradition and Reception.' *Histos*, 9, 2015, pp.174–98.
Zali, Vasiliki. 'Fate, Divine Phthonos, and the Wheel of Fortune: The Reception of Herodotean Theology in Early and Middle Byzantine Historiography.' *Histos Supplement*, 4, 2015, pp.85–126.
Zia-Ebrahimi, Reza. 'Self-Orientalization and Dislocation: The Uses and Abuses of the "Aryan" Discourse in Iran.' *Iranian Studies*, 44.4, 2011, pp.445–72.
Zia-Ebrahimi, Reza. *The Emergence of Iranian Nationalism: Race and the Politics of Dislocation*. Columbia University Press, 2016.

Index